Praise for *Understanding Natural Theology*

Christopher Brewer's new book can rightly be described as magisterial, and professional academics are as likely to derive benefit from reading it as are students relatively new to the field. The field is "nature" or "creation" and what kind of knowledge of God may be so derived without benefit of scriptural revelation. Teachers are commonly so convinced of their own approach (for example, "theology of creation" or analytic "proofs") that students often emerge from their classes totally unaware of alternatives. Brewer dispels such confusions by presenting five quite different approaches, with "natural religion" at one extreme and Karl Barth at the other, with equal attention given to background setting, critique, and defense. The presentation is admirably clear and in a lively, engaged style. Readers will not feel forced to endorse one particular view. Instead, they are given the tools to see clearly what is at stake through this impressive survey.

—DAVID BROWN, EMERITUS PROFESSOR, UNIVERSITY OF ST. ANDREWS

In this exploration of recent approaches, Chris Brewer expertly displays both the persistence of natural theology together with the variety of forms that it takes. In making the case for a necessary and complementary role, his account offers an acute but clear assessment of natural theology. Admirably generous in his acknowledgment of other writers, Brewer also brings his own distinctive voice to current debates.

—DAVID FERGUSSON, REGIUS PROFESSOR OF DIVINITY, UNIVERSITY OF CAMBRIDGE

After a century of stifling confusion and polemics, Brewer's *Understanding Natural Theology* is a lucid breath of fresh air. Useful for both teaching and research, this illuminating guide through five different approaches to natural theology clears the way for new possibilities to emerge.

—JOANNA LEIDENHAG, ASSOCIATE PROFESSOR OF THEOLOGY AND PHILOSOPHY, SCHOOL OF PHILOSOPHY, RELIGION, AND HISTORY OF SCIENCE, UNIVERSITY OF LEEDS, UK

This is a book that needed to be written. Debates about natural theology rarely pause to ask what, precisely, it is that is being debated about. Skillfully bringing both philosophical insight and theological depth to bear on this neglected question, along with an impressive research base, Brewer makes a real contribution by classifying and assessing five distinct approaches to the perennial human project of thinking about God. Showing that "natural theology" is a more complicated and vital concept than many suppose, this volume is now an essential reference point for future debates.

—ROBERT MACSWAIN, ASSOCIATE PROFESSOR OF THEOLOGY, SCHOOL OF THEOLOGY, UNIVERSITY OF THE SOUTH

Christopher R. Brewer has given us a commanding survey of natural theology, written with style. For years, Brewer has been rehabilitating this sometimes-maligned area of theology, and this book represents the culmination of his many years of much-needed research. I look forward to pushing this book into the hands of students.

—PHIL TALLON, ASSOCIATE PROFESSOR OF THEOLOGY, HOUSTON CHRISTIAN UNIVERSITY

Chris Brewer's *Understanding Natural Theology* is an excellent and urgently needed introduction into the developments and varieties of natural theology. It openly discusses the criticisms and counterarguments and invites the reader to join the conversation beyond the prejudices and polarizations in contemporary theology.

—STEPHAN VAN ERP, PROFESSOR OF FUNDAMENTAL THEOLOGY, KU LEUVEN AND AUSTRALIAN CATHOLIC UNIVERSITY

I heartily recommend this volume and celebrate its arrival. Readers will find an engaging and thoroughly informative combination here. While Brewer provides a timely and expert survey of the field—along with a set of immensely helpful categories and comparisons—readers will enjoy at the same time his own insights on the pressure points in natural theology. In these pages, Brewer has convened a sprawling dinner party for the most intriguing and invested cast of guests, and thus our good host offers here a much-needed reanimation of the discourse. He's done much to render the topic exhilarating once more.

—TAYLOR WORLEY, VISITING ASSOCIATE PROFESSOR OF ART HISTORY, WHEATON COLLEGE

UNDERSTANDING

Natural
Theology

UNDERSTANDING
Natural
Theology

Mapping the Terrain
of Recent Approaches

Christopher R. Brewer

ZONDERVAN
ACADEMIC

ZONDERVAN ACADEMIC

Understanding Natural Theology
Copyright © 2026 by Christopher R. Brewer

Published by Zondervan, 3950 Sparks Drive SE, Suite 101, Grand Rapids, MI 49546, USA. Zondervan is a registered trademark of The Zondervan Corporation, L.L.C., a wholly owned subsidiary of HarperCollins Christian Publishing, Inc.

Requests for information should be addressed to customercare@harpercollins.com.

Zondervan titles may be purchased in bulk for educational, business, fundraising, or sales promotional use. For information, please email SpecialMarkets@Zondervan.com.

ISBN 978-0-310-52269-0 (softcover)
ISBN 978-0-310-52270-6 (ebook)
ISBN 978-0-310-18279-5 (audio)

HarperCollins Publishers, Macken House, 39/40 Mayor Street Upper, Dublin 1, D01 C9W8, Ireland (https://www.harpercollins.com)

Cover design: Brian Bobel Design
Artist: © Alfonse Borysevicz Waters, 2010–15
Interior design: Denise Froehlich

Printed in the United States of America
25 26 27 28 29 LBC 5 4 3 2 1

I dedicate this book to my parents,
Gary and Kathy Brewer, and to
the memory of my forebears.
Montani Semper Liberi

Natural theology is not, and cannot be, a completed doctrine, something written down once and for all by a Thomas Aquinas or a Bishop Butler or some other distinguished worthy of the past. Natural theology, indeed, is a project rather than a doctrine, a process which in the nature of the case cannot be completed as long as time, and the debates of time, and our novelty-laden human experience shall continue. Natural theology is an essay in the art of communication, something which has to be renewed and rethought in every age, in the light of what the existing points of convergence happen to be at the time, and they certainly differ very greatly at different periods in the development of thought and civilization. Natural theology is always and necessarily contemporary theology.

—J. V. Langmead Casserley, *Graceful Reason*

Contents

Preface xi
Introduction: A Spectrum of Natural Theology 1

Part 1: Natural Religion

1. Natural Theology Informed by Natural Religion 29
2. Transforming Natural Religion: David Brown. 43

Part 2: Proof

3. Natural Theology as Proof/Argument. 59
4. Nice but Not Necessary: Alvin Plantinga 75

Part 3: Signals

5. Natural Theology as Signals of Transcendence 95
6. The Signs at the Core: C. Stephen Evans. 111

Part 4: Christian Natural Theology

7. Natural Theology as *Christian* Natural Theology 127
8. The Transformation of Natural Theology: Thomas F. Torrance 141

Part 5: Theology of Nature

9. Natural Theology as Theology of Nature. 153
10. The Key to the Secret of Creation: Karl Barth 165

Afterword. 179
Bibliography 183
Subject Index 197
Author Index 207

Preface

This book was born in the summer of 2013 at the St. Andrews Links Clubhouse in conversation with Katya Covrett. I was at that time a PhD candidate at the University of St. Andrews, and Katya was in town for the Society of Biblical Literature International Meeting. I had suggested that I would like to submit a proposal for a Counterpoints volume on natural theology. Katya responded that most people have no idea what natural theology is, let alone that there may be five views.[1] She suggested, instead, that I might write an introduction to natural theology along the lines of Edward W. Klink III and Darian R. Lockett's *Understanding Biblical Theology: A Comparison of Theory and Practice*. She then asked if I had any sense of the types I'd want to discuss. I rattled off five types on the spot. Those five types became the subject of the first chapter of my doctoral thesis, and they are the same five types elaborated in this book. This book is, then, a significantly expanded version of the first chapter of my doctoral thesis.[2]

---

1. Something along these lines has now been published: James K. Dew Jr. and Ronnie P. Campbell Jr., eds., *Natural Theology: Five Views* (Baker Academic, 2024).
2. Around that same time, I was invited—on extremely short notice—to contribute a chapter to a book on William Desmond and theology. Desmond's work was the subject of the second chapter of my doctoral thesis, and the paper submitted a sort of snapshot of my research at that point for my second and third chapters. The third chapter of my thesis would eventually be published in revised and expanded form as the introduction to Howard E. Root, *Theological Radicalism and Tradition: "The Limits of Radicalism" with Appendices*, ed. Christopher R. Brewer (Routledge, 2018), 1–38. That volume contains Howard E. Root's previously unpublished 1972 Bampton Lectures, which I discovered in an uncataloged box at Lambeth Palace Library. The fourth chapter of my thesis was published in revised form as "'Surely the Lord Is In This Place': Jacob's Ladder in Painting, Contemporary Sculpture and Installation Art," in *The Moving Text: Interdisciplinary Perspectives on David Brown and the Bible*, ed. Garrick V. Allen, Christopher R. Brewer, and Dennis F. Kinlaw III (SCM, 2018).

My first goal in writing this book is to problematize an all too easy advocacy or rejection of natural theology. As N. T. Wright wrote in the published form of his 2018 Gifford Lectures, "The phrase 'natural theology,' like all shorthand theological terms, is best understood as a drastically abbreviated version of a full sentence."[3] One can't espouse or reject natural theology *tout court*. One must instead acknowledge the existence of a wide variety of natural theologies, and these natural theologies must be patiently examined in turn. My second goal is to clear the ground for new forms of natural theology, even if they go by a different name. There is, as I will argue, a descriptive responsibility, but there is also prescriptive possibility. This book is concerned with the former as prerequisite to the latter.

Thanks to Katya for suggesting that I write this book and to Stan Gundry, who offered me the contract. Thanks also to my current editor David W. McNutt. Like so many authors, it has taken me longer to write this book than I'd initially planned, and this as the result of three international moves: from St. Andrews, Scotland, to Grand Rapids, Michigan, in 2015; from Grand Rapids to Nassau, The Bahamas, in 2018; and then—amid a global pandemic—back to Grand Rapids in 2021. I simply wouldn't have finished the book without the encouragement of my wife, Rachel, and my good friend Garrick Allen as well as several others—David Fergusson and Andrew Torrance among them—who, after noting the lack of a good, accessible introduction to the field encouraged me to get on with it. I am grateful to a number of readers who read and commented upon one or more chapters. These include Rachel, Garrick, and Andrew as well as Alfonse Borysewicz, David Brown, C. Stephen Evans, Robert MacSwain, Michael E. Wittmer, Nicholas Wolterstorff, and Taylor Worley. I am also grateful to Templeton Religion Trust for a grant that enabled me to write the second half of this book.

CHRISTOPHER R. BREWER

---

3. N. T. Wright, *History and Eschatology: Jesus and the Promise of Natural Theology* (SPCK, 2018), ix.

ADDITIONAL NOTE

Chris had been working on this book on and off for nearly fifteen years. We were both students when he signed the contract, and I remember being deeply jealous that someone had paid him for a book he had yet to write. Chris had always been ten steps ahead, an endless stream of ideas, strategies, and plans. He was a maximiser, squeezing the most out of every opportunity, never afraid to step outside of the expectations that came with his perceived station. I was always impressed that he could forge his own path, bring people together, and, as he would say, "shape the conversation." Chris was an ambitious, creative, and synthetic thinker. Characteristics of these qualities are infused throughout the pages of this book.

It is a sad irony then that shortly after submitting this manuscript Chris was diagnosed with terminal brain cancer, a reality that has kept him from polishing up the final form himself. To bring his mature work on the state of natural theology in the twenty-first century to fruition, I have edited the final version in conversation with his wife, Rachel, David McNutt (Chris's editor at Zondervan), and Chris himself as he was able. I have endeavored to preserve Chris's voice, trying to enable his vision of natural theology to be as clear as possible. I had counted Chris as one of my closest friends, and we have been in conversation about the topic of natural theology (and many other things) since we met as PhD students at the University of St. Andrews in 2012. I hope that this book is a monument to Chris's creative mind, incisive scholarship, sardonic wit, and his ability to see the forest for the trees. I know that my scholarship, theological thinking, and development as a person have benefitted immensely from our fifteen-year-long friendship, and I trust that readers of this book will be similarly gratified.

Chris concluded this book by sketching out a new metaphor for natural theology in conversation with the work of Gérard Genette—natural theology as paratext—noting that he planed to carry out this prescriptive work in a future book. He will not be able in the end to do this himself. But this book lays the groundwork for whoever has the courage to wade into the debate and sets a new, overdue agenda for reimagining the place of natural theology in contemporary research and Christian practice.

GARRICK ALLEN

Introduction

A Spectrum of Natural Theology

> Because the theoretical achievement does exist, it is a mistake
> to deny without qualification the possibility of a natural
> theology; and because the per se subject is just an abstraction,
> it is a mistake to affirm without qualification the concrete
> existence of a natural theology.[1]

—Bernard Lonergan

> If we continue to say that there are reasons for accepting one
> set of beliefs rather than another, we are that far committed
> to something which I should call metaphysics. But it will have
> to be a metaphysics which can somehow do justice not only to
> our desire for a Natural Theology but also to our religiously
> inspired distrust of Natural Theology. Just what it would
> look like is very much worth finding out.[2]

—Howard Root

---

1. Bernard Lonergan, *Method in Theology*, ed. Robert M. Doran and John D. Dadosky, Collected Works of Bernard Lonergan 14 (University of Toronto Press, 2017), 378.
2. Howard Root, "Metaphysics and Religious Belief," in *Prospect for Metaphysics: Essays of Metaphysical Exploration*, ed. Ian Ramsey (Allen & Unwin, 1961), 79.

Damned if you do, some say, and others, well, damned if you don't. Natural theology is, according to some, the loss of faith.[3] For others, it is that without which faith is lost.[4] For the latter, natural theology is the stuff of faith, a theological necessity. For the former, it is necessarily idolatrous.[5] Both parties think the other guilty of neglect. For those who think it the loss of faith, natural theology neglects the true God revealed exclusively in Christ. For those who think it the stuff of faith, they think these Christomonists who neglect natural theology in effect exclude God from action in our present wider world and could be said to evince an implicit deism and, in so doing, neglect God's revelation broadly conceived.[6] One asks, "What more than Christ is needed?" The other, advocating a theological variety of due diligence, replies, "Why ignore that which has been given?" Doing so risks alienating women and men whose experience of God is entirely beyond the walls of the church.

So natural theology: Yes or no? Well, that depends upon the answer to a more fundamental question: What is natural theology? Until this more fundamental question is answered, a response seems foolhardy. Yes or no to what? For Karl Barth, whose "No!" is the stuff of theological legend, natural theology was "an abyss into which it is inadvisable to step if one does not want to fall."[7] In a section that might just as easily have come from the pages of J. K. Rowling's *Harry Potter and the Chamber of Secrets*, Barth argues:

---

3. For the most well-known example, see Barth, *Church Dogmatics* I/1, 448–49; Barth, *Church Dogmatics* I/2, 522–23; Barth, *Church Dogmatics* II/1, 93–96. All citations of this work in this volume derive from Karl Barth, *Church Dogmatics*, ed. and trans. T. F. Torrance and G. W. Bromiley, 4 vols. in 13 parts (T&T Clark, 1932–1967).

4. See, e.g., H. E. Root, "Beginning All over Again," in *Soundings: Essays Concerning Christian Understanding*, ed. A. R. Vidler (Cambridge University Press, 1962), 6; Thomas Joseph White, OP, *Wisdom in the Face of Modernity: A Study in Thomistic Natural Theology* (Sapientia, 2009), xviii.

5. For an argument to the contrary, see Hugh Burling, "The Idolatry Argument Against Natural Theology: How It Works and Why It Fails," *Religious Studies* 51 (2015): 401–10.

6. For an example of this view, see David Brown, *Divine Generosity and Human Creativity: Theology Through Symbol, Painting and Architecture*, ed. Christopher R. Brewer and Robert MacSwain (Routledge, 2017), discussed most explicitly in my editor's introduction (vii–xiii).

7. Karl Barth, "No! Answer to Emil Brunner," in *Natural Theology: Comprising "Nature and Grace" by Professor Dr. Emil Brunner and the Reply "No!" by Dr. Karl Barth*, trans. Peter Fraenkel (Centenary, 1946), 75.

All one can do is to turn one's back upon it as upon the great temptation and source of error, by having nothing to do with it and by making it clear to oneself and to others from time to time why one acts that way. A real rejection of natural theology does not differ from its acceptance merely in the way which No differs from Yes. Rather are Yes and No, said, as it were, on different levels. Really to reject natural theology means to refuse to admit it as a separate problem. Hence the rejection of natural theology can only be a side issue, arising when serious questions of real theology are being discussed. . . . If you really reject natural theology you do not stare at the serpent, with the result that it stares back at you, hypnotises you, and is ultimately certain to bite you, but you hit it and kill it as soon as you see it![8]

For Barth, natural theology was no theology at all. It was a demon, an abyss, and a serpent that must not be named, for to name it would be to grant it a measure of autonomy. The very antithesis of theology, natural theology was for Barth, like evil, a nonthing, an impossibility. It had no autonomous existence. It could only be understood in terms of privation or lack, as something negative and without substance. That is why, according to Barth, "it cannot be the business of a Reformed theologian to raise so much as his little finger to support this undertaking in any positive way."[9] For Barth, natural theology was, plain and simple, "the transformation of the Christian Church into the temple of the German nature- and history-myth."[10] Barth's position may well seem extreme, but as Peter Berger has noted: "In a world full of Nazis one can be forgiven for being a Barthian."[11] Against the idea that Barth had

---

8. Barth, "No!," 75–76.
9. Karl Barth, *The Knowledge of God and the Service of God According to the Teaching of the Reformation: Recalling the Scottish Confession of 1560; The Gifford Lectures Delivered in the University of Aberdeen in 1937 and 1938*, trans. J. L. M. Haire and Ian Henderson (Hodder & Stoughton, 1938), 6. For a similar comment, see Barth, *Church Dogmatics* II/1, 85.
10. Barth, *Church Dogmatics* II/1, 173. For discussion, see Rodney Holder, *The Heavens Declare: Natural Theology and the Legacy of Karl Barth* (Templeton, 2012), 15–53.
11. Peter Berger, *A Rumour of Angels: Modern Society and the Rediscovery of the Supernatural* (Anchor, 1970), 18. See also Peter L. Berger, *The Heretical Imperative: Contemporary Possibilities of Religious Affirmation* (Anchor, 1980), 130: "As to Barthian Neo-orthodoxy, it should be given every credit for its historical nexus with Christian anti-Nazism. But it is not irrelevant to observe that many of the same theologians who were so clear-sighted about Nazism (Barth emphatically among them) were singularly obtuse when it came to understanding Communism after 1945."

good reason necessarily to relate natural theology and Nazism (*reductio ad Hitlerum*), however, Andrew Collier has argued: "Barth's linking of natural theology to Nazism is just one instance of that activity which few twentieth-century thinkers (particularly left-wing ones) have been able to resist: tarring their intellectual opponents with the brush of political perniciousness. But an intellectual position can lead to any number of political tendencies depending on which other beliefs it is combined with."[12] Along these same lines, Sarah Coakley has suggested: "If [Barth] were alive today, and setting out to counter the brash confidences of the New Atheists, I do wonder if his strategies would have been different."[13] In any case, Barth's refusal to admit natural theology as a separate subject leads to a number of problems, not least the difficulty in *understanding natural theology*.

Understanding Natural Theology

For those seeking to understand natural theology, the dictionary may well seem a good place to begin, and according to *The Oxford Dictionary of the Christian Church* natural theology is "the body of knowledge about God which may be obtained by human reason alone without the aid of Revelation and hence to be contrasted with 'Revealed Theology.'"[14] There it is in a nutshell. Natural theology is, according to this standard definition, a revelation-free, reason-informed theology most often associated with proofs for the existence of God. But, as the reader of this book will see, this

---

This leads him to conclude (rightly in my opinion): "*No particular theological position guarantees social or political clear-sightedness*" (131).

12. Andrew Collier, "Natural Theology, Revealed Theology and Religious Experience," in *Transcendence: Critical Realism and God*, ed. Margaret S. Archer, Andrew Collier, and Douglas V. Porpora (Routledge, 2004), 132–33. See also J. V. Langmead Casserley, *Graceful Reason: The Contribution of Reason to Theology* (Seabury, 1954), 57–58; Berger, *Heretical Imperative*, 142–44; David Brown, *God and Mystery in Words: Experience Through Metaphor and Drama* (Oxford University Press, 2008), 1.

13. Sarah Coakley, "Natural Theology and the Flat-Plane Fallacy," in *Darwinism and Natural Theology: Evolving Perspectives*, ed. Andrew Robinson (Cambridge Scholars, 2012), 97. See also Mark R. Lindsay, *Reading Auschwitz with Barth: The Holocaust as Problem and Promise for Barthian Theology* (Clarke, 2014), 8: "It is an open question whether or not the stridency of Barth's opposition is as necessary now as it was in the 1930s."

14. F. L. Cross and E. A. Livingstone, ed., *The Oxford Dictionary of the Christian Church*, 3rd rev. ed. (Oxford University Press, 2005), 1139. A similar definition is offered in Daniel Patte, ed., *The Cambridge Dictionary of Christianity* (Cambridge University Press, 2010), 857–58.

standard definition is noncomprehensive and so misleading. To cite just three examples confirming this claim: consider David Brown who argues "that the boundaries between natural and revealed theology were to a great extent artificial,"[15] C. Stephen Evans who (together with coauthor R. Zachary Manis) suggests that "the distinction between natural theology and revealed theology is not so easy to make as one might think,"[16] or Thomas F. Torrance who argues that "it is no longer possible to operate scientifically with a separation between natural theology and revealed theology any more than between geometry and physics."[17] Here we have three proponents of natural theology for whom the standard definition does not apply. Clearly, one cannot describe natural theology as revelation-free when natural theologians reject or question the distinction between natural and revealed. But if natural theology is not considered to be distinct from, or opposed to, revealed theology, then why does the standard definition persist? In a word: Barth.[18]

For Barth, natural theology is opposed to revelation because there is only one revelation: God in Jesus Christ. Natural theology is thus, for Barth, revelation-free. But what about general revelation? Does it not inform natural theology as its source?[19] Are there not, as Augustine said, two books—the book of nature and the book of Scripture—that correspond to general and special revelation?[20] Not for Barth, for whom there is no such thing as general

---

15. David Brown, *God in a Single Vision: Integrating Philosophy and Theology*, ed. Christopher R. Brewer and Robert MacSwain (Routledge, 2016), 3.

16. C. Stephen Evans and R. Zachary Manis, *Philosophy of Religion: Thinking About Faith*, 2nd ed. (InterVarsity, 2009), 56. George I. Mavrodes argues the point at length in *Revelation in Religious Belief* (Temple University Press, 1988), 3–38.

17. Thomas F. Torrance, *Space, Time and Incarnation* (T&T Clark, 1969), 69.

18. There may well be, and likely are, additional causes for the persistence of the standard definition, but it is no exaggeration to attribute the lack of understanding (or even misunderstanding) to the influence of Barth. See Barth, "No!," 76: "Real rejection of natural theology can come about only in the fear of God and hence only be a complete *lack* of interest in this matter. If this matter is allowed to become of interest, though but in order to be rejected, then interest is no longer centred [*sic*] upon theology." For additional discussion, see Charles E. Raven, *Natural Religion and Christian Theology: The Gifford Lectures 1951*, First Series: Science and Religion (Cambridge University Press, 1953), 2–3.

19. On the distinction between general revelation and natural theology, see G. C. Berkouwer, *General Revelation*, Studies in Dogmatics (Eerdmans, 1955). From my view, natural theology is a generative, constructive endeavor while general revelation is something that we receive, something we may or may not be able to interpret. The two are congruent but distinct.

20. See sermon 68.6 in Augustine, *Sermons (51–94) on the New Testament*, trans. E. Hill (New City,

revelation.[21] For Barth it is a zero-sum game, and special revelation always wins. Natural theology, from this perspective, has no basis in revelation. As G. C. Berkouwer explains: "[Barth's] offensive against natural theology is at the same time a denial of 'general' revelation. . . . For Barth *general* revelation and *natural* theology are inseparably united."[22] Now, whether or not one accepts Barth's damning critique of natural theology, his christological conception of revelation has, for the better part of a century, controlled our understanding of natural theology, and this is evidenced by the persistence of the standard definition, which accepts Barth's first premise—namely, a "christological" conception of revelation that excludes both general revelation and natural theology.[23] It is a prime example of a "hasty generalization."[24] Understanding natural theology cannot begin and end with Barth because natural theology is not in every case thought of as being revelation-free.

Nor should natural theology be limited to proofs for the existence of God. According to William Desmond, we need to get beyond or behind the idea of natural theology as "proofs" (i.e., "ways"), for proofs can only be understood in relation to their cultural context or worldview, or what Desmond calls "the ethos."[25] He argues that "we do an injustice to the 'proofs' if we abstract

---

1991), 225. For discussion, see Oskari Juurikkala, "The Two Books of God: The Metaphor of the Book of Nature in Augustine," *Augustinianum* 61 (2021): 479–98.

21. See, e.g., Barth, *Church Dogmatics* II/1, 99–116. To my mind, Barth's direct statements (here and elsewhere) speak for themselves in this context, even if some thematic readings of his entire corpus might push in other directions.

22. Berkouwer, *General Revelation*, 32–33. William J. Abraham argues that uniting general revelation and natural theology "is clearly a mistake." See his *Crossing the Threshold of Divine Revelation* (Eerdmans, 2006), 67n7.

23. I say "christological" because there are those like David Brown who have pointed out that "there is the whole question of what is meant by a christological criterion." Brown, *God in a Single Vision*, 75. See also Brown, *Discipleship and Imagination*, 400–402.

24. For a more helpful approach (with reference to natural theology), see Michael Sudduth, *The Reformed Objection to Natural Theology* (Ashgate, 2009), 54. Sudduth distinguishes between a "project objection" and a "model-specific objection."

25. William Desmond, "God, Ethos, Ways," *International Journal for Philosophy of Religion* 45 (1999): 13–30. This is, more specifically, what Desmond calls the second ethos. The first, or primal, ethos (i.e., "the between") is, according to Desmond, where metaphysical thinking takes shape. He distinguishes between the first ethos and the second, the latter of which is more or less synonymous with the term *worldview*. For additional discussion, see Christopher R. Brewer, "Rolling with Release into the Future: William Desmond's Donation to a Natural Theology of the Arts," in *William Desmond and Contemporary Theology*, ed. Christopher Ben Simpson and

them from the ontological context in which they are formulated; we have to acknowledge a complex interplay of ways and ethos."[26] What this means is that understanding natural theology encompasses understanding not only the proofs but also the enabling metaphysical conditions as well.

In seeking to draw attention to some other enabling feature related to the proofs, Desmond is not alone. According to C. Stephen Evans: "Many of the classical arguments for God's existence, such as the cosmological, teleological, and moral arguments, are grounded in . . . 'natural signs' that point to God's reality. These theistic arguments derive their force and enjoy whatever plausibility they possess from the signs that lie at their core."[27] I will discuss this at greater length in chapter 6, but for Evans, understanding natural theology means identifying foundational "natural signs." Another example is William J. Wainwright (who is explicitly following George Mavrodes) for whom proofs cannot be understood apart from the concept of "person-relativity."[28] So whether one follows Desmond on his "adventure of thought"[29] in an attempt to elucidate the enabling metaphysical conditions, Evans in his search for "natural signs," or Wainwright in his understanding of "person-relativity," the point is that natural theology in many cases has to do with much more than proofs for the existence of God.

So if natural theology is not necessarily revelation-free and need not deal with proofs for the existence of God, then what is it? To answer this question, I have identified a handful of key considerations, which like the frequency-specific faders on an equalizer might be adjusted or nuanced

Brennan Thomas Sammon (University of Notre Dame Press, 2017), 217–37.

26. Desmond, "God, Ethos, Ways," 14. See also Nicholas Wolterstorff, "The Migration of the Theistic Arguments: From Natural Theology to Evidentialist Apologetics," in *Rationality, Religious Belief, and Moral Commitment: New Essays in the Philosophy of Religion*, ed. Robert Audi and William J. Wainwright (Cornell University Press, 1986), 38–81.

27. C. Stephen Evans, *Natural Signs and Knowledge of God: A New Look at Theistic Arguments* (Oxford University Press, 2010), 2. See also 62: "It is important to recognize that there is no such thing as *the* cosmological argument or *the* teleological argument, although some philosophers have mistakenly assumed this to be the case. Many different versions of each of these arguments have been proposed, and some differ radically from others in the same category."

28. William J. Wainwright, *Reason, Revelation, and Devotion: Inference and Argument in Religion* (Cambridge University Press, 2016), 47. See also George Mavrodes, *Belief in God* (Random House, 1970), 45–47.

29. William Desmond, *Being and the Between* (State University of New York Press, 1995), xvi.

for a very different result. You might say that understanding natural theology means turning our attention from the stage (or soapbox), where definitive proclamations are made, to the soundboard, where each and every channel's gain (i.e., input volume), equalization, auxiliary output, and fader-controlled signal in the mix require nuanced decisions that collectively determine what is heard. What I am suggesting is that you might think of each of these key considerations as a channel on a large theological soundboard.

Key Considerations

Let me begin by saying that there is, in an important sense, no such thing as "natural theology" but instead only "natural theologies." As the Anglican priest and theologian J. V. Langmead Casserley (1909–78) said in 1951, "There are many 'natural theologies,' each taking its point of departure from some distinct strand or level of our secular experience. . . . The term 'natural theology' is a much wider and more inclusive one than most of those who make a great parade of rejecting all natural theology either realize or allow."[30] Quite right. This is why I argue that before we can understand these natural theologies we need to address a nexus of issues. There is, I would argue, a descriptive responsibility with reference to natural theology (hereafter, "the Descriptive Responsibility"), and it is a responsibility that we cannot neglect. At the forefront of these considerations are (1) one's definition of nature, (2) that from which nature and the natural are distinct, and (3) one's objective in approaching nature so defined, or, more simply, the function of natural theology.

NATURE

To understand *natural* theology we must understand the sense in which nature is being employed.[31] As Clement C. J. Webb has noted: "The history

---

30. J. V. Langmead Casserley, *The Retreat from Christianity in the Modern World* (Longmans, Green, 1952), 48. See also Casserley, *Graceful Reason*, 1, 160.

31. We must also be clear as to the referent, that is, the nature of what or whom? For a helpful discussion of the shift from natural theology as "the talk about God that corresponds to the nature of the divine itself" to that which is "in accordance with human nature," see Wolfhart

of philosophical terminology is full of the monuments of the intractability of words. And no word has been more intractable than the word Nature with its derivatives."[32] After a brief survey of usage, Webb concludes: "The ambiguities which thus beset the word Nature and its derivatives have introduced no little confusion into the use of the expression Natural Religion. It has never, I suppose, meant just the religion that actually exists; but its meaning has varied with all the other meanings of 'nature.'"[33]

It is for this very reason that Jeremy Begbie has more recently articulated four senses of the word: (1) *"the physical world,"* (2) *"the quintessentially human,"* (3) *"those constructive activities designated by the term 'culture',"* and (4) *"properly functioning human reason."*[34] The first sense is fairly straightforward, as is the fourth. My suspicion is that most people think natural theology to be "natural" in one of these two senses; that is to say, along the lines of the standard definition. The second sense is Begbie's preferred sense, and in the end he argues for a theologically (namely, christologically) controlled nature along the lines of Jüngel's *"more* natural theology."[35] I will have more to say about this later in the introduction, but here I want to highlight Begbie's third sense: culture.

It may seem strange to think of culture as nature, but this usage has a long lineage that goes all the way back to Cicero (106–43 BCE). Reflecting upon "the labours of men performed by their hands," including farming, metallurgy, forestry, seamanship, and irrigation, Cicero explained that "by the work of our hands we strive to create a sort of second nature within the

---

Pannenberg, *Systematic Theology*, vol. 1 (Eerdmans, 1991), 73–82, quotes from 77, 81.

32. Clement C. J. Webb, *Studies in the History of Natural Theology* (Clarendon, 1915), 6–7.

33. Webb, *History of Natural Theology*, 8–9. For discussion of nature in the Bible as well as the early church, see Raven, *Natural Religion*, 21–57. For a more general survey of meanings, see C. S. Lewis, *Studies in Words* (Cambridge University Press, 1960), 24–74. For a cultural history of the idea, see the relevant chapter in each volume of Sophia Rosenfeld and Peter T. Struck, eds., *A Cultural History of Ideas*, 6 vols. (Bloomsbury, 2022).

34. Jeremy Begbie, *Music, Modernity, and God: Essays in Listening* (Oxford University Press, 2013), 91–92.

35. Eberhard Jüngel, *Christ, Justice and Peace: Toward a Theology of the State in Dialogue with the Barmen Declaration*, trans. D. Bruce Hamill and Alan J. Torrance (T&T Clark, 1992), 26–27; quoted in Jeremy Begbie, "Natural Theology and Music," in *The Oxford Handbook of Natural Theology*, ed. Russell Re Manning (Oxford University Press, 2013), 573–74.

world of nature."[36] From a Christian (and more specifically, Reformed) per-spective, this idea is rooted in the cultural mandate of Genesis 1:28. In any case, nature includes culture (i.e., "second nature"). But there is also what might be called a "third nature," what Cicero refers to as "human reason" and "man's nature."[37] To summarize, drawing upon Cicero, there are three types of nature: first nature (N^1), or unworked nature; second nature (N^2), or worked nature; and third nature (N^3), or human reason.

Going further, Alister E. McGrath has argued that "[the observable world] is not viewed directly, but through a prism or interpretive frame-work. . . . An aspect of nature is thus 'seen' and interpreted through a lens which is a cultural or social artifact—but must still be regarded as being 'natural,' despite having been constructed."[38] For McGrath, N^1 entails N^3, with N^3 being understood as a particular activity of human reason—namely, interpretation. Now, this may well seem a bit too much at this stage, but the important point is that natural theology has to do with more than just science and the natural world (N^1). In fact, what are to my mind the most interesting varieties of natural theology being worked out today have to do with culture and interpretation (N^2 and N^3). Natural theology is, as Russell Re Manning has argued, "inherently interdisciplinary,"[39] and so in addition to science it includes culture and the arts.[40] In any case, understanding the

---

36. See *On the Nature of the Gods* 2.151–52. Translation from Cicero, *The Nature of the Gods*, trans. P. G. Walsh (Oxford University Press, 1998), 102. For discussion of this notion, see Clarence J. Glacken, *Traces of the Rhodian Shore: Nature and Culture in Western Thought from Ancient Times to the End of the Eighteenth Century* (University of California Press, 1967), 116–49. See also G. van der Leeuw, *Religion in Essence and Manifestation: A Study in Phenomenology*, trans. J. E. Turner, vol. 1 (Harper & Row, 1963), 52–53; Peter L. Berger, *The Sacred Canopy: Elements of a Sociological Theory of Religion* (Anchor, 1969), 10–11.

37. Cicero, *On the Nature of the Gods*, 2.152–53.

38. Alister E. McGrath, *The Open Secret: A New Vision for Natural Theology* (Blackwell, 2008), 128. For additional discussion with reference to landscape art, see David Brown, "Re-Conceiving the Sacramental," in *The Gestures of God: Explorations in Sacramentality*, ed. Geoffrey Rowell and Christine Hall (Continuum, 2004), 32–33.

39. Re Manning, introduction to Re Manning, *Oxford Handbook of Natural Theology*, 1.

40. For a variety of essays along these lines, see Re Manning, *Oxford Handbook of Natural Theology*, 523–610. For a recent essay in natural theology and the arts, see my essay, "From Apparently Finite to Infinite: Conceptual Art and Natural Theology," in *Christian Theology and the Transformation of Natural Religion: From Incarnation to Sacramentality; Essays in Honour of David Brown*, ed. Christopher R. Brewer (Peeters, 2018), 173–89.

sense in which nature is being employed is the first step to understanding a particular natural theology.

NATURAL OPPOSED TO . . . ?

Related to the first consideration, understanding a particular natural theology (and its accompanying sense of nature) means understanding that to which it is being opposed. This line of thinking has a long pedigree, going back to Marcus Terentius Varro (116–27 BCE), a Roman scholar whose work is discussed in Saint Augustine's *The City of God*.[41] Augustine tells us that, according to Varro, there are three types of theology: mythical (or fabulous), physical (or natural), and civic (or political). The first is the theology of the Greek poets and the theater, the second is the theology of the world, and the third is that of the city (i.e., state religion). With reference to Varro, William Fulton (1876–1952) has observed that "when we consider natural theology in its past relationships we find that the contrast involved in the phrase is virtually the contrast between the natural, or the scientific, or the rational, and the historical."[42] According to Fulton, then, natural theology is best defined when it is contrasted with "an historical form of theology," a designation which Fulton prefers to a "distinction and division between the natural and the revealed."[43] Here, Fulton is following Clement C. J. Webb, who twelve years earlier observed: "Normally the stories of the 'mythical' and the rites of the 'civil' theology would have gone more closely together; the two combined would have corresponded to the Revealed Theology of later times. Putting together, then, these two features of the contrast between the two antitheses, we see that the characteristic difference between the older view (which has been revived in more modern times) and the newer was a difference in the way of regarding *history* in relation to religion."[44] Both Webb and Fulton, then, contrast natural with historical types of theology.[45] Now, sorting out

---

41. See book 6 of Augustine, *City of God*.
42. William Fulton, *Nature and God: An Introduction to Theistic Studies, with Special Reference to the Relations of Science and Religion* (T&T Clark, 1927), 17.
43. Fulton, *Nature and God*, 17.
44. Webb, *History of Natural Theology*, 19.
45. It should be noted that Webb later nuances his position and refuses division. Webb, *History of Natural Theology*, 45, 50.

whether there are two (à la Webb and Fulton) or three (à la Varro) types of theology is not here my concern. Rather, my point is that natural theology has traditionally been defined by that to which it is opposed.[46]

Contrasting natural theology with revealed theology assumes a particular theology of revelation, one that could make rejecting natural theology, as Barth does, a foregone conclusion. William Temple (1881–1944) argued similarly (but as a proponent of natural theology): "The source of trouble is the uncritical acceptance by Natural Theologians of that distinction of the two spheres—Natural and Revealed Religion—which was itself drawn by the exponents of Revealed Theology."[47] If God reveals himself primarily (or even exclusively) in and through Christ, then any attempt to go around Christ can lead only to idolatry and so should be rejected. But if revelation itself includes reason and religious experience, then defining natural theology in terms of its opposition to revelation simply will not do. Surely, as Temple has argued: "If Natural Theology is restricted, or restricts itself, to the study of what has never been part of a supposed revelation, then it is concerned with what is very unimportant alike to its own students and to all mankind."[48] He thus advocates "the deliberate and total repudiation of any distinction of spheres as belonging respectively to Natural and Revealed Religion or Theology."[49] Whether or not one accepts Temple's repudiation, acting as if the distinction has not been questioned—with the result that natural theology is defined in each and every instance with the distinction in place—fails to do justice to the wide range of natural theologies and so fails to fulfill the Descriptive Responsibility.

Taking a slightly different approach, Patrick Sherry has argued that "theistic arguments are inverse forms of fundamental religious doctrines, e.g. Cosmological arguments reverse the doctrine of Creation, in that the latter claims that God brought the world into being and sustains it in being, whilst

---

46. For additional discussion and the suggestion of a fourth, "faithful" type, see Russell Re Manning, "Natural Theology Reconsidered (Again)," *Theology and Science* 15 (2017): 290–95. That said, Re Manning advocates a "faithless" variety of natural theology here (299) and elsewhere. See Russell Re Manning, "A Perspective from Continental Philosophy," in Re Manning, *Oxford Handbook of Natural Theology*, 266–69.

47. William Temple, *Nature, Man and God: Being the Gifford Lectures Delivered in the University of Glasgow in the Academical Years 1932–1933 and 1933–1934* (Macmillan, 1934), 10.

48. Temple, *Nature, Man and God*, 9.

49. Temple, *Nature, Man and God*, 16; cf. Root, "Beginning All over Again," 10.

the arguments seek to infer his existence from that of the world or from some very general feature of it."[50] Natural theology, in this sense, is the opposite or inverse of revealed theology rather than being opposed to or distinct from it. According to Sherry, "natural theology answers certain basic urges in human beings," and "is usually retrospective and apologetical."[51] And here Sherry raises the issue of function.

FUNCTION

While defining natural theology in terms of that to which it is opposed has a long and distinguished history, some scholars prefer to define natural theology in terms of function, answering the normative rather than the ontological question. The philosopher of religion Michael Sudduth, for example, begins by distinguishing "between natural theology as natural *knowledge* of God and natural theology as rational *proofs or arguments* for the existence and nature of God."[52] He refers to the former as natural theology *alpha* and to the latter as natural theology *beta*. He explains: "From this viewpoint, natural theology [*beta*] involves the conceptual clarification and reflective development of natural theology [*alpha*], a kind of formalization of an innate or spontaneously acquired knowledge of God. Hence we can think of natural theology [*beta*] as grounded in natural theology [*alpha*]."[53] Focusing upon natural theology *beta*, he identifies three functions: dogmatic, predogmatic, and apologetic.[54]

The dogmatic function is, one might say, the least controversial of the three functions. Situated within dogmatic theology, this function has to do with "(i) confirming and explicating the natural knowledge of God as a biblical datum, (ii) assisting the systematic development of biblically based doctrine of God, and (iii) strengthening and augmenting the Christian's knowledge of God."[55] Related to the discussion of the dogmatic function is

---

50. Patrick Sherry, "The Religious Roots of Natural Theology," *New Blackfriars* 84, no. 988 (2003): 301.
51. Sherry, "Religious Roots of Natural Theology," 304, 306.
52. Sudduth, *Reformed Objection to Natural Theology*, 4. See also David Fergusson, "Types of Natural Theology," in *The Evolution of Rationality: Interdisciplinary Essays in Honor of J. Wentzel van Huyssteen*, ed. F. LeRon Shults (Eerdmans, 2006), 380–93; Evans, *Natural Signs*, 10.
53. Sudduth, *Reformed Objection to Natural Theology*, 4.
54. Sudduth, *Reformed Objection to Natural Theology*, 53.
55. Sudduth, *Reformed Objection to Natural Theology*, 53.

Alvin Plantinga's claim that while "the believer does not need natural theology in order to achieve rationality or epistemic propriety in believing,"[56] "there *are* good theistic arguments—at least two dozen or so."[57] You might say that for Plantinga natural theology is *nice but not necessary* with reference to the rationality of religious belief.

More controversial is the predogmatic function, and this is because of its perceived independence from dogmatic theology. Natural theology in this sense is the rational foundation for dogmatic theology. Reason is thus elevated in relation to faith. The apologetic function, on the other hand, has to do with "[defending] theism against the objections of atheists and agnostics."[58] So whereas the predogmatic function plays offense in the establishing of faith, the apologetic function plays defense against faith's detractors.[59]

Turning from opposition to function is a particularly Protestant proclivity, one rooted in a need to account for the fall and, more specifically, total depravity. Some have argued that this is the dividing line between Protestants and Roman Catholics on this issue.[60] In any case, the function of a particular natural theology will be related to (or better yet, controlled by) one's doctrine of sin or, put positively, some construal of nature and grace.

All this being said, I realize that introducing the beginner to a concept by problematizing its definition may well confuse rather than disabuse, but just as learning the basics of biblical Greek requires the student to work through "the fog" of case endings and so forth, understanding natural theology requires an awareness of the aforementioned key considerations.[61] And just

---

56. Alvin Plantinga, "Reason and Belief in God," in *Faith and Rationality: Reason and Belief in God*, ed. Alvin Plantinga and Nicholas Wolterstorff (University of Notre Dame Press, 1983), 65.

57. Alvin Plantinga, "Appendix: Two Dozen (Or So) Theistic Arguments," in *Alvin Plantinga*, ed. Deane-Peter Baker (Cambridge University Press, 2007), 203. See also Jerry L. Walls and Trent Dougherty, eds. *Two Dozen (Or So) Arguments for God: The Plantinga Project* (Oxford University Press, 2018).

58. Sudduth, *Reformed Objection to Natural Theology*, 53.

59. I have avoided the language of *positive* and *negative* (despite Sudduth's use of *positive* with reference to the predogmatic function) to avoid confusion with positive and negative apologetics, both of which would fall under Sudduth's apologetic function. For discussion of these two varieties of apologetics, see Michael J. Murray, "Reason for Hope (in a Postmodern World)," in *Reason for the Hope Within*, ed. Michael J. Murray (Eerdmans, 1999), 15.

60. See, e.g., Thomas Woolford, "Natural Theology and Natural Philosophy in the Late Renaissance" (DPhil diss., Trinity College, University of Cambridge, 2011), 85–149.

61. William D. Mounce, *Basics of Biblical Greek*, 3rd ed. (Zondervan Academic, 2009), 39, 69.

as the student of biblical Greek, after having spent time in their grammar, can make some sense of a text in the Greek New Testament, the student of natural theology will, after having familiarized themselves with these key considerations—what might be called "the grammar" of natural theology—be able to make some sense of a text discussing natural theology. But an important question remains: If there is, in an important sense, no such thing as natural theology and instead a wide range of natural theologies, how are we to proceed?

The Challenge of Definition

Responding to what David Fergusson has referred to as "the elasticity of the concept of natural theology,"[62] it seems we might proceed in one of five ways: (1) ignore the diversity, (2) embrace the diversity, (3) replace the designation, (4) replace the definition, or (5) define the term by a taxonomy of various types. The first response treats natural theology univocally, that is, as if it had only one, unambiguous meaning. Here, the American philosophers William Lane Craig and J. P. Moreland are representative, and their approach is characteristically analytic.[63] But surely there is more to natural theology than the natural theology of analytic philosophy, and we need look no further than *The Oxford Handbook of Natural Theology* to confirm this suspicion. There, the philosopher of religion Russell Re Manning explains that "one of the primary aims of this *Handbook* [is] to highlight the rich diversity of approaches to, and definitions of, natural theology."[64] Thirty-eight chapters follow, each one highlighting a different approach (or series of approaches). Embracing the diversity is certainly superior to ignoring the same, for at the very least it acknowledges the reality of a wide variety of definitions. Nevertheless, Re Manning's equivocal conclusion leaves us hanging. Do we not still ask: What is natural theology?

---

62. Fergusson, "Types of Natural Theology," 389n19.
63. William Lane Craig and J. P. Moreland, introduction to *The Blackwell Companion to Natural Theology* (Blackwell, 2009), ix–xii.
64. Re Manning, introduction to *Oxford Handbook of Natural Theology*, 1. See also Eugene Thomas Long, introduction to *Prospects for Natural Theology*, ed. Eugene Thomas Long, Studies in Philosophy and the History of Philosophy 25 (Catholic University of America Press, 1992), 22.

For some, the plurality of designations cannot be ignored with Craig and Moreland, nor embraced with Re Manning. One example of this third approach is Begbie, who wants to replace the designation.[65] While I understand the impulse, this approach is fraught with problems. To name but one, that the term *natural theology* might "smuggle in . . . questionable characteristics . . . or . . . particular assumptions" may be so, but so too does Begbie's suggested "one responsibility of a theology of creation," elsewhere "'natural theology' (appropriately conceived),"[66] as well as the other he mentions: Colin Gunton's "theology of nature" or Eberhard Jüngel's "*more* natural theology." If Craig and Moreland's approach is univocal, and Re Manning's equivocal, then Begbie's might be described as dialectical or self-mediating.[67] It is a reintegration of the other from the side of the same. The song remains the same, so to speak. Natural theology has been subsumed. This is natural theology as Christology or, in other words, natural theology with each of these new descriptors supposedly read in the light of explicitly Christian belief. But this is sleight of hand.

A fourth way maintains the designation "natural theology," but replaces its definition and, having done so, it more or less reverts to the first, univocal approach. Along these lines, the Northern Irish theologian and Anglican priest Alister E. McGrath comments:

> The notion of "natural theology" has proved so conceptually fluid, resistant to precise definition, that its critics can easily present it as a subversion of divine revelation, and its supporters, with equal ease, as its obvious outcome. Instead of perpetuating this unsatisfactory situation, there is much . to be said for beginning all over again, in effect setting aside past definitions, preconceptions, judgments, and prejudices, in order to allow a fresh examination of this fascinating and significant notion.[68]

---

65. Begbie, "Natural Theology and Music," 573–74. See also Eberhard Jüngel, *Christ, Justice and Peace*, 26–27. Begbie reiterates the point in Begbie, *Music, Modernity, and God*, 94.

66. Begbie, "Natural Theology and Music," 579.

67. For additional discussion of these responses to otherness, see William Desmond, *Desire, Dialectic, and Otherness: An Essay on Origins*, 2nd ed. (Cascade, 2014), 7–12.

68. McGrath, *Open Secret*, 3. It should be noted that McGrath does, in addition to replacing the definition, replace the designation (4). More recently still, McGrath has identified six approaches in his *Re-Imagining Nature: The Promise of a Christian Natural Theology* (Wiley-Blackwell, 2017), 18–22.

The strengths of this approach is that it acknowledges the plurality of definitions, but as previously mentioned there is the danger of reverting to the first, univocal approach once a satisfactory definition has been set forth, and this definition will no doubt be subject to the same criticisms that McGrath levels at previous definitions.

A fifth option is to group together and describe a wide variety of approaches with some system of classification. The earliest example of a taxonomy of natural theology that I have come across is that of J. V. Langmead Casserley: (1) natural theology as a natural, Godward tendency; (2) natural theology as argument; (3) natural theology as theology of nature; and (4) natural theology as analogy (à la Joseph Butler). To cite another, more recent example, John Macquarrie (1919–2007) distinguished between old-style and new-style natural theology, the latter being "more fundamental in going to the very sources of religious conviction, that it is descriptive in its method rather than deductive, and that it is existential rather than rational."[69] That said, according to Macquarrie, this new-style-natural theology "will perform the same basic function as the old natural theology. It will provide a bridge between our everyday thinking and experience and the matters about which the theologian talks: it will relate religious discourse to all the other areas of discourse."[70] More recently, Fergusson has identified five types of natural theology in terms of function.[71] These functions are as follows: foundational (or type 1, à la John Locke), deistic (or type 2, à la Matthew Tindal), one "that reflects the divinely bestowed powers of reason" (or type 3, à la Thomas Aquinas), apologetic (or type 4), and the closely related "vocation of attesting that Christian faith can coexist with the best insights from other fields of knowledge" (or type 5, à la Edward Farley).[72] In addition to these five types, Fergusson mentions two more: a "variant" of type 3, "which we might call 3b," the "*praeparatio evangelii*,"[73] and a more or less Barthian approach of

---

69. John Macquarrie, *Principles of Christian Theology*, rev. ed. (SCM, 1977), 57. For a recent attempt along these lines, see Guy Bennett-Hunter, *Ineffability and Religious Experience*, Pickering Studies in Philosophy of Religion (Pickering & Chatto, 2014).

70. Macquarrie, *Principles of Christian Theology*, 57.

71. Fergusson, "Types of Natural Theology," 384.

72. Fergusson, "Types of Natural Theology," 388. The examples given (e.g., Aquinas) are from Fergusson.

73. Fergusson, "Types of Natural Theology," 387.

"witness."[74] All of this being said, advocates of these types recall the parable of the blind men and the elephant, each one feeling a different part of the elephant and mistaking it for the whole. But what is the whole? What, in other words, is natural theology?

The Book Itself

As the reader will by now have realized, answering this question "What is natural theology?" is difficult because understanding natural theology entails a host of related conversations ranging from the Bible, biblical criticism, and the exegesis of particular texts to questions of metaphysics and theological language, theological method, and the evolution of the meaning of words. To appropriate a comment from George Pattison: "It is only on the basis of what will often be difficult interpretive work that we will know what we are doing when we say Yes or No . . . by which point a simple Yes or No may no longer be the most interesting thing to say."[75] Given the complex narrative of natural theology's developing tradition as well as the key considerations discussed above, it seems most prudent, after having rejected a more selective, inaccurate, and untrue version of the tale of natural theology's truncation and disintegration, to proceed by considering various types of natural theology governed by the previously discussed key considerations—including, but not limited to, one's definition of nature, that to which nature and the natural are opposed, and function—with reference to particular individuals and their natural theologies. It is my hope that by focusing on the understanding of the term in the writings of specific individuals, readers will find it much easier to comprehend the kind of substantial issues that are raised, whatever kind of definition one adopts.

What follows is akin to a master verb chart, and although it is not comprehensive, it nevertheless begins to fulfill—in a manner sufficient for introduction—what I have previously called the "Descriptive Responsibility," in that it seeks a greater degree of clarity in describing these various types

---

74. Fergusson, "Types of Natural Theology," 393.

75. George Pattison, *God and Being: An Enquiry* (Oxford University Press, 2011), 7–8. Pattison is, to be clear, in this passage discussing one's response to Heidegger's thesis, but the logic applies equally here.

of natural theology. The advantage of this clarification is that one can then explore the corresponding "Prescriptive Possibility." One or more types may be a dead end for any number of reasons, but as Sudduth has pointed out, there is a difference between a "project objection" that applies to all types of natural theology and a "model-specific objection" that applies to only one type or, I might add (following Desmond), to only one configuration of that one type. The bottom line is that more specificity is needed when discussing natural theology—whether for or against—to avoid confusion of one particular version of natural theology with another or one particular version of natural theology for the so-called whole.

THE TYPES

I begin with natural theology as natural religion (NT1), which stands at the opposite end of the spectrum from natural theology as theology of nature (NT5). While it would of course be helpful to identify poles at each extreme—such as religion/theology, nature/grace, reason/revelation, antecedent/consequent, incarnational/christological, immanent/transcendent, inclusivist/exclusivist, continuity/discontinuity (i.e., with reference to general/special revelation)—any such identification would be contested by one or more of the type's proponents. To give one example, while some might think Barth's view of the relationship between nature and grace is discontinuous and so characterize NT5 along these lines, the American theologian Keith L. Johnson has argued that, for Barth, "a relationship of continuity exists between nature and grace, but he believes that it is an *unveiled* continuity that can be known only retrospectively in the light of knowledge of the saving work of Jesus Christ on the cross."[76] That is to say, in consequent perspective, continuous. But, one could ask, what is a *veiled* continuity in antecedent perspective? Is the answer not discontinuous? I would say so (and in so doing, disagree with Johnson), and if this is the case, is this not an attempt to have one's cake and eat it too? And would this not contrast with David Brown and others for whom there is, at the very least, *more* continuity? In any case, the reader would do well to bear these various poles in mind as

---

76. Keith L. Johnson, "When Nature Presupposes Grace: A Response to Thomas Joseph White, O.P.," *Pro Ecclesia* 20 (2011): 280.

	Description	Representative Figure(s)
NT1	Natural Theology Informed by Natural Religion	David Brown
NT2	Natural Theology as Proof/Argument	Richard Swinburne, Alvin Plantinga
NT3	Natural Theology as Signals of Transcendence	C. Stephen Evans
NT4	Natural Theology as *Christian* Natural Theology	Alister McGrath, Anthony Monti
NT5	Natural Theology as Theology of Nature	Karl Barth

they, together with the previously mentioned key considerations, function like soundboard controls that can be adjusted or nuanced for a very different result. And now, without further ado, these are the five types.[77]

NT1: Natural Theology Informed by Natural Religion

The first type of natural theology is the one most closely associated with natural religion (as natural human religiousness).[78] Drawing upon the Greeks, Enlightenment thinkers known as the deists argued not only for the sufficiency but also the superiority of natural religion as well as the corresponding superfluousness of revealed religion. Against deism, David Brown has advocated for a *transformed* natural religion, one less concerned with proofs or arguments than with revelatory, religious experience understood along sacramental lines. I will have more to say about Brown's project in chapter 2, but the important point here is that, for Brown, "revealed religion builds on natural religion rather than wholly subverts it."[79] Unlike the deists, Brown thinks revealed religion and theology legitimate, but unlike Barth (NT5) Brown thinks religion, and natural religion in particular, are relevant to the Christian theologian's task as well as a constituent part of religious practice, theology, and faith.

---

77. It should be noted, however, that as H. Richard Niebuhr pointed out with reference to his own taxonomy of Christ and culture, "we are always left with a large number of examples of mixture." H. Richard Niebuhr, *Christ and Culture* (HarperSanFrancisco, 1951), 116.

78. Like natural theology, natural religion can be understood in a variety of ways. For further discussion, see Peter Byrne, *Natural Religion and the Nature of Religion: The Legacy of Deism* (Routledge, 1989), 1–10, 8–10 in particular.

79. David Brown, *God and Mystery in Words*, 1.

NT2: Natural Theology as Proof/Argument

As with NT1, proponents of NT2 highlight the preparatory function of natural theology. Pope Leo XIII, for example, wrote in an 1879 encyclical that "philosophy, if rightly made use of by the wise, in a certain way tends to smooth and fortify the road to true faith, and to prepare the souls of its disciples for the fit reception of revelation; for which reason it is well called by ancient writers sometimes a steppingstone to the Christian faith, sometimes the prelude and help of Christianity, sometimes the Gospel teacher."[80] The primary difference between NT1 and NT2 is that whereas someone like Brown focuses upon potentially revelatory, religious experience (i.e., natural religion),[81] proponents of NT2 are more likely to be interested in rational demonstrations of God's existence.[82] Sometimes called "proofs" and other times referred to (in more chastened language) as "arguments," "ways to God," or simply "ways," these demonstrations are, in either case, rooted in human reason and seek to defend, among other things, the coherence of theism. Perhaps the most well-known British proponent of this type is Brown's erstwhile colleague at Oriel College (Oxford), Richard Swinburne, who has argued: "If they are to believe, those others need to have explained to them what the theist's claims mean. They often doubt the coherence of these claims. If the religious man could show the claims to be coherent, he would remove a stumbling-block which stands in the way of the conversion of the unbeliever."[83] I will have more to say about Swinburne in chapter 3, but, in general, proponents of this type are committed to formal proofs or arguments, viewing natural theology as the removal of stumbling blocks or, more positively, a stepping stone along the path to faith.

---

80. See §4 of Leo XIII, *Aeterni Patris: Encyclical of Pope Leo XIII on the Restoration of Christian Philosophy*, http://w2.vatican.va/content/leo-xiii/en/encyclicals/documents/hf_l-xiii_enc_04081879 _aeterni-patris.html.
81. For discussion of "The Collapse of Theistic Arguments and the Appeal to Religious Experience," see Brown, *Divine Generosity and Human Creativity*, 26–29.
82. See R. Garrigou-Lagrange, *God: His Existence and Nature; A Thomistic Solution of Certain Agnostic Antinomies*, trans. Dom Bede Rose, 2 vols. (Herder, 1949). For a more recent defense and survey of this type, and the language of *proofs* in particular, see Matthew Levering, *Proofs of God: Classical Arguments from Tertullian to Barth* (Baker Academic, 2016), 3–7 (for defense), 7ff. (for survey).
83. Richard Swinburne, *The Coherence of Theism*, rev. ed. (Oxford University Press, 1993), 6.

NT3: Natural Theology as Signals of Transcendence

In some ways a combination of the previous types, this third type high-lights "signals of transcendence" and signs or experiences that lie at the core of the traditional arguments for the existence of God. Drawing upon Thomas Reid (1710–96), the American philosopher C. Stephen Evans, who is this type's chief contemporary proponent, explains: "The natural signs that point to God's reality are signs that can be interpreted in more than one way and thus are sometimes misread and sometimes not even perceived as signs. They point to God but do not do so in a coercive manner."[84] From this, Evans draws upon two Pascalian principles: wide accessibility and easy resistibility. Regarding the former, Evans wants to say that the knowledge of God is not restricted but widely available, and, regarding the latter, that despite the knowledge of God being unrestricted, it is not forced on people. Evans focuses upon the experience of cosmic wonder (cosmological), ben-eficial order (teleological), and moral accountability or the intrinsic worth of human beings (moral). More generally, he speaks of the enterprise of natural theology itself as "a sign that we should look for other sources of knowledge about God."[85]

NT4: Natural Theology as *Christian* Natural Theology

Proponents of NT4 typically read Barth through the Scottish theologian and Presbyterian minister T. F. Torrance (1913–2007), who argued that, accord-ing to Barth, "natural theology is included *within* revealed theology, where we have to do with actual knowledge of God as it is grounded in the intelligible relations in God himself."[86] Torrance argued that Barth's primary objection to the traditional type of natural theology was its independent character.[87] It was, in other words, a model-specific objection rather than a general project objection. This reading has rightly been contested by the American Catholic

---

84. Evans, *Natural Signs*, 2.
85. Evans, *Natural Signs*, 190.
86. T. F. Torrance, *The Ground and Grammar of Theology: Consonance Between Theology and Science* (T&T Clark, 2001), 91. For his use of "*Christian natural theology*," see p. 107.
87. Torrance, *Ground and Grammar of Theology*, 92. See also T. F. Torrance, "The Problem of Natural Theology in the Thought of Karl Barth," *Religious Studies* 6 (1970):121–35.

theologian Paul Molnar,[88] and for this reason, I have distinguished between NT4 and NT5. Contemporary proponents of NT4 include McGrath, whose "scientific theology" takes Torrance as its prolegomena,[89] as well as Anthony Monti, who explores natural theology with reference to the arts.[90] However, these Torrance-inspired readings of Barth are, as Fergusson has rightly noted, a "revision of Barth,"[91] and as such, are distinct from NT5.

NT5: Natural Theology as Theology of Nature

Following Barth, proponents of NT5 say "No!" to natural theology because "theology will really be theology . . . when from beginning to end it is Christology."[92] There is no room for so-called *natural* theology, for any such theology claims to know something impossible to know without God's revelation in Jesus Christ. That said, Barth maintained, in a well-known and much-discussed section of *Church Dogmatics*, that "important human words are spoken, bright lights are set up in the human sphere and great and little revelations occur."[93] However, this must be understood in context. As the American theologian George Hunsinger explains: "There is no way, Barth wants to say, from the words to the Word, but only from the Word to the words."[94] There is, from Barth's perspective, no such thing as natural theology. There is only theology, and by theology Barth means Christology.

Given Barth's rejection of natural theology, one might wonder why I have included him here as a proponent of NT5. I answer, with reference to Barth, that natural theology "appear[s] necessarily . . . at the edge of theology as its

---

88. Paul D. Molnar, "Natural Theology Revisited: A Comparison of T. F. Torrance and Karl Barth," *Zeitschrift für Dialektische Theologie* 21 (2005): 53 83; cf. W. Travis McMaken, "The Impossibility of Natural Knowledge of God in T. F. Torrance's Reformulated Natural Theology," *International Journal of Systematic Theology* 12 (2010): 319–40.

89. For discussion of the connection with Torrance, see Benjamin Myers, "Alister McGrath's Scientific Theology," in Alister E. McGrath, *The Order of Things: Explorations in Scientific Theology* (Blackwell, 2006), 2–3.

90. Anthony Monti, *A Natural Theology of the Arts: Imprint of the Spirit* (Ashgate, 2003); Begbie, "Natural Theology and Music," 566–80; Begbie, *Music, Modernity, and God*, 73–105.

91. Fergusson, "Types of Natural Theology," 393n27.

92. Karl Barth, "Fate and Idea in Theology," in *The Way of Theology in Karl Barth: Essays and Comments*, trans. by George Hunsinger, ed. H. Martin Rumscheidt (Pickwick, 1986), 60.

93. Barth, *Church Dogmatics* IV/3.1, 97.

94. George Hunsinger, *How to Read Karl Barth: The Shape of His Theology* (Oxford University Press, 1991), 257. See also Jüngel, *Christ, Justice and Peace*, 27–29.

necessary limit."[95] But if that is the case, then surely the reverse is also true. Theology appears at the edge of natural theology, and so whether Barth's project is theology, as he would have it, or natural theology, as the Scottish Old Testament scholar James Barr (1924–2006) and Brown would have it, Barth might be placed at the edge of the spectrum as I have proposed. Having now described each of the five types in overview, I turn from the "Descriptive Responsibility" to the "Prescriptive Possibility."

The Prescriptive Possibility

Consideration of the wide range of natural theologies leads from description to prescription, for having explored and described the various types of natural theology, possibilities are discovered as opportunities that invite further reflection. The critiques of natural theology, whether philosophical or theological, do not apply to every type (past, present, or future). That being said, the project of natural theology need not be abandoned, even if some or most of the models are left behind. Like theology, natural theology is an ever-renewing, developing tradition, and so the time is always ripe for reconfiguration in response to the culture in which we find ourselves. I mentioned Evans's argument for wide accessibility and easy resistibility. I would add a third principle: persistent possibility.[96]

I suspect that, in our increasingly secular society, the task facing the natural theologian has less to do with rational demonstrations of the credibility of theistic belief—as important as these may be—and more to do with confronting a widespread failure of imagination. Belief no longer seems plausible, whether individuals or societies are in view. We are, in many cases, *beyond* belief, and this because of the collapse of what Peter Berger has called "the plausibility structure for a religiously legitimated world."[97] I will have more

---

95. Barth, "No!," 76.

96. Evans acknowledges this possibility in an earlier work. See Evans and Manis, *Philosophy of Religion*, 62.

97. Berger, *Sacred Canopy*, 48. It should be noted that I am not here arguing for the "secularization thesis" but instead noting, with reference to the phenomenology of faith, that belief versus unbelief is now a daily decision, what the poet Christian Wiman has described as a "vertiginous inward to-and-fro with God." See Christian Wiman, *My Bright Abyss: Meditation of a Modern Believer* (Farrer, Straus & Giroux, 2013), 27–28.

to say about this in the epilogue, but anticipating my discussion there I will argue that the categories of predogmatic and dogmatic natural theology are no longer sufficient. What is needed, in addition to these, is natural theology as *postdogmatic recovery*, but I am getting ahead of myself. Description comes before prescription.

PART 1

Natural Religion

CHAPTER 1

Natural Theology Informed by Natural Religion

In present theological conditions, one who is called upon to discourse concerning "natural religion as it is commonly called and understood by divines and learned men" finds himself embarrassed at the outset by the difficulty of defining his subject in accordance with the requirement.[1]

—W. W. Fenn

The idea of natural religion is one of those arresting ideas which never get fully defined but which nevertheless excite reflection and even controversy when they appear. . . . Natural religion has been appealed to as a touchstone of rationality and it has been attacked as illegitimate if not actually blasphemous. An idea capable of producing such reactions cannot be ignored.[2]

—John E. Smith

Like natural theology, natural religion is tough to define once and for all. In some cases, natural theology and natural religion are used

---

1. W.W. Fenn, "Concerning Natural Religion," *Harvard Theological Review* 4 (1911): 460.
2. John E. Smith, "The Permanent Truth in the Idea of Natural Religion: The Dudleian Lecture for 1960," *Harvard Theological Review* 54 (1961): 1.

interchangeably—as in *The Stanford Encyclopedia of Philosophy*[3]—and while they are no doubt closely related, they are by no means equivalent in meaning. Using natural theology and natural religion interchangeably further confuses what are already two hard-to-pin-down concepts. After distinguishing between these two concepts in the first part of this chapter, I will then discuss one particular variety of natural theology: *natural theology informed by natural religion* (NT1). This type of natural theology is, of the five types discussed, most closely allied with the concept of natural religion. Finally, in the chapter's third part I discuss the most prominent critic of this type: Karl Barth.

Natural Religion and Natural Theology

As Wilde Lecturer in Natural and Comparative Religion, the English theologian and philosopher Clement C. J. Webb (1865–1954) suggested that "we may . . . take it as agreed that Natural Theology must stand in the closest possible relation to Natural Religion; that it must denote the reasoned and articulated account of what is implied in the existence of natural religion."[4] While it would be easy to read Webb as saying that natural religion and natural theology are one and the same, that is not the case. Two things are actually being said: First, natural theology and natural religion are closely related but distinct, for only distinct entities can be in relation. Second, natural theology is reasoned and explicit rather than implicit like natural religion.

The Scottish philosopher Edward Caird (1835–1908) argued similarly in his Gifford Lectures delivered at the University of Glasgow. His first lecture was explicitly concerned with "The Relation of Religion to Theology."[5] He claims:

---

3. Andrew Chignell and Derk Pereboom, "Natural Theology and Natural Religion," *The Stanford Encyclopedia of Philosophy*, last revised March 18, 2025, https://plato.stanford.edu/entries/natural -theology/. See also Peter Byrne, *Natural Religion and the Nature of Religion: The Legacy of Deism* (Routledge, 1989), 1. Byrne describes natural religion and natural theology as "allied," suggesting recognition of distinction with relation, but then—in his fourfold taxonomy of the concept of natural religion—refers to "natural religion (theology)" and for the most part uses the terms interchangeably.

4. Clement C. J. Webb, *Studies in the History of Natural Theology* (Clarendon, 1915), 1.

5. Edward Caird, *The Evolution of Theology in the Greek Philosophers: The Gifford Lectures Delivered in the University of Glasgow in Sessions 1900–1 and 1901–2*, vol. 1 (MacLehose, 1904), 1–30. The

Theology is not religion; it is at best philosophy of religion, the reflective reproduction and explanation of it; and, as such, it is the product of a time that has outgrown simple faith and begun to feel the necessity of understanding what it believes. Early religion does not trouble itself about its own justification: it does not even seek to make itself intelligible. It manifests itself in a ritual rather than a creed.[6]

Religion, according to Caird, has to do with ritual and theology with reflection. Natural religion, he continues, "is intuitive rather than reflective, practical rather than speculative, conscious rather than self-conscious."[7] At work here is the idea that religion and theology have evolved from faith to reason and, related to this, that religions tend to move from the local and particular to the universal (e.g., from Israel to the world). Regardless of whether one accepts this evolutionary account of religion, what is clear is that religion and theology are related but distinct concepts. The two should not be confused or used interchangeably, for that would be to mistake relation for identity.[8] That said, we need to get a better sense of natural religion in its historical context before discussing NT1.

Rather than attempting to give a comprehensive overview of the various types of natural religion—a task well beyond the scope of this book—I will focus upon one particular type: natural religion as natural human religiousness,[9] and more specifically the early modern articulation of natural religion as not only original but also sufficient apart from revealed religion. From this perspective, revealed religion is a corruption of natural religion and is ultimately superfluous. This was the view taken by thinkers collectively referred to as the deists. Deism is, like natural theology and natural religion,

---

Gifford Lectures are a significant source for natural theology because, as Stanley L. Jaki has observed, "The philosophy known as natural theology received a quasi-institutional forum in the Gifford Lectureship." Stanley L. Jaki, *Lord Gifford and His Lectures: A Centenary Retrospect* (Scottish Academic Press, 1986), 37.

6. Jaki, *Lord Gifford and His Lectures*, 3.
7. Jaki, *Lord Gifford and His Lectures*, 3.
8. For additional discussion, see Wolfhart Pannenberg, *Systematic Theology*, vol. 1 (Eerdmans, 1988), 95.
9. Byrne identifies four senses of natural religion (theology), and natural human religiousness is Byrne's fourth type. For discussion of this type, see Byrne, *Natural Religion*, 8–10. For discussion of this type with reference to the cognitive science of religion, see Helen De Cruz and Johan De Smedt, *A Natural History of Natural Theology: The Cognitive Science of Theology and Philosophy of Religion* (MIT Press, 2015), chapter 2 in particular.

difficult to define, but rather than enter into that debate here, I will for the sake of introduction accept Peter Harrison's succinct description of deism as "the extreme manifestation of the rationalising tendency within the thought of seventeenth- and early eighteenth-century England."[10] Going further, he writes: "This desire to demonstrate the reasonableness of religion becomes deism when doubt is cast upon the adequacy of revelation as a medium of religious truth."[11] Responding to the "scandal of particularity,"[12] Lord Herbert of Cherbury (1583–1648),[13] the so-called father of deism, argued that natural religion could be found in those notions common to the positive religions,[14] and also that natural religion could stand alongside these other religions—having "won its freedom"[15]—as itself another legitimate religious option. This reason-driven, lowest common denominator approach was, to Herbert's way of thinking, the only path to "true religion."

Taking a slightly different approach, the deists who came after Herbert— Charles Blount (1654–93) for example—argued that it was the church's priests who had corrupted the original, natural religion,[16] and so, as Harrison explains, they "bent their efforts not towards establishing the universality of any set of beliefs, but rather the universality of priestcraft."[17] According to these deists, natural religion had been corrupted by priestly deception, result- ing in an unnatural religious pluralism that included Judaism, Christianity,

---

10. Peter Harrison, *"Religion" and the Religions in the English Enlightenment* (Cambridge University Press, 1990), 62; cf. S. J. Barnett, *The Enlightenment and Religion: The Myths of Modernity* (Manchester University Press, 2003), 11–44.

11. Harrison, *Religions in the English Enlightenment*, 62.

12. This is the idea that endorsing specific religions as alone salvific seemed to that age to result in a very unjust God, arbitrarily sending millions to hell through no fault of their own.

13. See, for biographical details, Edward Herbert, *The Autobiography of Edward, Lord Herbert of Cherbury: With Introduction, Notes, Appendices, and a Continuation of the Life*, ed. Sidney L. Lee (Nimmo, 1886; repr., Cambridge University Press, 2013). For additional discussion of Herbert, see Webb, *History of Natural Theology*, 344–58; Harrison, *Religions in the English Enlightenment*, 61–73.

14. For discussion of Herbert's "five common notions," see Harrison, *Religions in the English Enlightenment*, 65–73.

15. Webb, *History of Natural Theology*, 358.

16. The same might be said more recently with even Pope John Paul II being accused of ignoring the problem (in the case of Theodore E. McGarrick). See John Horowitz, "Vatican Report Places Blame for McCarrick's Ascent on John Paul II," *The New York Times*, November 10, 2020, https://www .nytimes.com/2020/11/10/world/europe/theodore-mccarrick-vatican.html. One might just as easily mention Protestants such as Carl Lentz, the former pastor of Hillsong Church in New York.

17. Harrison, *Religions in the English Enlightenment*, 73.

and Islam. These irrational interlopers were, not surprisingly, deemed super-fluous. Here again, the deists called for a return to the more primitive and original natural religion.[18]

Against the deists, Joseph Butler (1696–1752) argued that revealed religion was not corruption but rather a clarification of and supplement to natural religion.[19] In *The Analogy of Religion* (1736), Butler maintained that the difficulties associated with revealed religion had analogies in nature and were therefore no reason for rejecting the former in favor of the latter. He begins with probability rather than proof, famously suggesting that "probability is the very guide of life."[20] This leads to discussion of analogy as an argument along these lines, with Butler summarizing the argument of the book as follows:

> The design then of the following Treatise will be to show, that the several parts principally objected against in this moral and Christian dispensation, including its scheme, its publication, and the proof which God has afforded us of its truth; that the particular parts principally objected against in this whole dispensation, are analogous to what is experienced in the constitution and course of nature, or Providence; that the chief objections themselves which are alleged against the former, are no other than what may be alleged with like justness against the latter, where they are found in fact to be inconclusive; and that this argument from analogy is in general unanswerable, and undoubtedly of weight on the side of religion, notwithstanding the objections which may seem to lie against it, and the real ground which there may be for difference of opinion, as to the particular degree of weight which is to be laid upon it.[21]

---

18. J. V. Langmead Casserley provides a more sympathetic response that I think correct. He writes: "Thus the rather superficial lapse of the eighteenth-century deists and unitarians, and nineteenth-century romantics, into natural religion is at least to some extent explained and excused by the extraordinary tendency of a good many post-Reformation—and also post-Counter-Reformation—worthies to interpret and present the Christian faith as a frankly unnatural religion." J. V. Langmead Casserley, *The Retreat from Christianity in the Modern World* (Longmans, Green, 1952), 52.

19. For additional detail, see David Brown, "Butler, Joseph," in *The SPCK Handbook of Anglican Theologians*, ed. Alister E. McGrath (SPCK, 1998), 99–102.

20. Joseph Butler, *The Analogy of Religion: Natural and Revealed to the Constitution and Course of Nature*, ed. W. E. Gladstone, Butler's Works 1 (Clarendon, 1896), 5.

21. Butler, *Analogy of Religion*, 18.

Revealed religion is, in other words, analogous to natural religion, insofar as the chief objections levied by the deists against the former apply also to the latter. If the deists reject revealed religion, says Butler, then they must also reject natural religion. The argument against revealed religion is, therefore, inconclusive. According to Butler, natural religion anticipates revealed religion, and revealed religion builds upon and completes natural religion.[22] They are not exclusive but complementary. Natural reason has its place, but revealed religion can teach us something new.[23]

Having now briefly discussed this particular variety of natural religion (i.e., natural human religiousness) in its historical context—Butler and the deists being seen as two sides of the same coin, insofar as both acknowledge the reality and role of natural religion—I now turn to the first of the five types of natural theology.

Natural Theology Informed by Natural Religion (NT1)

This first type of natural theology is the one most closely associated with natural religion. This almost goes without saying, but natural theologies of this type acknowledge the reality and role of (and are in this sense informed by) natural religion, which is just another way of saying that they ascribe a central role to reason and take religious experience seriously. As John E. Smith (1921–2009) argued in his 1960 Dudleian Lecture:

> In supposing that man could answer the religious question and complete
> the religious quest merely through the exercise of his reason, the advocates
> of natural religion went too far. But in their demand that religious truth be

---

22. According to John Henry Cardinal Newman, "The distinction between natural religion and revealed lies in this, that one has a subjective authority, and the other an objective. . . . Thus, what conscience is in the system of nature, such is the voice of Scripture, or of the Church, or of the Holy See, as we may determine it, in the system of Revelation." John Henry Cardinal Newman, *An Essay on the Development of Christian Doctrine*, 6th ed. (University of Notre Dame Press, 1989), 86. In the spirit of Butler, William J. Abraham writes: "Special revelation, rather than cancelling nature, corrects and enriches it." See William J. Abraham, *Crossing the Threshold of Divine Revelation* (Eerdmans, 2006), 106.

23. For an assessment of Butler's arguments with reference to contemporary deism, see David Brown, "Butler and Deism," in *Joseph Butler 1692–1752: Philosopher, Theologian, and Pastor*, ed. Christopher Cunliffe (Oxford University Press, 1992), 7–28.

intelligible, they saw that if the unity and integrity of the human self is to be preserved, *the doctrines of religion cannot be left in a sphere totally foreign to human reason and general experience.* We cannot be religious animals by parts and we cannot seal off the knowledge we gain from our participation in general experience from religious truths which we receive through an historical tradition. The two must interpret each other.[24]

For proponents of NT1, there is no interpretation without experience, no theology without religion.[25] It is clear that these proponents view (natural) religion and theology as distinct but intimately related, and though, as Smith admits, "the advocates of natural religion went too far," they maintain that human reason and religious experience cannot be neglected.

Since the church fathers, theologians have described revelation using the metaphor of "the two books": the book of nature (i.e., God's works) and the book of Scripture (i.e., God's words).[26] These complementary sources are two texts that can be "read" with knowledge of God as the result. The notions of general revelation and special revelation correspond to these two books, with natural religion drawing upon the former and revealed (i.e., historical) religion drawing upon the latter. Proponents of NT5 reject the metaphor because they reject the notion of general revelation.[27] Proponents of NT1, however, see the natural world as a place where, as David Brown puts it, "God can be encountered, and encountered often."[28] This is because, as Brown explains elsewhere, "grace is intrinsic to the creation itself as part of the divine generosity that defines God as goodness itself."[29] Given this understanding of

---

24. Smith, "Permanent Truth," 9 (italics mine).

25. See, e.g., Charles E. Raven, *Natural Religion and Christian Theology: The Gifford Lectures 1951*, First Series: Science and Religion (Cambridge University Press, 1953), 17–18.

26. After the descriptive challenge, I think this the greatest challenge facing natural theology today. Turning from description to prescription, I think natural theology needs a new metaphor and, along these lines, would prefer to draw upon Gérard Genette to extend the metaphor and speak of natural theology as a "paratext"—and so paratextual theology—that precedes, accompanies, and mediates the text of Scripture. See Gérard Genette, *Paratexts: Thresholds of Interpretation*, trans. Jane E. Lewin (Cambridge University Press, 1997).

27. For discussion of Barth's rejection, see G. C. Berkouwer, *General Revelation* (Eerdmans, 1955), 21–33.

28. David Brown, *God and Enchantment of Place: Reclaiming Human Experience* (Oxford University Press, 2004), 9.

29. David Brown, *God in a Single Vision: Integrating Philosophy and Theology*, ed. Christopher R. Brewer and Robert MacSwain (Routledge, 2016), 15.

nature, proponents of NT1 tend to emphasize continuity rather than discontinuity between natural and revealed theology.[30] Any attempt to do away with natural religion disrupts the whole.[31] For Charles E. Raven (1885–1964), the separation of theology from religion is the symptom of a theological illness, to wit, the separation of God from the realm of everyday experience. According to Smith, this separation "shows impiety toward the divine creation."[32] To neglect reason and religious experience is, according to these proponents of NT1, to run the risk of heresy, impiety, and ultimately, irrelevance.

Moving on from nature (and that to which it is opposed) to the third of the three key considerations, NT1's function has less to do with proof than it does with probability (à la Butler) or possibility. As Macquarrie explains:

> The basic function of natural theology may be something quite different from devising a watertight proof, and the fact that our traditional natural theology has been formulated in terms of logical demonstration may be due only to the operation of certain historical and cultural factors in the West. We could say that the function of natural theology was to provide a *connection* between our ordinary everyday discourse about the world or even our scientific discourse on the one side, and theological discourse on the other.[33]

Natural theology along these lines is more like criticism, a reasoned consideration of everyday experience that involves study, interpretation, and evaluation.[34] More than theological cultural analysis, NT1 acknowledges the reality and role of natural religion, an experience that requires interpretation. It is to some extent an exercise in dot connecting but also has to do with world making.[35] Brown suggests that "it is a matter of favorable

---

30. See, e.g., John Macquarrie, *Thinking About God* (SCM, 1975), 136; John Macquarrie, *In Search of Deity: An Essay in Dialectical Theism* (SCM, 1984), 12–13.

31. See Raven, *Natural Religion*, 19–20. See also David Brown, *Invitation to Theology* (Blackwell, 1989), 31; Brown, *God in a Single Vision*, 3.

32. Smith, "Permanent Truth," 19.

33. Macquarrie, *Thinking About God*, 137 (italics mine). It should be noted that Macquarrie was no advocate of natural religion, but his new-style natural theology was, nevertheless, in many ways like what I am here describing as NT1.

34. For an excellent discussion of criticism (that highlights the need for evaluation) with reference to art, see Noël Carroll, *On Criticism* (Routledge, 2009).

35. Nelson Goodman, *Ways of Worldmaking* (Hackett, 1978).

conditions being set under which experience of the divine does at least become a realistic possibility."[36] For the sake of context, Brown believes "that the Church has made a number of serious errors in withdrawing from theological engagement with large areas of human experience that were once religion's concern."[37] This is related to Weber's notion of the disenchantment of the world, and the previously mentioned "favorable conditions," with recovery or reenchantment.

This dynamic has been described in numerous, analogous ways. For Paul Ricoeur (1913–2005), the movement is from a precritical "primitive naïveté" (i.e., received beliefs) to "criticism" and then to a postcritical "second naïveté."[38] The movement from "primitive naïveté" to "criticism" is one from faith to understanding, and the movement from "criticism" to "second naïveté" is a movement from understanding to faith. For Charles Taylor, "the conditions of belief" have shifted from "a society where belief in God is unchallenged and indeed, unproblematic, to one in which it is understood to be one option among others, and frequently not the easiest to embrace."[39] The movement here is from the enchanted world of "naïve understanding" to "disenchantment," from "the porous self" to "the buffered self," from transcendence to "the immanent frame."[40] For William Desmond, the movement is from "porosity" to a clogged "postulatory finitism," a closed system in which God is no longer an option. However it is expressed, the point is that proponents of NT1 acknowledge these conditions and see natural theology as stage building for the recovery of religion in a secular age.[41] Whether or not one espouses NT1, this preparatory (i.e., contextual) function, which extends beyond the individual to society as a whole, seems essential to the recovery of natural theology.

---

36. David Brown, *God and Grace of Body: Sacrament in Ordinary* (Oxford University Press, 2007), 293–94.

37. Brown, *God and Enchantment of Place*, 5.

38. Paul Ricoeur, *The Symbolism of Evil*, trans. Emerson Buchanan (Beacon, 1967), 349. See also Richard Kearney, "Ricoeur and Biblical Hermeneutics: On Post-Religious Faith," in *Ricoeur Across the Disciplines*, ed. Scott Davidson (Continuum, 2010), 30–43.

39. Charles Taylor, *A Secular Age* (Belknap, 2007), 3.

40. Taylor, *Secular Age*, 30, 539–93.

41. To be clear, I am not arguing that Ricoeur, Taylor, and Desmond are proponents of NT1 but instead that proponents of NT1 often accept some version of the enchantment/disenchantment/reenchantment narrative.

At this point, however, many Protestants ask, "What about sin?"[42] Is this not a limiting factor in the conversation of natural theology's function? Brown responds, rightly in my view:

> The doctrine of Original Sin applies to us all. For too long it has been used to yield selective negative verdicts only on what happens outside the Church. Indeed, despite the prominent position given to the Fall in the opening chapters of Genesis, it is salutary to remind ourselves of how seldom that story is subsequently alluded to later in Scripture and by contrast how often a positive verdict is recorded on the natural world as a mediator of divine knowledge.[43]

Going further, Macquarrie argues that "to hold that our intellect is so perverted that we just cannot think straight is to fall into a skepticism so bottomless that further discussion becomes pointless."[44] Of course sin is a factor, insofar as it may affect our ability to reason, but for proponents of NT1, reason is not opposed to revelation, and the function of natural theology reaches beyond condemnation.

In summary, NT1 prioritizes reason and takes religious experience seriously. Proponents seek to make connections between theology and the everyday, and this reaches beyond the walls of the church and even into other religions. Nature is graced, and God is everywhere available. There is continuity between natural and revealed theology, so much so that proponents of NT1 regularly question the distinction. Sin is a constant rather than a variable, and so it applies to us all, but it does not have the final word. The church and its theologians must reach beyond its walls, for as Howard E. Root writes: "The great problem of the Church (and therefore of its theologians) is to establish or re-establish some kind of vital contact with that enormous majority of human beings for whom Christian faith is not so much unlikely

---

42. For discussion, see Thomas Woolford, "Natural Theology and Natural Philosophy in the Late Renaissance" (DPhil thesis, Trinity College, University of Cambridge, 2011), 85–149.

43. David Brown, "Re-Conceiving the Sacramental," in *The Gestures of God: Explorations in Sacramentality*, ed. Geoffrey Rowell and Christine Hall (Continuum, 2004), 29.

44. John Macquarrie, *Principles of Christian Theology*, rev. ed. (SCM, 1977), 50. I am, on this point, with Macquarrie and Brown.

as irrelevant and uninteresting."[45] NT1 affirms religious experience, and not only because it might well be revelatory but also for the sake of relevance. Not as a reductive concession but in order to speak of things about which the church once had something to say and could once more. Reason. Religious experience. Relevance. These are key words for NT1, but according to Barth NT1 misses the point.

The Heresy of Natural Religion?

Natural religion is, according to Barth, a heresy, for it substitutes religion for revelation.[46] Barth explains: "The real catastrophe of modern Protestant theology was not as it has often been represented. . . . The real catastrophe was that theology lost its object, revelation in all its uniqueness. And losing that, it lost the seed of faith with which it could remove mountains, even the mountain of modern humanistic culture. That it really lost revelation is shown by the very fact that it could exchange it, and with it its own birthright, for the concept of 'religion.'"[47] Revelation and religion are, for Barth, distinct, and "concession to religionism"[48] is the end of faith or, as Barth dramatically states, "a war lost at the very outset."[49] Contrast this with Brown, who argues for the legitimacy of religion as revelation, which, lest one think Brown beyond the pale, is rooted in an incarnational logic.[50] I will have more to say about Brown's logic in chapter 2, but for Barth revelation has everything to do with Jesus Christ, or, some might prefer to say, a particular understanding of Jesus Christ. Theology is Christology, and so natural theology as natural religion, which, from Barth's perspective, seeks "an autonomous being and status over against revelation,"[51] is nonsensical. How does one learn of

45. Howard E. Root, "Beginning All over Again," in *Soundings: Essays Concerning Christian Understanding*, ed. A. R. Vidler (Cambridge University Press, 1962), 6.
46. See §17 in Barth, *Church Dogmatics* I/2, 280–361, 292 in particular. For discussion of various theologians critical of religion, see Macquarrie, *Principles of Christian Theology*, 157–61, 159–60 in particular (for discussion of Barth's view).
47. Barth, *Church Dogmatics* I/2, 294.
48. Barth, *Church Dogmatics* I/2, 295.
49. Barth, *Church Dogmatics* I/2, 294. Barth continues: "We always have to speak about revelation from the very outset if we really want to speak about it later and not about something quite different" (296).
50. See Brown, *Invitation to Theology*, 26–42, 28 in particular.
51. Barth, *Church Dogmatics* I/2, 294.

the true God revealed in Christ through that which has nothing to do with Christ and so, *ipso facto*, nothing to do with revelation? Barth's critique of natural theology flows from his rejection of the notion of autonomous religion. One cannot begin with religion and end with theology, for religion can, according to Barth, only be understood theologically.[52] Religion, in other words, can only be understood in light of "the christological doctrine of the *assumptio carnis*" (i.e. the assumption of flesh).[53] Responding to Barth and his ilk, Brown confesses:

> My own personal belief in the Incarnation is no less firm than theirs, but for that very reason I find their convictions strange. Could a God who involves himself with the world to the degree that is implied in this doctrine really abandon the world in every other respect? It is precisely for that reason that my Christianity demands belief in a God who expresses himself in other religions and also in secular culture, though obviously as a Christian I believe this only reaches its fullest expression in Christ.[54]

Clearly, the differences between NT1 and NT5 are significant and complex, but the primary difference between these two types has less to do with the incarnation or some supposed (and undefined) christological criterion than it does with rival conceptions of creation and their attendant notions of revelation. In any case, proponents of NT1 would want us to remember Macquarrie's warning that "even those who in the name of faith or revelation rebel against religion do not escape from it. They produce their own version of religion, and this can turn out to be more distorted than the version they have rejected."[55] Religion is an inescapable reality.

So there are those who, like the deists, thought natural religion to be the one and only true religion, and revealed religion to be corrupt and false; those who, like Butler, argued that revealed religion builds upon natural religion (which is true insofar as it goes); and those who, like Barth, thought so-called

---

52. Barth, *Church Dogmatics* I/2, 296–97.
53. Barth, *Church Dogmatics* I/2, 297.
54. Brown, *Invitation to Theology*, 28. For further discussion with reference to Judaism and Islam, see David Brown, *Tradition and Imagination: Revelation and Change* (Oxford University Press, 1999), 106–67.
55. Macquarrie, *Principles of Christian Theology*, 161.

natural religion idolatrous and false and only revealed religion to be true. For Brown, Barth failed to do justice to human experience. He writes: "Barth's great strength is his insistence that God as the transcendent Other should never be seen as subject to human manipulation, but his weakness in my view is his failure to engage adequately with the messiness of the world."[56] Wherever your sympathies may lie, the crux of the issue has been nicely outlined by Byrne, who explains:

> The more natural knowledge is played down, the more Christianity appears to be an abrupt intervention into human religious history. If no preparation for Christ's proclamation is allowed in the general history of thought, the more it appears to be a new and local disclosure and the more arbitrary and capricious the God behind it appears to be. Yet if its message is made more reasonable by being likened to ancient and long-known truths, it will seem far from unique. It will appear an unnecessary repetition of what the best minds have already taught.[57]

Like theology, natural theology didn't fall from the sky. It has been forged in history by the church and its theologians as an interpretation of experience. At its very heart, it has to do with (perceived) faithfulness to the gospel and Christian witness. In the next chapter I will focus upon Brown, a proponent of NT1 whose work embodies this claim.

---

56. David Brown, *Divine Generosity and Human Creativity: Theology Through Symbol, Painting and Architecture*, ed. Christopher R. Brewer and Robert MacSwain (Routledge, 2017), 16.
57. Byrne, *Natural Religion*, 12.

CHAPTER 2

Transforming Natural Religion: David Brown

Without some natural theology it is impossible to see why revelation should be of interest. It only becomes so when we see that there are certain questions posed by human experience to which it could possibly be the answer.[1]

—David Brown

In chapter 1, I described natural theology informed by natural religion (NT1), and in this chapter I will discuss one contemporary proponent of this type: the British theologian David Brown.[2] While some might think taxonomies to be artificial impositions and so view my use of "proponent" to describe Brown (as well as the other theologians discussed in the remaining even numbered chapters) with skepticism, Brown is explicit and thereby justifies my use of the word in this case with the following admission: "The exercise upon which I am engaged is in effect a form of what used to be called

---

1. David Brown, *Continental Philosophy and Modern Theology: An Engagement* (Blackwell, 1987), 13–14.
2. Full disclosure: Brown was my doctoral supervisor, and I was his last PhD student. He is also godfather to my two boys, John and Samuel, whose godmother was Ann Loades (1938–2022). For the details of Brown's biography, see my editor's introduction to *Christian Theology and the Transformation of Natural Religion: From Incarnation to Sacramentality; Essays in Honour of David Brown*, ed. Christopher R. Brewer (Peeters, 2018), 7–12. See also Christopher R. Brewer, "David W. Brown (1948–)," in *Twentieth Century Anglican Theologians: From Evelyn Underhill to Esther Mombo*, ed. Stephen Burns, Bryan Cones, and James Tengatenga (Wiley-Blackwell, 2021), 185–94.

natural religion."[3] This exercise has primarily taken the form of three books that "seek to expand and transform what used to be called natural religion."[4] More specifically, Brown is seeking to draw attention to a broad range of human experience once thought relevant by the church and its theologians. The tragedy, from Brown's point of view, is that the church has willfully abandoned this wider range of religious experience, leaving individuals with the void of nothing more than a spiritual-but-not-religious explanatory framework, the legitimacy of which the church then questions. The church has, in other words, artificially constricted the realm of what is theologically relevant, and then wonders why individuals choose their once-relevant experience over the church (to whom these individuals return the charge of irrelevance).

Brown's solution to this rather unfortunate situation is for the church and its theologians to readmit this experience by returning to earlier notions of sacramentality, extending beyond the now official Protestant two, or Roman Catholic seven, to the world at large. Giving some indication of the expansive nature of this theological vision, he writes:

> Sport, drama, humour, dance, architecture, place and home, the natural world are all part of a long list of activities and forms of experience that have been relegated to the periphery of religious reflection, but which once made invaluable contributions to a human perception that this world is where God can be encountered, and encountered often.[5]

This is, in a nutshell, Brown's notion of natural religion, but in order to understand the adjustments being made on Brown's theological soundboard I will begin with an overview of his thought followed by some discussion of the associated understanding of nature and also the other two key considerations. With this context in mind, I will then describe Brown's natural

---

3. David Brown, *God and Enchantment of Place: Reclaiming Human Experience* (Oxford University Press, 2004), 8.
4. Brown, *God and Enchantment of Place*, 9. See also David Brown, *God and Grace of Body: Sacrament in Ordinary* (Oxford University Press, 2007); David Brown, *God and Mystery in Words: Experience Through Metaphor and Drama* (Oxford University Press, 2008).
5. Brown, *God and Enchantment of Place*, 9.

theology of symbol. I conclude the chapter with a preliminary assessment of Brown's version of NT1.

David Brown in Context

Brown begins with divine generosity, on the one hand, and human freedom, on the other.[6] To get a sense of what he means by divine generosity, we need to start with creation and, more specifically, God's reason or motivation for creating the world. Against theologians who see reasons as inappropriate (e.g., Friedrich Schleiermacher, Karl Barth) as well as those who advocate for reasons such as divine fiat (e.g., Martin Luther, John Calvin) or divine need (e.g., Dorothee Sölle, Jürgen Moltmann), Brown argues for divine goodness and beauty. The first of these two reasons is particularly relevant here. Drawing upon Duns Scotus, Pseudo-Dionysius, and Thomas Aquinas, Brown sees "good of its very nature being diffusive of itself."[7] What this means is that God's goodness is by nature generous, and that, in Brown's words, "it is of the nature of goodness to share and so, if God is good, he must also share his being with others."[8] God created the world because he is good, and the nature of divine goodness is to share without any expectation of return. This goodness is then extended from God to the world, with Brown concluding that "this approach implies that grace is intrinsic to creation itself as part of the divine generosity that defines God as goodness itself."[9] This last bit is more controversial.

With the claim that grace is intrinsic to creation itself, Brown is planting his flag on one side of the nature-grace debate. I can hardly do justice to that debate here,[10] but it should be noted that for Brown there is no nature before or without grace, for God is always already given and everywhere available.

---

6. Brown's approach could be seen as a "priestly discourse" (i.e., "y") insofar as he begins with "divine availability". Wesley A. Kort, *Bound to Differ: The Dynamics of Theological Discourses* (Penn State University Press, 1992), 85. Kort classifies Barth as a "prophetic discourse" (i.e., "x").
7. David Brown, *God in a Single Vision: Integrating Philosophy and Theology*, ed. Christopher R. Brewer and Robert MacSwain (Routledge, 2016), 14.
8. Brown, *God in a Single Vision*, 14.
9. Brown, *God in a Single Vision*, 14–15.
10. For an introduction to the debate, see Fergus Kerr, *After Aquinas: Versions of Thomism* (Blackwell, 2002), 134–48.

Connecting the dots between divine generosity, human freedom, and nature/grace, Brown explains:

> For God remains the unique source of all goodness as its first instigator and as such he has done all he lovingly can do to bring it about, compatible with respect for human freedom. Indeed, for this view nature without grace is what Karl Rahner calls a 'remainder concept' (*Restbegriff*), a mere intellectual abstraction which has no independent existence. For God's grace is always seen as prevenient, and so there never can be a time or place where nature is to be found in complete isolation from it.[11]

Rejecting the idea of "pure nature," Brown aligns himself with Rahner, for whom this notion was nothing more than an intellectual abstraction conceivable only by way of a thought experiment: imagine graced nature sans grace. That which remains is "pure nature," but this "nature" has no real, autonomous existence. It is purely theoretical. Because grace precedes nature, nature cannot be seen apart from grace. Rather, we always and everywhere, since the creation of the world, see nature through grace and grace as being intrinsic to creation.

For this reason, Brown resists opposing nature and grace, reason and revelation. He argues that "we should not think of revelation and reason as necessarily two mutually exclusive vehicles towards reaching the truth about God. Thus it may well be the case that all the revelatory process does is enable a particular individual to grasp a truth that could also have been independently ascertained and confirmed by reason."[12] This is classic NT1 language. Reason takes its place alongside revelation, and both are said to yield knowledge of God.[13] But this raises an important question: What does Brown mean by revelation?

---

11. David Brown, *Continental Philosophy and Modern Theology: An Engagement* (Blackwell, 1987), 108.
12. Brown, *Continental Philosophy and Modern Theology*, 81. See also David Brown, *Invitation to Theology* (Blackwell, 1989), 31.
13. For additional discussion with reference to Butler, see Robert MacSwain, "The Tradition of Reason: David Brown, Joseph Butler, and Divine Hiddenness," in Brewer, *Transformation of Natural Religion*, 21–35.

Unlike Barth or Bonhoeffer, Brown takes religion to be revelatory,[14] and this as a logical consequence of divine generosity. He reasons that if God is indeed omnipresent, then revelation need not always be understood as God, the transcendent Other, intervening in this world, but might also be understood immanently as "a disclosure of what might otherwise have remained hidden from view."[15] Brown thus begins with revelation through the world and its symbols before turning to revelation through texts,[16] arguing that "the very symbols we use of God in the Bible often come from this shared universal experience of God [in the natural order]."[17] He mentions heaven and sacrifice as two examples and explains with reference to the former:

> People often speak patronizingly of primitive cultures as though the sky was populated with gods simply because these early societies didn't know any better, but Christians ought to be a little more careful, especially when they recall that the Lord's Prayer itself opens with the invocation "Our Father who art in Heaven," and heaven is just another word for the sky. . . . The point is that the sky or heavens are seen as particularly revelatory of the nature of God, as a vehicle through which God symbolizes what he is truly like.[18]

The bottom line for Brown is that we can't understand revelation through texts without revelation through the world and its symbols (i.e., natural theology).[19]

Turning now to revelation through texts, it should first be noted that Brown rejects the notion of a Bible that contains "the detailed, specific and literal words of God."[20] According to Brown, "In describing a particular text as revelatory, one is saying that it has a peculiar power for disclosing

---

14. Brown, *Invitation to Theology*, 26ff.
15. Brown, *Invitation to Theology*, 27. Brown explains that "talk of God's transcendence or immanence (of him being beyond or in the world) turn out to be metaphors, which can easily bewitch us into drawing illegitimate conclusions" (26).
16. Brown, *Invitation to Theology*, 27–33.
17. Brown, *Invitation to Theology*, 29.
18. Brown, *Invitation to Theology*, 29.
19. Here again I mention paratextuality as a useful metaphor to describe natural theology.
20. Brown, *Invitation to Theology*, 32.

the divine."[21] Second, Brown argues for a "moving text" that encompasses not only the scriptural canon but also the interpretive canon (i.e., tradition, including art). He develops this line of thinking in *Tradition and Imagination*, arguing that "Christians must disabuse themselves of the habit of contrasting biblical revelation and later tradition, and instead see the hand of God in a continuing process that encompasses both."[22] Suffice it here to say that, by revelation, Brown means religion, and for him this includes the natural world and its symbols as well as the "moving text," which includes Scripture and also tradition.[23]

Closely related to all of this is religious experience, for, as Brown notes, "any religious experience must also be a revelation, in that to experience the divine or some other form of transcendent reality must also mean that one is in receipt of an 'unveiling' or 'disclosure' from that other realm."[24] According to Rudolph Otto (1869–1937) these nonconceptual (and so nonrational) feelings have to do with a particular moment, one in which the individual comes into contact with the holy. By *holy*, Otto means something more than goodness, and it is this "something more"—"This 'extra' in the meaning of 'holy' above and beyond the meaning of goodness"[25]—that Otto refers to as the "numinous." The numinous is experienced as a feeling, and Otto refers to this feeling as *mysterium tremendum*."

The Dutch historian and philosopher of religion Gerard van der Leeuw (1890–1950) preferred to speak of "Power" (the experience of potency) as the basis of religion, and this is more or less equivalent to Otto's notion of the holy (i.e., numinous), insofar as it occasions amazement and fear. Explaining this experience, van der Leeuw writes:

> For whoever is confronted with potency clearly realizes that he is in the presence of some quality with which in his previous experience he was

---

21. Brown, *Invitation to Theology*, 32.
22. David Brown, *Tradition and Imagination: Revelation and Change* (Oxford University Press, 1999), 1. See also Garrick V. Allen, Christopher R. Brewer, and Dennis F. Kinlaw III, eds., *The Moving Text: Interdisciplinary Perspectives on David Brown and the Bible* (SCM, 2018).
23. Brown develops this idea even further in David Brown, *Gospel as Work of Art: Imaginative Truth and the Open Text* (Eerdmans, 2024).
24. David Brown, "Response," in Brewer, *Transformation of Natural Religion* 235.
25. Rudolph Otto, *The Idea of the Holy: An Inquiry into the Non-Rational Factor in the Idea of the Divine and Its Relation to the Rational*, 2nd ed., trans. John W. Harvey (Oxford University Press, 1950), 6.

never familiar, and which cannot be evoked from something else but which . . . can be designated only by religious terms such as "sacred" and "numinous." All these terms have a common relationship in that they indicate a firm conviction, but at the same time no definite conception, of the completely different, the absolutely distinct. The first impulse aroused by all this is avoidance, but also seeking: man should avoid Power, but he should also seek it.[26]

It seems to me that this dynamic pair—avoidance and seeking—characterizes natural theology in general but tends to be subjectively inflected in NT1.

For Brown, the roots of religion (i.e., awe and wonder) have everything to do with God's revelation, for God is everywhere present and "always taking initiatives to draw us closer to himself."[27] Religion, religious experience, reason, and revelation are, in other words, not only related but overlapping categories for Brown. While some would argue that the knowledge of God yielded by reason is, at best, vague or confused, Brown wonders: "Why should the vagueness of an experience make it less connected to God?"[28] I wonder the same. Those who take an all-or-nothing approach to the knowledge of God are, from Brown's perspective, part of the problem, for they deny God's revelation and, in so doing, marginalize those individuals with whom God interacts beyond the walls of the church.

The function of natural theology in this context is primarily educative, insofar as it seeks to uncover latent natural religion, what Brown in one place describes as a "residual sense of God."[29] The notion of a residual sense of God is interesting for at least two reasons, which I will only mention briefly. First, and with reference to the individual, it could mean anything from John Calvin's *sensus divinitatus* (sense of divinity) to Richard Kearney's

---

26. G. van der Leeuw, *Religion in Essence and Manifestation: A Study in Phenomenology*, trans. J. E. Turner, vol. 1 (Harper & Row, 1963), 47–48.

27. Brown, *Invitation to Theology*, 27.

28. David Brown, *Divine Generosity and Human Creativity: Theology Through Symbol, Painting and Architecture*, ed. Christopher R. Brewer and Robert MacSwain (Routledge, 2017), 14. See also David Brown and Gavin Hopps, *The Extravagance of Music* (Palgrave Macmillan, 2018), 294. Using the distinction between *formal* and *material*, Denys Turner takes a similar position in *Faith, Reason and the Existence of God* (Cambridge University Press, 2004), 18–9.

29. Brown, *Divine Generosity and Human Creativity*, 16.

"anatheism."[30] The former is more familiar, but the latter more relevant in a posteverything world. After the death of God and religion (in the cultural consciousness), is it possible to return to God? With so many "nones" and "dones" in our midst,[31] this question needs answering or at the very least some attention. As Kearney writes: "The choice of faith is never taken once and for all. It needs to be repeated again and again—every time we speak in the name of God or ask God why he has abandoned us."[32] Second, while some might tend to think of the individual with a residual sense of God, I think the idea more productive with reference to the group or culture. Blurring the lines between nature and culture, as well as between individual and community, one might think of a residual sense of God that resides in the extended mind of a culture.[33] This might also be thought of with reference to Hans-Georg Gadamer's notion of "effective history" or along sociological lines with Peter Berger. In any case, the idea is that society, culture (i.e., worked nature), and/or history are carriers of meaning and perhaps also knowledge of God.

Returning now to Brown, there is a persistent emphasis upon the goodness of creation (including not only nature but also culture),[34] and this is bolstered by the incarnation, which Brown takes to be God's endorsement of material reality.[35] If God so chose to identify with his creation, reasons Brown, then surely we can expect to see a similar incarnational logic at work more generally in the world. Brown thus argues for a sacramental world in which God is active beyond the walls of the church.[36] According to Brown,

---

30. See Calvin, *Institutes*, 1.3.1; Richard Kearney, *Anatheism: Returning to God After God* (Columbia University Press, 2010). All citations of Calvin's *Institutes* in this volume are from John Calvin, *Institutes of the Christian Religion*, ed. John T. McNeill, trans. Ford Lewis Battles, 2 vols. (Westminster, 1960).

31. Joshua Packard, "Meet the 'Dones,'" *Christianity Today*, Leadership Journal Summer 2015 Issue, https://www.christianitytoday.com/pastors/2015/summer-2015/meet-dones.html.

32. Kearney, *Anatheism*, 16; cf. Christian Wiman, *My Bright Abyss: Meditation of a Modern Believer* (Farrar, Straus & Giroux, 2013), 27–28, 61; T. M. Luhrmann, *How God Becomes Real: Kindling the Presence of Invisible Others* (Princeton University Press, 2020), xi.

33. See Andy Clark and David Chalmers, "The Extended Mind," *Analysis* 1 (1998): 7–19.

34. See Brown, *God and Enchantment of Place*, 33.

35. See Brown, *God in a Single Vision*, 6.

36. See David Brown, "Reconceiving the Sacramental: Valuing the Useless," in *The Gestures of God: Explorations in Sacramentality*, ed. Geoffrey Rowell and Christine Hall (Continuum, 2004), 21–36; Brown, "Sacramentality," in *The Oxford Handbook of Theology and Modern European Thought*, ed. Nicholas Adams, George Pattison, and Graham Ward (Oxford University Press, 2013), 615–31; Brown, "A Sacramental World: Why It Matters," in *The Oxford Handbook of Sacramental Theology*, ed. Hans Boersma and Matthew Levering (Oxford University Press, 2015), 603–15.

this transformed natural religion (or sacramentality) is the central means for interaction between a generous God and his free creatures. With this context in mind, I turn now to Brown's natural theology of symbol.

A Natural Theology of Symbol

Brown discusses natural theology explicitly at several points, the first time in his second book, *The Divine Trinity* (1985).[37] This was followed by discussions in his *Continental Philosophy and Modern Theology* (1987)[38] and then his *Invitation to Theology* (1989).[39] As previously noted, Brown is committed to divine interactionism and human freedom, but balancing God's agency with human freedom is challenging to say the least, as God's intervention might well encroach upon human freedom or, if one gives priority to human freedom, frustrate the divine purpose. Brown's solution is to explore the role of symbols with reference to divine dialogue. He argues "that symbols exercise a crucial role in God's dialogue" with humanity for three reasons,[40] the third of which is most relevant here. Symbols have to do with the subconscious, and this is "important because it makes it a medium through which God can act upon us, without destroying our freedom in the process."[41] Symbols, in other words, are the means by which God interacts with humans while preserving their freedom.[42]

"Symbols are," according to Brown, "but enacted metaphors,"[43] and they are "two not unrelated ways of achieving the same goal, of helping the hearer or viewer to move from one form of perception to another."[44] Here we begin to see natural theology as having to do with possibility or porosity rather than proof, the point being that through symbols (indirectly presented in

---

37. David Brown, *The Divine Trinity* (Open Court, 1985), 32–51, 60–62.

38. Brown, *Continental Philosophy and Modern Theology*, 1–10, 78–79, 201–3.

39. Brown, *Invitation to Theology*, 27–31.

40. David Brown, "God and Symbolic Action," in *Divine Action: Studies Inspired by the Philosophical Theology of Austin Farrer*, ed. Brian Hebblethwaite and Edward Henderson (T&T Clark, 1990), 115. Now available in *Scripture, Metaphysics, and Poetry: Austin Farrer's The Glass of Vision with Critical Commentary*, ed. Robert MacSwain (Ashgate, 2013), 142.

41. Brown, "God and Symbolic Action," 116, 143.

42. A slightly different version of this paragraph appeared in my introduction to Brown, *Divine Generosity and Human Creativity*, xi.

43. Brown, *God and Mystery in Words*, 9.

44. Brown, *God and Mystery in Words*, 18.

nature and the arts) the individual can think through the work to a new reading of reality. Brown explains:

> Wherever metaphor and symbol occur they help to draw apparently different aspects of reality closer together and so help generate a more inclusive conception of the world that we inhabit, and so hint, however tentatively, at a single enfolding reality that lies in God as their common creator. Let me put it another way. Fundamental to religious belief is the conviction that, however much the divine has put of itself into the creation, it remains of a fundamentally different order. So, in trying to conceptualize God, words must necessarily resort to images and metaphors that in the nature of the case draw unexpected connections between different aspects of reality, and indeed derive much of their power precisely from the fact that they are unexpected.[45]

To be clear, Brown is here describing the potential for religious experience through the arts, and it is precisely these kinds of experiences that he has in mind when he speaks of a "natural theology of symbolism" with reference to the architecture of Durham Cathedral.[46] Worth noting in this context is that, according to Brown, the symbol is more than a sign (i.e., "a mere pointer elsewhere rather than inherently valuable in itself")[47] and so stands in contrast to Evans's natural theology of signs (to be considered more fully in chapter 6), insofar as Brown thinks of the world as a place where the divine presence can be encountered.

Assessment

A significant achievement, Brown's transformed natural religion nevertheless presents noteworthy, yet-to-be answered questions and will, due to a number

---

45. Brown, *God and Mystery in Words*, 20.
46. David Brown, "Durham Cathedral as Theology," paper presented at the Society for the Study of Theology, Durham, April 4–6, 2016 (for which I ran the PowerPoint). This paper has now been published as "Durham Cathedral and the Jerusalem Temple: Let Sacred Buildings Speak," *International Journal for the Study of the Christian Church* 16 (2016): 93–107.
47. Brown, *Divine Generosity and Human Creativity*, 56.

of factors, be difficult for many evangelicals to take on board.[48] That said, he raises important issues, particularly with reference to NT1.

From Brown's perspective, the advent of proofs for the existence of God is closely tied to the separation of nature from grace. When precisely that separation occurred is the subject of debate, but some would say that it began with Aquinas and his Aristotle-influenced theology. According to Brown, "The problem begins when religious belief comes to be seen as an *inference* from something else rather than itself directly experienced as part of the air we breathe, as it were."[49] Everything about his transformed natural religion seeks to reverse the trend. In this sense Brown's natural theology has more to do with possibility or porosity than proof. As he explains: "The primary focus on formal arguments was a mistake not least because this was not where the great mass of believers in the past had located God. Instead, the entire range of human experience could be seen to be shot through with the possibility of God."[50] This connects with my discussion in the first chapter of Max Weber's notion of the disenchantment of the world with reference to Paul Ricoeur, Charles Taylor, and William Desmond.

For Brown, the enchantment-disenchantment-reenchantment story arc has everything to do with reclaiming human experience through the theological lens of the sacramental and, more specifically, with recovering notions of sacramentality prevalent in the first millennium when, he argues, "the term could be applied to almost any material reality that symbolically mediated the divine presence."[51] God was once everywhere available, according to Brown, through this expansive understanding of the sacramental. This understanding was progressively restricted to the point that people no longer expect to encounter God in the world and, perhaps as a result, no longer go to church where "authorized" experience of God is on offer. The solution, from Brown's perspective, is to highlight the ways God interacts sacramentally through a wide range of religious experience beyond the walls of the

---

48. For Brown's self-assessment, see Brown, *God and Mystery in Words*, 277–78.
49. Brown, *Divine Generosity and Human Creativity*, 26. To be clear, Brown is saying that NT2 is part of the problem.
50. David Brown, "Sacramentality and Public Theology: Pursuing Stephan van Erp's Vision," *Louvain Studies* 39 (2015–16): 167. See also Brown, *God and Enchantment of Place*, 411.
51. Brown, "Sacramentality," 615.

church, and this includes nature explored through not only the sciences but also the arts and culture.

Whereas Ricoeur spoke of primitive naïveté, criticism, and second naïveté, Brown sees the movement as one from sacramental interaction to deism (or natural religion) and secularism to a reconceived notion of the sacramental (or *transformed* natural religion). Whether or not one accepts Brown's approach, what cannot be denied from a purely descriptive perspective is that the field of natural theology isn't limited to formal arguments (as in some examples of NT2), proof, or probability. For Brown, natural theology has more to do with the possibility of God and the porosity of religious experience than it does with faith seeking understanding. It is, to use Sudduth's categories mentioned in the introduction, a predogmatic (or antecedent) natural theology, insofar as it has to do with the conditions of belief (i.e., the conditions in which belief become possible).

One final point: Brown sees the incarnation as God's endorsement of material reality. For Brown, this means an argument from the greater to the lesser. He explains: "Modern biblical scholarship suggests that the incarnation involved a more radical kenosis than Christianity has assumed throughout most of its history, with Jesus very much conditioned by the culture of which he was part. But if this was true at the point of God's deepest disclosure and involvement with humanity, then *a fortiori* one would expect matters to proceed similarly elsewhere in revelation, and this is in fact what we find as we study the origin of the various biblical ideas."[52] Along these same lines (and in the same book) he writes: "To put the matter at its simplest, if God was willing to subject himself to such restraints at the point of his most concrete and definitive engagement with the world, it seems probable that *a fortiori* this is how in general his relation with that world should be characterized."[53] By contrast, Barth and his followers take a so-called christological approach (NT5) that operates from a christological criterion. Jeremy Begbie is a contemporary defender of that view and a persistent critic of Brown's approach, which he takes to be operating without sufficient theological (that is, christological) criteria. Gavin Hopps has rightly challenged Begbie on this front,

---

52. Brown, *Tradition and Imagination*, 7–8.
53. Brown, *Tradition and Imagination*, 109.

highlighting the fact that Begbie's approach "begins by abstracting from the New Testament a list of Christological criteria (although the criteria according to which these criteria are determined are not themselves presented for inspection)."[54] This leads Hopps to conclude that "[Begbie's] christological approach is neither as neutral nor as intrinsically Christian as he seems to assume."[55] The point is that while Brown's approach doesn't solve every problem, it is not the only approach in need of further articulation (or justification). That said, his broad-minded approach is rooted in the Christian tradition, more specifically the doctrine of the incarnation, and seeks to do justice to human experience.

---

54. Brown and Hopps, *Extravagance of Music*, 190.
55. Brown and Hopps, *Extravagance of Music*, 191.

PART 2

Proof

CHAPTER 3

Natural Theology as Proof/Argument

*Proofs of God today have lost much of their force but little
of their fascination. They continue to exercise a silent,
secret attraction on thinking people. Does God exist? It
must be possible to prove this. There must be a proof that
is irrefutable, rational, obvious to everyone. It may be that
the proofs of God have failed as proofs today, that they are
perhaps dead. But even as failed and dead proofs, they
demand respect from those born in later times.[1]*

—Hans Kung

We turn now from natural theology informed by natural religion (NT1)
to natural theology as proof/argument (NT2). But what is proof? To
prove is to demonstrate the truth or existence of something. And how does
one demonstrate? Demonstration is accomplished through argument and/
or evidence. But how does one prove God? Dale Kohler, the young computer
scientist in John Updike's novel *Roger's Version*, thinks he can prove God
by computer, describing his project as follows: "*To demonstrate from existing
physical and biological data, through the use of models and manipulations on the
electronic digital computer, the existence of God, i.e. of a purposive and determining intelligence behind all phenomena.*"[2] That's the sort of project many of us

---

1. Hans Kung, *Does God Exist? An Answer for Today*, trans. Edward Quinn (Collins, 1980), 529.
2. John Updike, *Roger's Version* (Random House, 1986), 79–80.

think of when we think of natural theology. Data. Demonstration. Sherlock Holmes.[3]

For Anselm (1033–1109), proof began with prayer: "Come then, Lord my God, teach my heart where and how to seek You, where and how to find You."[4] This was faith seeking understanding.[5] And the proof? God, "that-than-which-a-greater-cannot-be-thought," exists not only in the mind but also in reality, for to exist in reality is greater than to exist only in the mind. But how could this be so? Anselm explains: "If then that-than-which-a-greater-cannot-be-thought exists in the mind alone, this same that-than-which-a-greater-*cannot*-be-thought is that-than-which-a-greater-*can*-be-thought. But this is obviously impossible. Therefore there is absolutely no doubt that something-than-which-a-greater-cannot-be-thought exists both in the mind and in reality."[6] That is the ontological argument: an argument for God from the very definition of God. Moving from conception

---

3. Contrast this approach with Annie Dillard's observational approach in *Pilgrim at Tinker Creek* (HarperCollins, 1974). In chapter 2, titled "Seeing," Dillard embarks on the *via positiva*, describing a newly sighted (i.e., no longer blind) girl who "saw 'the tree with the lights in it'" (35–36). There is beauty and goodness in the world. As Dillard explains, "The book's first half, the *via positiva*, accumulates the world's goodness and God's" (270–80). She continues: "The second half of the book starts down the *via negativa* with 'Fecundity,' the dark side of intricacy. This half culminates in 'Nothing' . . . , in which the visible world empties, leaf by leaf" (280). The world is full of beauty—"the tree with the lights in it"—and death, and Dillard invites us to sit with that.

4. Anselm of Canterbury, "Proslogion," in *The Major Works*, ed. Brian Davies and G. R. Evans (Oxford University Press, 1998), 84–85. For a book-length discussion of natural theology as proof/argument including Anselm, see Stephen T. Davis, *God, Reason and Theistic Proofs* (Eerdmans, 1997).

5. It is often argued that because Anselm's faith seeking understanding begins with prayer (i.e., within the dogmatic context of faith) and is primarily intended for those who already believe, it is no natural theology at all. But this is a misreading of Anselm, for, as Thomas Williams has argued, "although the theistic proofs are borne of an active love of God seeking a deeper knowledge of the beloved, the proofs themselves are intended to be convincing even to unbelievers." Thomas Williams, "Saint Anselm," *The Stanford Encyclopedia of Philosophy*, last revised January 21, 2015, https://plato.stanford.edu/archives/spr2016/entries/anselm/. Williams explains: "Thus Anselm opens the *Monologion* with these words: 'If anyone does not know, either because he has not heard or because he does not believe, that there is one nature, supreme among all existing things, who alone is self-sufficient in his eternal happiness, who through his omnipotent goodness grants and brings it about that all other things exist or have any sort of well-being, and a great many other things that we must believe about God or his creation, I think he could at least convince himself of most of these things by reason alone, if he is even moderately intelligent.' (*M* 1) And in the *Proslogion* Anselm sets out to convince 'the fool,' that is, the person who 'has said in his heart, "There is no God"' (Psalm 14:1; 53:1)."

6. Anselm, "Proslogion," 88.

to necessary existence, this *a priori* argument is a concise, clever, and rather controversial proof.

Thomas Aquinas (1225–74) took a different approach, arguing from effect to cause. He explains: "When we argue from effect to cause, the effect will take the place of a definition of the cause in the proof that the cause exists; and this is especially if the cause is God."[7] So, rather than reasoning *a priori* from definition to existence as Anselm did, Aquinas argued *a posteriori* from effects, such as change or motion, to their cause: God.[8] Those are two of the most well-known proofs for the existence of God: the ontological and the cosmological.

After Aquinas, René Descartes (1596–1650) resurrected the ontological argument,[9] but rather than arguing from definition to necessary existence as Anselm did, he argued to necessary existence from the innate idea of God. He explains:

> Certainly, the idea of God, or a supremely perfect being, is one which I find within me just as surely as the idea of any shape or number. And my understanding that it belongs to his nature that he always exists is no less clear and distinct than is the case when I prove of any shape or number that some property belongs to its nature. Hence, even if it turned out that not everything on which I have meditated in these past days is true, I ought still to regard the existence of God as having at least the same level of certainty as I have hitherto attributed to the truths of mathematics.[10]

---

7. Thomas Aquinas, *Summa Theologiae*, ed. and trans. Timothy McDermott, OP, vol. 2 (Cambridge University Press, 2006), Ia, Q. 2, Art. 2. For a comprehensive discussion of Aquinas's proofs, see Jules Bansnee, "Thomas Aquinas's Proofs of the Existence of God Presented in Their Chronological Order," in *Philosophical Studies in Honor of the Very Reverend Ignatius Smith, O. P.*, ed. John K. Ryan (Newman, 1952), 29–64.

8. For an excellent discussion of "Ways of Reading the Five Ways," see Fergus Kerr, *After Aquinas: Versions of Thomas* (Blackwell, 2002), 52–72. See also Thomas Joseph White, OP, *Wisdom in the Face of Modernity: A Study in Thomistic Natural Theology* (Sapientia, 2009), 76–96.

9. For a more recent example of resurrecting the ontological argument, consider Paul Tillich (1886–1965), according to whom the cosmological arguments represent the dissolution of the Augustinian solution—that is, the ontological argument—advanced by Anselm. Tillich therefore advocated a return to, and renewal of, the ontological approach. See Paul Tillich, "The Two Types of Philosophy of Religion," in *Theology of Culture*, ed. Robert C. Kimball (Oxford University Press, 1959), 10–29.

10. René Descartes, *Meditations on First Philosophy: With Selections from the Objections and Replies*, 2nd ed., trans. and ed. John Cottingham (Cambridge University Press, 2017), 52.

This marks a significant turning point from medieval forms of rationality to Enlightenment rationalism. How does one prove God? Intuition, deduction, innate knowledge, and innate concepts. These are the stock in trade of rationalists like Descartes, who argue from thought to reality. Contrast this with John Locke (1632–1704), who advocated an empirical approach rooted in sense experience.[11] How does one prove God according to Locke? Evidence.

Taking account of these developments, Nicholas Wolterstorff has observed that "the medieval project of natural theology was profoundly different from the Enlightenment project of evidentialist apologetics. It had different goals, presupposed different convictions, and was evoked by a different situation."[12] These are significant observations, and I take them to mean that criticism of one model or type of natural theology need not apply to every model or type, let alone the entire project.[13] Wolterstorff's observation thus excludes some varieties of natural theology from criticism leveled at a different kind of natural theology, that is, what Wolterstorff refers to as evidentialist apologetics. Wolterstorff's argument is, then, primarily an argument for distinction and against conflation. Having differentiated two varieties of natural theology, he then exempts the medieval variety from Barth's criticism of natural theology.

In this chapter, I will extend Wolterstorff's argument by situating it within William Desmond's discussion of ethos and ways. Desmond's discussion goes beyond comparing two versions of natural theology to explain the more complex interplay of ethos and ways.[14] Remember, there is no such thing as natural theology in a strict, essentialist sense, and Wolterstorff's analysis, while helpful, could be read as suggesting that evidentialist apologetics was

---

11. John Locke, *An Essay Concerning Human Understanding*, 2 vols. (Clarendon, 1844).

12. Nicholas Wolterstorff, "The Migration of the Theistic Arguments: From Natural Theology to Evidentialist Apologetics," in *Rationality, Religious Belief, and Moral Commitment: New Essays in the Philosophy of Religion*, ed. Robert Audi and William J. Wainwright (Cornell University Press, 1986), 39. For a more critical take on medieval arguments for the existence of God, see Graham Oppy, "Arguments for the Existence of God," in *The Oxford Handbook of Medieval Philosophy*, ed. John Marenbon (Oxford University Press, 2012), 687–704.

13. Along these lines, and as previously noted, Michael Sudduth differentiates between a "*model-specific objection*" and "a *project objection*." See Sudduth, *The Reformed Objection to Natural Theology* (Ashgate, 2009), 6, 54.

14. What Desmond describes as "the ethos" and, more specifically, as "the second ethos," Wolterstorff refers to as "a vast change of mentality." Wolterstorff, "Migration of the Theistic Arguments," 79. Note also p. 80: "change of mentality."

an aberration or deviation from natural theology in its pure form.[15] But there is no "pure" form. As with theology, natural theology is developed in history and so culturally situated.[16] That is just another way of saying that development has taken (and is taking) place, but this is no limitation. Rather, it is, as I have said previously, a persistent possibility. Natural theology preserves (and I would go so far as to say that it *better* preserves) that character of theology which John Henry Newman so aptly described: "To live is to change, and to be perfect is to have changed often."[17] Natural theology is always and everywhere beginning all over again,[18] continually resurrected in the complex interplay of ethos and ways.

Ethos and Ways

According to Desmond, "the ways" (i.e., proofs/arguments) cannot be abstracted from "the ethos" (i.e., "the ontological ethos," "the between").[19] He argues that "we do an injustice to the 'proofs' if we abstract them from the ontological context in which they are formulated; we have to acknowledge a complex interplay of ways and ethos. The result is not only a task for

---

15. A point also made by Hunter Brown in "Alvin Plantinga and Natural Theology," *International Journal for Philosophy of Religion* (1991): 13: "Plantinga perhaps ought not so sweepingly to identify natural theology as 'the attempt to prove or demonstrate the existence of God' and claim in quite so unqualified a way that the process so described has a 'long and impressive history' as if to suggest that it constitutes the very essence of the long tradition of natural theology. The relation between experience of the natural order and religious understanding in the longer history of christian [*sic*] natural theology is too complex to allow for such generalizations." Precisely. And this is why Brown goes on to "question . . . the adequacy of the view of natural theology which is rejected by Plantinga" (14). Brown's question with reference to Plantinga is mine with reference to any who reject truncated views of natural theology without taking into account the "many-sided diversity" of natural theology. Quotation (in relation to the ontological argument) from Alvin Plantinga, *God Freedom, and Evil* (Eerdmans, 1974), 104. Recall the Descriptive Responsibility.
16. For discussion, see David Fergusson, *Faith and Its Critics: A Conversation* (Oxford University Press, 2009), 39ff.
17. John Henry Newman, *An Essay on the Development of Christian Doctrine* (University of Notre Dame Press, 1989), 39.
18. See H. E. Root, "Beginning All over Again," in *Soundings: Essays Concerning Christian Understanding*, ed. A. R. Vidler (Cambridge University Press, 1962), 3–19.
19. This section draws and expands upon an earlier essay: Brewer, "Rolling with Release into the Future: William Desmond's Donation to a Natural Theology of the Arts," in *William Desmond and Contemporary Theology*, ed. Christopher Ben Simpson and Brennan Thomas Sammon (University of Notre Dame Press, 2017), 217–37. Used with permission. I am grateful to Christopher Ben Simpson for his feedback on this revised version, and my analogy in particular.

rethinking the ways; it is also a task for more adequate metaphysical reflection on the ontological character of the ethos."[20] All too often, natural theology is thought to be synonymous with ways or proofs, but Desmond calls for a deeper mindfulness, that is, a mindfulness of the ethos.

But what is the ethos? The ethos (or "the between") is where metaphysical thinking takes shape.[21] Desmond explains: "Ethos is more primordial; a way formulates a more definite passage of thinking out of the overdetermination of ethos; a way also makes determinate what otherwise is indefinite in the ethos."[22] In addition to this primal ethos, Desmond names a second ethos, what he refers to as "the reconfigured ethos." One might thus speak of the ancient ethos, the modern ethos, and so forth. In any case, it is this second ethos that the ways all too often reflect. More fully, Desmond explains:

> There is first an ontological ethos of what I call the between; we are in this between and our participation shapes its form. Our participation contributes to this *second* ethos which is the *reconfigured* ethos, in light of our fundamental perception and presuppositions, and basic sense of good and evil, and so on. Then there are ways, arguments, proofs; most of these reflect the second ethos; not many put their roots into the primal ethos; and if they do not, they will tend to reflect, shall we say, the preoccupations of the *Zeitgeist*, perhaps the idolatries and bewitchments.[23]

The problem, it seems, is that natural theologians have failed to mind the first ethos. Desmond is thus concerned to recover a deeper mindfulness of this ethos.

Jumping into Desmond's work can be challenging,[24] but consider this analogy. A particular way/argument is something like the kitchen in my previous home. For eight years, my family and I lived in a house built about 1900

---

20. William Desmond, "God, Ethos, Ways," *International Journal for Philosophy of Religion* 45 (1999): 14.
21. William Desmond, *Being and the Between*, SUNY Series in Philosophy (State University of New York Press, 1995), 44.
22. Desmond, "God, Ethos, Ways," 23.
23. Desmond, "God, Ethos, Ways," 23.
24. For a helpful introduction to Desmond, see Christopher Ben Simpson, ed., *The William Desmond Reader* (State University of New York, 2012).

in the Dutch colonial revival style.[25] When we moved in, the kitchen, clearly remodeled in the 1970s, desperately needed updating. It no longer served the needs of a twenty-first-century family. Function aside, the kitchen was in a sad state. It was literally falling apart, and remodeling it meant peeling off the layers of wallpaper and linoleum to get back to something more original—old-growth studs and red pine flooring in this case.

Returning now to Desmond, our remodeled kitchen is a determinate articulation of, or way of expressing so as to make the connection more explicit, what Desmond calls the second ethos. The second ethos is more or less equivalent to a worldview: perhaps the ancient ethos, the modern ethos, or in the case of our new kitchen, the early twenty-first-century ethos. Whereas the kitchen originally had several doors separating it from the rest of the house, two of these doors have now been removed because of changes in kitchen design as well as in American life. Kitchens were once closed off from the rest of the house, but they have increasingly become more open and integrated with the rest of the floor plan. No longer a workroom for the cook (read: housewife or, at the time of our home's construction, servant), kitchens are now the hub of the home. These kinds of changes in attitude make up the second ethos. The corresponding first ethos is, according to Desmond, the more primal, overdeterminate milieu of being. Back to the analogy of my kitchen, you might think of the first ethos as the context in which "we live and move and have our being" (Acts 17:28), with all the promise of possibility. Reconfiguring the space of our kitchen—staying true to this promise[26]—has required a good deal of attention to this context.

To review: there is the overdeterminate first ethos, the more determinate second ethos, and the determinate ways of thinking or expressing the second ethos. The proofs or ways are often confused with the second ethos, but it is through interplay with the first ethos that the ways are remodeled, recharged, or reconfigured. Like a rechargeable battery, the project of natural theology as well as its various models or types need to be plugged into the ontological ethos regularly, and this to be not only recharged but also reconfigured.

---

25. We now live in a house designed in the vernacular, albeit with heavy Greek revival influences, and built in 1903.
26. See William Desmond, *Ethics and the Between* (State University of New York Press, 2001), 17.

Perhaps natural theology is, in this sense, like an iPhone that needs regular updates, and some updates are better than others.

Natural Theology as Proof/Argument (NT2)

From the introduction, the reader will recall that natural theology is, according to the standard definition, a revelation-free, reason-informed theology most often associated with proofs for the existence of God. I have to this point been concerned to argue that natural theology should be more broadly conceived, but this natural theology as proof/argument (NT2) is, of the five types, closest to the standard definition, insofar as it is concerned with proof/argument for the nature and existence of God.

I have already mentioned Anselm and Aquinas, two of the most frequently cited (and contested) proof protagonists. The most well-known advocates of NT2 on the contemporary scene are Richard Swinburne and Alvin Plantinga.[27] Like Aquinas, Swinburne prefers *a posteriori* to *a priori* arguments. He explains: "I think that ontological arguments for the existence of God are very much mere philosophers' arguments and do not codify any of the reasons that ordinary people have for believing that there is a God. The greatest theistic philosophers of religion have on the whole rejected ontological arguments and relied on *a posteriori* ones."[28] Plantinga, on the other hand, thinks these arguments unsuccessful and instead favors a modal version of the ontological argument.[29] Neither Swinburne nor Plantinga are particularly interested in proof. Swinburne is concerned with probability and explanatory power, while Plantinga is concerned with rational acceptability and permissibility.[30] For Plantinga, natural theology is, one might say, nice but not necessary. One need not argue for God's existence given that belief in God is properly basic.

---

27. See Richard Swinburne, "The Vocation of a Natural Theologian," in *Philosophers Who Believe: The Spiritual Journeys of 11 Leading Thinkers*, ed. Kelly James Clark (InterVarsity, 1993), 179–202; and Alvin Plantinga, "A Christian Life Partly Lived," in Clark, *Philosophers Who Believe*, 45–82.
28. See Richard Swinburne, *The Existence of God*, 2nd ed. (Oxford University Press, 2004), 9.
29. See Alvin Plantinga, *The Nature of Necessity* (Oxford University Press, 1974); and Plantinga, *God, Freedom, and Evil* (Eerdmans, 1974).
30. See Plantinga, *God, Freedom, and Evil*, 112. For natural theology as proof, see Matthew Levering, *Proofs of God: Classical Arguments from Tertullian to Barth* (Baker Academic, 2016); and Edward Feser, *Five Proofs for the Existence of God* (Ignatius, 2017).

Turning now to the key considerations, Swinburne elaborates nature in terms of "the quintessentially human" (i.e., Begbie's second sense).[31] Plantinga, however, describes nature in terms of proper function (i.e., Begbie's fourth sense). Proper function is related to warrant, that is, "that which distinguishes knowledge from mere true belief."[32] According to Plantinga, "A necessary condition of a belief's having warrant for me is that my cognitive equipment, my belief-forming and belief-maintaining apparatus or powers, be free of such [i.e., cognitive] malfunction. A belief has warrant for you only if your cognitive apparatus is functioning properly, working the way it ought to work, in producing and sustaining it."[33] So to argue for rational permissibility with reference to justified true belief, one must, according to Plantinga, begin with proper function. Related to this is what Plantinga refers to as the "Design Plan," that is, "the way the thing in question is 'supposed' to work, the way in which it works when it is functioning as it ought to, when there is nothing wrong with it, when it is not damaged or broken or nonfunctional."[34] This understanding of nature—proper function and the design plan—is fundamental to Plantinga's argument that belief in God is properly basic. As Plantinga explains, "A belief has warrant just if it is produced by cognitive processes or faculties that are functioning properly, in a cognitive environment that is propitious for that exercise of cognitive powers, according to a design plan that is successfully aimed at the production of true belief."[35] Suffice to say, there is, according to Plantinga, a natural knowledge of God. We are, by nature, believers. This natural belief—what John Calvin referred to as the knowledge of God the Creator in the first book of his *Institutes*—is distinct from and opposed to the knowledge of God the Redeemer according to Plantinga. In other words, nature is distinct from and opposed to "Scripture and the testimony of the Holy Spirit," that is, "a special divine response to our (unnatural) sinful condition."[36] I will later refer to this

---

31. See Jeremy Begbie, *Music, Modernity, and God: Essays in Listening* (Oxford University Press, 2013), 91–92. To be human, according to Swinburne, is to be body and soul. See Richard Swinburne, *The Christian God* (Clarendon, 1994), 16–25.

32. Alvin Plantinga, *Warrant: The Current Debate* (Oxford University Press, 1993), 3.

33. Alvin Plantinga, *Warrant and Proper Function* (Oxford University Press, 1993), 4.

34. Plantinga, *Warrant and Proper Function*, 21.

35. Alvin Plantinga, *Warranted Christian Belief* (Oxford University Press, 1998), xi.

36. Calvin, *Institutes*, 1.14.21.

pair—nature and that to which it is opposed—as Plantinga's knowledge of God "tag team."

Swinburne takes a different approach. While speaking of "nature" (i.e. Begbie's first sense: the physical world) as well as "the laws of nature"[37] and, it should be noted, discussing a wide range of evidence and arguments from the natural world,[38] Swinburne is particularly interested in human nature or "the nature and evolution of man."[39] According to Swinburne, "Humans consist of two separate substances, body and soul."[40] I have no intention of getting into the details of Swinburne's argument for "soft dualism."[41] However, I do want to note that he moves from the existence of the soul (or mind) and, more specifically, the connection(s) that exist(s) between body and soul (or mind), to an argument for the existence of God. This is the argument from consciousness,[42] one of several elaborated by Swinburne as part of a cumulative case.[43]

When it comes to the second key consideration (i.e., that to which nature is opposed), Swinburne more or less accepts the traditional formulation— "Revealed theology, as opposed to natural theology (which is knowledge of God and his purposes available from the study of publicly available evidence of the natural world)"[44]—but acknowledges that "the division between natural and revealed theology cannot be a sharp one."[45] Citing James Barr, Swinburne notes that the Bible itself contains natural theology.[46]

Moving on from nature and that to which it is opposed to the function of natural theology, we might observe that Swinburne advocates for what Michael Sudduth has referred to as "the *predogmatic function*,"[47] while Plantinga rejects this in favor of the "*apologetic function*."[48] Sudduth explains:

---

37. See, e.g., Richard Swinburne, *The Evolution of the Soul*, rev. ed. (Oxford University Press, 2007), 198; Swinburne, *Faith and Reason*, 2nd ed. (Oxford University Press, 2005), 91–92.
38. For a brief summary of "the evidence of natural theology" discussed, see Richard Swinburne, *Revelation: From Metaphor to Analogy*, 2nd ed. (Oxford University Press, 2007), 80.
39. Swinburne, *Evolution of the Soul*, 4.
40. Swinburne, *Evolution of the Soul*, ix.
41. Swinburne, *Evolution of the Soul*, 10.
42. See Swinburne, *Existence of God*, chap. 9; and Swinburne, *Evolution of the Soul*, 198–99.
43. See Swinburne, *Existence of God*, 12ff.
44. Swinburne, *Revelation*, 1.
45. Swinburne, *Revelation*, 1.
46. Swinburne, *Faith and Reason*, 111–12.
47. Swinburne's ramified natural theology is the dogmatic complement.
48. Sudduth, *Reformed Objection to Natural Theology*, 53.

"According to the former, theistic arguments are parts of a system of theology that is independent of dogmatic theology and serves as its rational foundation. According to the latter, theistic arguments are used to defend theism against the objections of atheists and agnostics."[49] It is difficult to do justice to the variety of NT2 models. My brief discussions of Plantinga and Swinburne are here meant to illustrate this variety with reference to the divide between those who prefer ontological or cosmological approaches. Their definitions of nature, construals of nature and that to which it is opposed, and notions of function should not be taken as representative of every version of NT2. Rather, they should encourage the reader to think more carefully about how these key considerations operate within a given thinker's framework.

Shifting now from these two thinkers to more general observations, it is important to keep several things in mind. First, proof has to do with cogency, but proofs or arguments need not compel universally. Proof is, as George Mavrodes and others have argued, person-relative.[50] As Kelly James Clark explains: "There is an irreducibly psychological or sociological element in persuasion. In a successful proof the premises not only must be true, the unbeliever must understand and accept the premises."[51] Second, and related to this, proofs and arguments function in concert. No one proof or argument does it all.[52] Rather, as Swinburne argues, it is the cumulative case that matters, and this case includes not only ontological and cosmological arguments but also teleological and moral arguments, the previously mentioned argument from consciousness and, as Robert MacSwain has more recently argued, the argument from human holiness.[53] Just as a proof or argument may not convince everyone, one proof or argument cannot do everything, but when considered alongside all of the other proofs and arguments, it may

---

49. Sudduth, *Reformed Objection to Natural Theology*, 53.
50. George Mavrodes, *Belief in God* (Random House, 1970), 45–47; discussed in Kelly James Clark, *Return to Reason* (Eerdmans, 1990), 42.
51. Clark, *Return to Reason*, 42.
52. As Mavrodes notes: "We are, of course, especially interested in whether there is any argument that will prove God's existence to everyone. Such an argument has apparently not yet been invented.... The invention of such an argument would, of course, be a wonderful thing, just as would be the development of a drug that would cure all diseases. But there is not much reason to believe that either of these in possible." From Mavrodes, *Belief in God*, 46.
53. Otherwise known as the hagiological argument, this argument comes in several forms. See Robert MacSwain, *Saints as Divine Evidence* (Cambridge University Press, 2025).

well be that we have a very strong *cumulative* case in favor of theistic belief, and indeed I believe this to be so. Third, while the proofs retain much of their fascination, many philosophers and theologians have increasingly shied away from the language of proof, and while some, including Edward Feser and Matthew Levering, protest more chastened language, I think the move from proofs and universal reason to arguments, person-relativity, and the cumulative case represents a positive development, but perhaps this has as much to do with my own personality as it does with objective reasoning.

Fourth, NT2 has as much to do with probity (or permeability) and possibility (i.e., the enabling metaphysical conditions) as it does proof and probability. As Desmond has argued, proofs probe.[54] All of this being said, it should now be apparent that proofs and arguments are not static things, flies trapped in amber. They come in many forms and are, like my kitchen or garden, constantly being reworked. That is part of the dynamic interplay between ethos and ways previously discussed. Even so, we must consider the objections to NT2, even if these objections apply only to some, perhaps earlier formulations.

Philosophical Critiques: Hume and Kant

The project of natural theology was challenged by David Hume (1711–1776) who, in his posthumously published *Dialogues on Natural Religion* (1779), argued (through Philo)[55] that one cannot reason from natural effect to supernatural cause based upon the similar case of natural effect and natural cause.[56] A natural cause may well lead to a natural effect, but one cannot upon that basis argue that just as a natural effect requires a natural cause. So too a natural effect requires a supernatural cause. This is because in the latter case the species of cause is different than the species of effect. Hume's Philo explains:

---

54. Desmond, "God, Ethos, Ways," 24.

55. The extent to which Hume is expressing his own opinions through Philo is the subject of debate. See Robert J. Fogelin, *Hume's Presence in the Dialogues Concerning Natural Religion* (Oxford University Press, 2017).

56. Interestingly enough, Hume's mausoleum in Old Calton Cemetery (Edinburgh, Scotland) is kitty-corner from Adam Lord Gifford's grave. Gifford was the benefactor of the Gifford Lectures, established in 1887, which promote natural theology. For more information, see https://giffordlectures.org/.

If we see a house . . . , we conclude, with the greatest certainty, that it had an architect or builder; because this is precisely that species of effect, which we have experienced to proceed from that species of cause. But surely you will not affirm, that the universe bears such a resemblance to a house, that we can with the same certainty infer a similar cause, or that the analogy is here entire and perfect. The dissimilitude is so striking, that the utmost you can here pretend to is a guess, a conjecture, a presumption concerning a similar cause; and how that pretension will be received in the world, I leave you to consider.[57]

What this means is that we cannot, according to Hume's Philo, argue from natural cause to supernatural effect, from "parts to the whole,"[58] from finite to the infinite, from imperfect to the perfect, or from mortal to the immortal. In other words, we are limited by partial, imperfect experience, and weak analogies will not save us. As Philo cries out, "Our experience, so imperfect in itself, and so limited both in extent and duration, can afford us no probable conjecture concerning the whole of things."[59] We cannot argue from nature to God, says Hume.

Following closely on the heels of Hume, Immanuel Kant (1724–1804) argued that reality includes not only observable phenomena (i.e., appearances) but also the distinct realm of noumena (i.e., the things themselves) that lies beyond human cognition. According to Kant, we cannot argue from phenomena to noumena. Kant begins with a critique of the ontological argument. Remember that, according to Anselm's ontological argument, to exist in reality is greater than to exist only in the mind. But according to Kant, this is nonsense: "Being is obviously not a real predicate, i.e. a concept of something that could add to the concept of a thing. It is merely the positing of a thing or of certain determinations in themselves."[60] What Kant is saying is that adding "Being" to the concept of a thing doesn't make it greater; it *makes* it, that is, it posits the thing itself. This leads him to conclude: "The concept

---

57. David Hume, *Dialogues Concerning Natural Religion* (Routledge, 1991), 110.
58. Hume, *Dialogues Concerning Natural Religion*, 115.
59. Hume, *Dialogues Concerning Natural Religion*, 139.
60. Immanuel Kant, *Critique of Pure Reason*, Cambridge Edition of the Works of Immanuel Kant (Cambridge University Press, 1998), 567.

of a highest being is a very useful idea in many respects; but just because it is merely an idea, it is entirely incapable all by itself of extending our cognition in regard to what exists."[61] Having critiqued the ontological argument, Kant turns to the cosmological argument.

According to Kant, while the cosmological proof begins with experience, "it is really only the ontological proof from mere concepts that contains all the force of proof in the so-called cosmological proof; and the supposed experience is quite superfluous."[62] He explains:

> In order to ground itself securely, this proof gets a footing in experience, and thereby gives itself the reputation that it is distinct from the ontological proof, which puts its whole trust solely in pure concepts *a priori*. But the cosmological proof avails itself of this experience only to make a single step, namely to the existence of a necessary being in general.[63]

What this means is that, in Kant's estimation, the cosmological proof relies upon the ontological proof, and because he thinks the ontological proof unsuccessful, he also thinks the cosmological proof unsuccessful. Having dispensed these two proofs in one fell swoop, Kant turns to the physico-theological proof, arguing that the physico-theological proof depends upon the cosmological, and the cosmological depends upon the ontological. According to Kant, the ontological proof is not sound, and so neither are the cosmological nor physico-theological proofs. And that is how you kill three birds with one stone. Or is it?

In the wake of Hume and Kant, Pope Leo XIII argued for the restoration of Christian philosophy, more specifically for the natural theology of Aquinas.[64] This led to a Thomistic renaissance in the twentieth century with theologians such as Denys Turner arguing that "the existence of God is rationally demonstrable, as a dogmatic decree of the first Vatican Council

---

61. Kant, *Critique of Pure Reason*, 568.
62. Kant, *Critique of Pure Reason*, 571.
63. Kant, *Critique of Pure Reason*, 571.
64. See Leo XIII, *Aeterni Patris: Encyclical of Pope Leo XIII on the Restoration of Christian Philosophy*, http://www.vatican.va/holy_father/leo_xiii/encyclicals/documents/hf_l-xiii_enc_04081879_aeterni-patris_en.html.

says."[65] Against what are from his perspective revisionist readings (e.g., *nouvelle théologie*), Turner maintains the "Thomas of rational proof."[66] Although he acknowledges "that the 'five ways' are . . . proposed as proofs within a context of faith and of Christian practice,"[67] Turner denies that "their character *as proofs* depends logically upon that context's being presupposed to them."[68] But what of the critiques of Hume and Kant?

According to Plantinga, "There is really nothing in Kant to suggest that we can't think or talk about God."[69] In fact, Plantinga thinks Kant's argument is self-defeating, for how can one identify something that, apparently, we cannot refer to or think about? Swinburne is equally dismissive of Kant's arguments, for, as he notes, "Kant's claim, derived from Hume, that the only causes of things which we can know are precedent observable phenomena, is quite implausible. It would rule out in advance most of the great achievements of science since his day. For science has been able to explain observable phenomena . . . in terms of unobservable causes (the movements of such fundamental particles as electrons, protons, and positrons)."[70] All of this to say that the arguments of Hume and Kant were by no means final, and even if their critiques stand, they would only be applicable to some models or types of natural theology, not the entire project, whether synchronically or diachronically. The conversation is always, must always, and has moved on.

To understand NT2, we need to understand the relationship between these contextual currents and the proofs and arguments trying to make their way through what might be called the "Northwest Passage of natural theology." An apt metaphor, the Northwest Passage between the Atlantic and Pacific Oceans was for years no more than a dream. Numerous expeditions set sail from England, and many never returned, but in 1854 Robert McClure and his crew traversed the Northwest Passage, completing the journey over the Arctic ice by sled, and in 1906 Roald Amundsen and his crew

---

65. Denys Turner, *Faith, Reason and the Existence of God* (Cambridge University Press, 2004), ix.

66. Turner, *Existence of God*, xi. That said, Turner suggests that "for Thomas, to prove the existence of God is to prove the existence of a mystery, that to show God to exist is to show how, in the end, the human mind loses its grip on the meaning of 'exists'" (xiv).

67. Turner, *Existence of God*, 16.

68. Turner, *Existence of God*, 17.

69. Plantinga, *Warranted Christian Belief*, 31. This claim follows a thorough discussion of Kant's claims (9–30).

70. Swinburne, *Faith and Reason*, 103–4.

made it through the entire passage by sea. Since 2007, the route has been, due to climate change, ice free. Navigating the Northwest Passage today is very different than it was in 1497 when John Cabot set out from Bristol, the first European to make the attempt. Unsuccessful, Cabot made a second attempt in 1498 but never returned. The history of the search for the Northwest Passage is filled with tragedy, but in 2016 a cruise ship filled with tourists made the trip. The conditions have changed. The same could be said for natural theology as proof/argument, particularly with reference to Plantinga, whose approach is the subject of the next chapter.

CHAPTER 4

Nice but Not Necessary: Alvin Plantinga

The Christian does not need natural theology, either as the source of his confidence or to justify his belief.[1]

—Alvin Plantinga

One can be justified and rational in accepting theistic belief, even if one doesn't accept theism on the basis of arguments and even if in fact there aren't any good theistic arguments. . . . That said, of course, it doesn't follow that there aren't any good theistic arguments, and as a matter of fact . . . there are good theistic arguments—at least two dozen or so.[2]

—Alvin Plantinga

Before Alvin Plantinga, theistic belief was in a tough spot, or so the story goes.[3] In 1980, *Time* referred to him as "America's leading orthodox

---

1. Alvin Plantinga, "Reason and Belief in God," in *Faith and Rationality: Reason and Belief in God,* ed. Alvin Plantinga and Nicholas Wolterstorff (University of Notre Dame Press, 1983), 67.
2. Alvin Plantinga, "Appendix: Two Dozen (Or So) Theistic Arguments," in *Alvin Plantinga,* ed. Dean-Peter Baker, Contemporary Philosophy in Focus (Cambridge University Press, 2007), 203.
3. A different story could, of course, be told. See, e.g., Richard Swinburne, "The Revival of Natural Theology," *Archive di Filosofia* 75 (2007): 303–22. For Plantinga's intellectual biography, see Alvin Plantinga, "Self-Profile," in *Alvin Plantinga,* ed. James E. Tomberlin and Peter van Inwagen, Profiles (Reidel, 1985), 3–97. For his spiritual autobiography, see Alvin Plantinga, "A Christian Life Partly Lived," in *Philosophers Who Believe: The Spiritual Journeys of 11 Leading Thinkers,* ed.

Protestant philosopher of God,"[4] and this was well before he delivered the Gifford Lectures at the University of Aberdeen in 1986–87, published his *Warrant* trilogy (1993–2000),[5] delivered his second series of Gifford Lectures in 2005 in St. Andrews, or won the Templeton Prize in 2017.[6] Plantinga has had an enormous impact, to be sure, but his view of natural theology can be difficult to pin down. As Graham Oppy has noted, "Plantinga himself has given different accounts of 'natural theology' at different points in his career."[7] Understanding Plantinga's view of natural theology is in this sense no different than defining natural theology more generally. In his first two books, he both critiques natural theology and atheology *and* advances new arguments (e.g., God and other minds) as well as new versions of traditional arguments (e.g., the modal ontological argument). At the same time, he argues that the believer has no need for natural theology in relation to the justification of or warrant for theistic belief, making his view of natural theology particularly challenging to grasp. Is he for *it* or against *it*? For Plantinga, it comes down to the function

---

Kelly James Clark (InterVarsity, 1993), 45–82. See also James F. Sennett, ed., *The Analytic Theist: An Alvin Plantinga Reader* (Eerdmans, 1998).

4. "Religion: Modernizing the Case for God," *Time*, April 7, 1980, 65–66, https://content.time.com /time/subscriber/article/0,33009,921990-3,00.html.

5. Alvin Plantinga, *Warrant: The Current Debate* (Oxford University Press, 1993); Plantinga, *Warrant and Proper Function* (Oxford University Press, 1993); and Plantinga, *Warranted Christian Belief* (Oxford University Press, 2000). For a "shorter and . . . more user-friendly version" of the third volume, see Plantinga, *Knowledge and Christian Belief* (Eerdmans, 2015), vii.

6. Published as Alvin Plantinga, *Where the Conflict Really Lies: Science, Religion, and Naturalism* (Oxford University Press, 2011).

7. Graham Oppy, "Natural Theology," in *Alvin Plantinga*, ed. Deane-Peter Baker (Cambridge University Press, 2007), 41. Oppy continues: "When he supposes that natural theology is the project of showing that the claim that the God of the Judaeo-Christian tradition exists follows deductively or inductively from propositions that are obviously true and accepted by nearly every sane man, together with propositions that are self-evident or necessarily true, he consistently takes the view that natural theology is a failure, and he also consistently takes the view that the reasonableness of belief in God is quite independent of the success or failure of natural theology. When he supposes that natural theology is the project of showing that religious belief is rationally acceptable, his thought moves in two different directions. On the one hand, there are various places where he has given arguments whose conclusion *seems* to be that religious belief is rationally acceptable *tout court*— for example, in the 'different approach' of *God and Other Minds*, and in the 'victorious' modal ontological argument of *God, Freedom, and Evil* and *The Nature of Necessity*; on the other hand, there are places where he argues that religious belief is rationally acceptable *provided* that theism is true—for example, in 'Reason and Belief in God' and in *Warranted Christian Belief*. When he supposes that natural theology is the project of providing arguments for the existence of God, then his view seems quite consistently to be that there are various senses in which there are numerous good arguments for the existence of God, that is, arguments that can serve to 'bolster' or 'confirm' the beliefs of reasonable but wavering theists (and perhaps do other things as well)" (41–42).

of natural theology, but before getting into Plantinga's discussion of the prospects for natural theology, I begin with an overview of his work. One must read carefully and pay attention to changes along the way.

Alvin Plantinga in Context

In his first book, *God and Other Minds*, Plantinga examines natural theology (part 1) and natural atheology (part 2), deeming both unsuccessful.[8] He then argues for analogy between belief in God and belief in other minds (part 3). This leads him to conclude: "If my belief in other minds is rational, so is my belief in God. But obviously the former is rational; so, therefore, is the latter."[9] Several things are worth noting here. First, Plantinga takes arguments seriously. The cosmological, ontological, and teleological arguments receive chapter-length and, in the case of the ontological argument, two chapter-length treatments. His conclusion "that natural theology does not provide a satisfactory answer to the question with which we began: Is it rational to believe in God?"[10] comes after more than one hundred pages of careful analysis. Second, Plantinga looks not only at the arguments of natural theology but also those of natural atheology, and here again his conclusion comes only after pages of careful analysis: "Natural atheology seems no better than natural theology as an answer to the question 'Are religious beliefs rationally justified?'"[11] Third, Plantinga calls the entire enterprise into question by shifting the focus from the arguments for and against belief to the epistemological question to which these arguments are a response. If the question is unfair, an answer may not be needed. Why must the believer justify belief in God when belief in other minds is taken for granted?

In his second and third books, *The Nature of Necessity* and *God, Freedom, and Evil*,[12] Plantinga returns to natural theology and natural atheology,

---

8. Alvin Plantinga, *God and Other Minds: A Study of the Rational Justification of Belief in God* (Cornell University Press, 1967), 111 (natural theology), 183 (natural atheology).
9. Plantinga, *God and Other Minds*, 271.
10. Plantinga, *God and Other Minds*, 111.
11. Plantinga, *God and Other Minds*, 183.
12. Alvin Plantinga, *The Nature of Necessity* (Clarendon, 1974); and Plantinga, *God, Freedom, and Evil* (Eerdmans, 1974). The former is, according to Plantinga, "more rigorous and complete" (*Nature of Necessity*, 4).

taking up the latter in part 1 of *God, Freedom, and Evil*, with particular attention given to the problem of evil. Part 1 concludes: "Natural atheology doesn't work."[13] In part 2, Plantinga examines the cosmological, teleological, and ontological arguments for the existence of God and once again finds them wanting (in their considered forms).[14] Plantinga then presents "A Modal Version of the Argument"[15] that, as he explains, "establishes, not the *truth* of theism, but its rational acceptability. And hence it accomplishes at least one of the aims of traditional natural theology."[16] This is significant, insofar as it accomplishes this task and shows that Plantinga, who has argued that the Christian does not need natural theology, nevertheless advances (in one book from 1967 and then again in two books from 1974) arguments that could legitimately be characterized as natural theology.[17] Once again, Plantinga takes the arguments seriously and, once again, he looks not only at the arguments of natural theology and atheology. And here again, in the final pages, he offers a powerful argument for theistic belief, but whereas his argument in *God and Other Minds* was that the believer needs no argument for theistic belief, his argument in *The Nature of Necessity* and *God, Freedom, and Evil* is a reformulated version of a traditional argument.[18] Here, however, the purpose or function of the argument has to do not with truth but with rational acceptability. Recall the key considerations (outlined in the introduction) that, like the frequency-specific faders on an equalizer, might be adjusted or nuanced for a very different result.

Fast-forward six years. In 1980 Plantinga delivered a lecture (published later that year) titled: "The Reformed Objection to Natural Theology."[19]

---

13. Plantinga, *God, Freedom, and Evil*, 73.
14. Plantinga, *God, Freedom, and Evil*, 80 (cosmological), 84 (teleological), and 104 (ontological).
15. Plantinga, *God, Freedom, and Evil*, 104.
16. Plantinga, *God, Freedom, and Evil*, 112.
17. According to Deane-Peter Baker, "The heart of [Plantinga's] argument in *God and Other Minds* is that the arguments of natural theology are *no worse than* the arguments for the existence of other minds, and that therefore we have as much reason to belief in God as in other minds." Deane-Peter Baker, introduction to Baker, *Alvin Plantinga*, 9.
18. In this sense Plantinga is no different than William Desmond, who also sees the need for reformulation. But whereas Plantinga reformulates proofs, Desmond reformulates proof (as "probes"). See William Desmond, *God and the Between*, Illuminations: Theory and Religion (Blackwell, 2008), 131–32. In that sense, Desmond is more like C. Stephen Evans (whose signs serve a similar function as Desmond's hyperboles), the subject of chapter 6.
19. Alvin Plantinga, "The Reformed Objection to Natural Theology," *Proceedings of the American Catholic Philosophical Association* 15 (1980): 49–63.

Plantinga's claim, the so-called Reformed objection, is that thinkers in the Reformed tradition haven't pursued natural theology for this reason: Unlike classical foundationalists, who claim to argue from indubitable principles to all subsequent claims, these Reformed thinkers simply take belief as basic. Theistic belief is, according to Plantinga, something you argue from, not to, and natural theology is nice but not necessary.[20]

Plantinga begins "The Reformed Objection to Natural Theology" with a definition: "Suppose we think of Natural Theology as the attempt to prove or demonstrate the existence of God."[21] After citing Thomas Aquinas as "the natural starting point for Christian philosophical reflection,"[22] he then writes:

> Many Christians, however, have been less than totally impressed. In particular Reformed or Calvinist theologians have for the most part taken a dim view of the enterprise. A few Reformed thinkers—B. B. Warfield, for example—endorse theistic proofs; but for the most part the Reformed attitude has ranged from indifference, through suspicion and hostility, to outright accusations of blasphemy. And this stance is initially puzzling. It looks a little like the attitude some Christians adopt towards faith healing: it can't be done, but even if it could, it shouldn't be.[23]

After this brief introduction, Plantinga quotes from Herman Bavinck and, then more extensively, from John Calvin—"As good a Calvinist as any"[24]— before concluding: "The Christian doesn't *need* natural theology, either as the source of his confidence or to justify his belief. Furthermore, the Christian *ought* not to believe on the basis of argument; if he does, his faith is likely to be unstable and wavering."[25]

---

20. Plantinga's approach is in some ways similar to Cornelius Van Til's presuppositional apologetic, though when I asked Plantinga what he made of the comparison at his lake cottage in 2006, he replied that unlike Van Til, he wasn't a fideist. For a detailed discussion of points of similarity and difference, see James Anderson, "If Knowledge Then God: The Epistemological Theistic Arguments of Alvin Plantinga and Cornelius Van Til," *Calvin Theological Journal* 40 (2005): 49–75.
21. Plantinga, "Reformed Objection to Natural Theology," 49.
22. Plantinga, "Reformed Objection to Natural Theology," 49.
23. Plantinga, "Reformed Objection to Natural Theology," 49.
24. Plantinga, "Reformed Objection to Natural Theology," 50.
25. Plantinga, "Reformed Objection to Natural Theology," 53.

Plantinga develops this line of argument further in a well-known 1983 essay, doubling down on his claim that the problem with natural theology is that it is a response to the evidentialist objection that emerges from a faulty epistemological framework: classical foundationalism.[26] According to Plantinga, "Classical foundationalism is both false and self-referentially incoherent; it should therefore be summarily rejected."[27] And if classical foundationalism is rejected, the evidentialist objection to theistic belief may well disappear, and if so, natural theology is no longer needed to justify theistic belief (i.e., as a response to the evidentialist objection emerging from classical foundationalism). But if classical foundationalism is rejected, what takes its place?

Reformed Epistemology and the Prospects for Natural Theology

Reformed (or Calvinist) epistemology rejects classical foundationalism as a viable epistemological option.[28] This entails a criticism of the evidentialist objection to theistic belief, the Thomistic conception of faith and reason, and natural theology. This criticism is said to be all but explicit in the language of the Reformers.

By classical foundationalism, Plantinga means to include ancient, medieval (e.g., Aquinas), and modern foundationalists.[29] A classical foundationalist might be understood as someone for whom a proposition is properly basic

---

26. Describing the evidentialist objection, Plantinga writes: "Many philosophers—W. K. Clifford, Brand Blanshard, Bertrand Russell, Michael Scriven, and Anthony Flew, to name a few—have argued that belief in God is irrational and unreasonable or not rationally acceptable or intellectually irresponsible or somehow poetically below par because, as they say, there is *insufficient evidence* for it." See Plantinga, "Reason and Belief in God," 17. On the same page he writes: "I shall argue that the evidentialist objection and the Thomistic conception of faith and knowledge can be traced back to a common root in *classical foundationalism*—a pervasive and widely accepted picture or total way of looking at faith, knowledge, belief, rationality, and allied topics."

27. Plantinga, "Reason and Belief in God," 17.

28. This section draws from Christopher R. Brewer, "Is Reformed Epistemology Reformed? The Nature and Function of the *Sensus Divinitatus* in the Writings of John Calvin and Alvin Plantinga" (MA thesis, Grand Rapids Theological Seminary, Cornerstone University, 2005). Plantinga regrets "having referred to this project, half in jest, as 'Reformed Epistemology' or 'Calvinist Epistemology'; some didn't realize this was supposed to be just a clever title, not a gauntlet thrown at the feet of Catholic philosophers." See Plantinga, "Christian Life Partly Lived," 67. Despite his regretting having referred to this project as Reformed epistemology, it is nonetheless, in his own estimation, a development of Calvin's insights. See Plantinga, "Reason and Belief in God," 16.

29. Brewer, "Is Reformed Epistemology Reformed?," 58–59.

only if it is either self-evident, incorrigible, or evident to the senses. Plantinga has, however, argued that the classical foundationalist's criteria for proper basicality are neither comprehensive nor coherent. That is, first of all, they do not explain things we commonly accept as basic (i.e., propositions about the past, propositions entailing the existence of persons distinct from myself) and are thus not comprehensive. Furthermore, he argues that these criteria are self-referentially incoherent because none of the criteria are themselves either self-evident, incorrigible, or evident to the senses.[30] Therefore, Plantinga argues that classical foundationalism should be rejected as a viable epistemological option. As a result, Plantinga places less emphasis upon natural theology, at least to the extent that it is needed to justify one's beliefs. Instead, Plantinga argues, belief in God may be taken as properly basic.

According to Plantinga, basic beliefs are those beliefs that I "accept but do not accept on the basis of any other beliefs."[31] In other words, one does not accept these beliefs (e.g., the belief that God exists) "on the evidential basis of other propositions" but instead takes them as a starting point.[32] To understand more fully what Plantinga means by basic beliefs, some grasp of the concept of justification and the discussion of what it means for a belief to have warrant is necessary. According to Plantinga, justification is a term of epistemic appraisal. Plantinga explains: "To say that a belief is *warranted* or *justified* for a person is to evaluate it or him (or both) *positively*; his holding that belief in his circumstances is *right*, or *proper*, or *acceptable*, or *approvable*, or *up to standard*."[33] Furthermore, Plantinga notes: "We appraise not only the belief itself, but also the *degree* to which it is accepted."[34] Defining justification is no easy task. According to Plantinga, there is "a wide and indeed confusing assortment of alternatives."[35] Suffice it to say that justification is a term of epistemic appraisal, that being justified is not "up to us,"[36] and that the notion of basic beliefs is intricately associated with the concept of justification and warrant.[37]

30. For the details of Plantinga's argument regarding "the collapse of foundationalism," see Brewer, "Is Reformed Epistemology Reformed?," 59–63.

31. Brewer, "Is Reformed Epistemology Reformed?," 46.

32. Plantinga, *Warranted Christian Belief*, 176–77.

33. Plantinga, *Warrant: The Current Debate*, 3.

34. Plantinga, *Warrant: The Current Debate*, 4.

35. Plantinga, *Warrant: The Current Debate*, 7.

36. Plantinga, *Warrant: The Current Debate*, 15.

37. For a more complete discussion of justification and its relationship to knowledge and warrant

The belief that God exists is not only basic but also properly basic, in that a person may be "*justified* in holding it in a basic way . . . within his epistemic rights . . . not irresponsible . . . violating no epistemic or other duties in holding that belief in that way."[38] Yet belief in God is not groundless,[39] nor is it some version of fideism.[40] Rather, it is among the deliverances of reason. According to Plantinga, this is what Calvin, Kuyper, Bavinck, and Barth held.[41] Furthermore, "theistic belief produced by the *sensus divinitatus* can also be *properly basic with respect to warrant*."[42] Thus, for Plantinga, belief in God is immediate and occasioned by a variety of circumstances (i.e., basic), epistemically responsible (i.e., justified), and when produced in

---

see Plantinga, *Warrant: The Current Debate*, 3–29; and Plantinga, *Warranted Christian Belief*, 67–107, 177–79.

38. Plantinga, *Warranted Christian Belief*, 178. Elsewhere, he notes: "One who takes belief in God as basic is not thereby violating any epistemic duties or revealing a defect in his noetic structure; quite the reverse. The correct or proper way to believe in God, [the Reformers] thought, was not on the basis of arguments from natural theology or anywhere else; the correct way is to take belief in God as basic." Plantinga, "Reason and Belief in God," 72.

39. See Plantinga, "Reason and Belief in God," 78–82.

40. See Plantinga, "Reason and Belief in God," 87–91; and Plantinga, *Warranted Christian Belief*, 263–64. On this point Plantinga clearly differs from Van Til, Barth, and Kierkegaard. While followers of Van Til, such as John Frame, claim that Christian presuppositions are *rationally* grounded in revelation (John M. Frame, *Cornelius Van Til: An Analysis of His Thought* [P&R, 1995], 137), they, like Van Til, "prefer assertion over argument." See Kelly James Clark, "A Reformed Epistemologist's Response," in *Five Views on Apologetics*, ed. Steven B. Cowan (Zondervan, 2000), 256. Clark continues: "Perhaps the presuppositionalists are right. . . . But making the case that this is so requires an enormous amount of research, thought, and argument" (256).

41. Plantinga, "Reason and Belief in God," 71–72. Barth would certainly share Plantinga's sentiments with regard to natural theology as well as the necessity of *starting with* belief in God. However, that he would accept Plantinga's understanding of the *sensus divinitatus* is rather dubious. Barth clearly states: "We lack the capacity both to establish His existence and to define His being" (Barth, *Church Dogmatics* II/1, 187). In all fairness, Barth may be referring to "capacity" as something we actually possess (as he does elsewhere, see *Church Dogmatics* IV/1, 539) rather than a potential cognitive capacity in the sense that Plantinga argues, but this is not altogether apparent. If anything, Barth argues just the opposite. Elsewhere he notes: "The concept of a 'capacity' of man for God has therefore to be dropped." See Karl Barth, "No! Answer to Emil Brunner," in *Natural Theology: Comprising "Nature and Grace" by Professor Dr. Emil Brunner and the Reply "No!" by Dr. Karl Barth*, trans. Peter Fraenkel (Centenary, 1946), 89. Either way, Barth would argue that Jesus Christ is "the first and proper Subject of the knowledge of God" (Barth, *Church Dogmatics* II/1, 252). Thus, even if Barth agreed with Plantinga with regard to the nature and function of the *sensus divinitatus*, he would reject any epistemology that does not begin with revelation *in Christ*. It is not enough to begin with God. One must begin with God as he is revealed *in Christ*. For Barth the knowledge of God is his (i.e., Christ's) own knowledge (Barth, *Church Dogmatics* II/1, 252). We do not have the capacity to "establish His existence" or "to define His being." Instead, our knowledge of God is derivative by way of the fellowship we have in Jesus Christ.

42. Plantinga, *Warranted Christian Belief*, 178–79.

accordance with God's design plan by a properly functioning *sensus divinitatus* (i.e., sense of divinity), it may also be properly called knowledge (i.e., warranted Christian belief). This is, according to Plantinga, consistent with Calvin.[43]

According to Plantinga, warrant is that which separates knowledge from mere true belief.[44] It is also an appraisal of the favorability of that belief.[45] Thus warrant is what separates knowledge from mere true belief, a sort of appraisal of the belief itself as well as an appraisal of the degree to which it is accepted. In addition, it "involves the notion of proper function, which involves or presupposes the idea of a *design plan*."[46] An important part of this design plan is the *sensus divinitatus*, which I will now discuss in more detail.

How can a person who takes belief in God as basic know that God exists? More fundamentally, how can belief in God be basic? For Plantinga, the *sensus divinitatus* delivers the belief that God exists, and, for reasons discussed above, this belief is basic. But, according to Plantinga, how exactly does the *sensus divinitatus* function? In this section, I will address four questions concerning Plantinga's understanding of the *sensus divinitatus* including: What is the *sensus divinitatus*? What is the role of the *sensus divinitatus* as a part of natural revelation? Does the *sensus divinitatus* function in the nonbeliever? And what are the consequences of sin upon the *sensus divinitatus*?

For Plantinga, the *sensus divinitatus* is a capacity or disposition to form the belief that God exists in certain circumstances (i.e., grounds). As I have already mentioned, Plantinga's understanding of the *sensus divinitatus* and grounds might be understood as a sort of natural revelation "tag team" that produces true beliefs (i.e., the knowledge of God the Creator) that anticipate the knowledge of God the Redeemer. However, these beliefs should be thought of not as premises for the conclusion that God exists but rather as the circumstances that occasion those beliefs.[47] It is in this sense that the

---

43. Plantinga, "Reason and Belief in God," 73.

44. He notes: "Warrant is a normative, possibly complex quantity that comes in degrees, enough of which is what distinguishes knowledge from mere true belief." Plantinga, *Warrant: The Current Debate*, 4.

45. Plantinga, *Warrant: The Current Debate*, 4.

46. Plantinga, *Warrant and Proper Function*, 21. See also Plantinga, *Warranted Christian Belief*, xi.

47. Plantinga, *Warranted Christian Belief*, 175.

beliefs produced by the natural revelation "tag team" are immediate. They "just arise within us."[48]

Plantinga argues, by way of analogy, that the *sensus divinitatus* is a basic starting point just like perception, memory, or *a priori* belief.[49] Following Bavinck,[50] he notes:

> It isn't a matter of making a quick and dirty inference from the grandeur of the mountains or the beauty of the flower or the sun on the treetops to the existence of God; instead, a belief about God spontaneously arises in those circumstances, the circumstances that trigger the operation of the *sensus divinitatus*. This belief is another of those starting points for thought; it too is basic in the sense that the beliefs in question are not accepted on the evidential basis of other beliefs.[51]

Therefore, the *sensus divinitatus* delivers these theistic beliefs in an immediate rather than inferential way. The belief that God exists is a spontaneous deliverance of the *sensus divinitatus*. But how does the *sensus divinitatus* relate to natural revelation?

The *sensus divinitatus* is certainly *a part of* natural revelation, but the two should not be thought of as synonymous. That is, they are related as a part is to the whole, not as identical designations for the same concept. For Plantinga, the *sensus divinitatus* is an *internal* variety of natural revelation that serves as a sort of capacity. This capacity is then filled by what Plantinga calls grounds, which are the complementary *external* variety of natural revelation. Together, they function to produce theistic belief. The *sensus divinitatus* and grounds are, therefore, a theistic belief producing "tag team" that cooperate to produce the knowledge of God the Creator. Taken together, they anticipate the knowledge of God the Redeemer that comes by way of a second "tag team" (i.e., Scripture and the internal instigation of the Spirit) as a result of faith.[52]

---

48. Plantinga, *Warranted Christian Belief*, 175.
49. Plantinga, *Warranted Christian Belief*, 175–76.
50. See Herman Bavinck, *The Doctrine of God*, trans. William Hendricksen (Eerdmans, 1951), 78–79, quoted in Plantinga, "Reason and Belief in God," 64.
51. Plantinga, *Warranted Christian Belief*, 176.
52. Plantinga, *Warranted Christian Belief*, 180, 243–44, 252. Plantinga's "three-tiered cognitive process" is what I have been calling the second "tag team."

For Plantinga then, the *believer* is entirely rational in starting with belief in God, and the one who takes belief in God as basic (i.e., the believer) can *know* that God exists. But what about the nonbeliever? Does the nonbeliever have what it takes to believe in God? According to Plantinga, the believer "who takes belief in God as basic can *know* that God exists," but the nonbeliever has only a "tendency or nisus, in certain situations . . . to apprehend God's existence and to grasp something of his nature and actions."[53] In other words, even the nonbeliever has this capacity (i.e., the *sensus divinitatus*) that is triggered in certain circumstances, resulting in a tendency toward belief in God. This tendency or nisus, however, "can be and is suppressed by sin." Nonetheless, "we human beings typically have at least some knowledge of God, and some grasp of what is required of us; this is so even in the state of sin and even apart from regeneration."[54] The reason we resist the deliverances of the *sensus divinitatus*, says Plantinga, is that the fall had *affective* as well as cognitive consequences. He acknowledges that there has been "a failure of proper function," resulting in "a sort of madness of the will."[55] This has, in turn, perverted what would have been a natural inclination toward the knowledge and love of God. Elsewhere, he notes: "It is no part of the model, however, to hold that the *sensus divinitatus* is never subject to malfunction; perhaps it is sometimes diseased or even inoperative. It can also be impeded in the usual ways, and its deliverances can perhaps sometimes be extinguished by the wrong kind of nurture."[56] Yet, whatever the condition of the *sensus divinitatus*, it can be healed by faith and the work of the Spirit.[57] To summarize: the *sensus divinitatus* has suffered certain consequences as a result of sin but is nonetheless functional, and this despite our affective disorders, which result in a failure to accept the deliverances of the *sensus divinitatus*.

According to Plantinga, the *sensus divinitatus* is, in certain circumstances, a "reliable belief-producing mechanism." Taken together, the *sensus divinitatus* and these circumstances (i.e., grounds) function as a sort of natural revelation "tag team." Furthermore, everyone, including believer and

---

53. Plantinga, "Reason and Belief in God," 90.
54. Plantinga, *Warranted Christian Belief,* 210.
55. Plantinga, *Warranted Christian Belief,* 208.
56. Plantinga, *Warranted Christian Belief,* 173n.
57. Plantinga, *Warranted Christian Belief,* 186.

nonbeliever alike, has this capacity, but the nonbeliever continues to resist the deliverances of the *sensus divinitatus* because of sin. Nevertheless, they do have "some knowledge of God, and some grasp of what is required . . . even in the state of sin and even apart from regeneration."[58] Last, though the *sensus divinitatus* has admittedly been "damaged and corrupted by sin," it may be "partly healed and restored to proper function" as a result of "faith and the concomitant work of the Holy Spirit." Thus the *sensus divinitatus* should not be thought of as functioning properly in any exclusive sense (i.e., apart from the work of the second "tag team").[59] For Plantinga, the notion of warranted Christian belief presupposes the regenerating work of the Holy Spirit, which repairs the *sensus divinitatus* so that we might "with the aid of spectacles . . . begin to read distinctly . . . gathering up the otherwise confused knowledge of God in our minds."[60] Prior to regeneration, in certain circumstances the *sensus divinitatus* may well produce theistic beliefs, but these beliefs are suppressed. After regeneration, however, "we can see God and be put in mind of him in the sorts of situations in which that belief-producing process is designed to work."[61] For Plantinga the *sensus divinitatus* and grounds certainly play a role in theistic-belief production (i.e., the knowledge of God the Creator), but they do not deliver distinctly Christian beliefs (i.e., the knowledge of God the Redeemer). Those beliefs (i.e., the great truths of the gospel) come "by way of the work of the Holy Spirit" as a "supernatural gift," and the believer who has come to know God as Creator and Redeemer in this manner "will of course be justified."[62]

With this context in mind, we can now consider what Plantinga has to say about the prospects for natural theology. Is there prescriptive possibility from his perspective? Plantinga begins his 1991 essay "The Prospects for Natural Theology" with a question: "What is natural theology, and what is it for?"[63] Recall the Descriptive Responsibility. Plantinga answers: "As to what it *is*, for present purposes we may take it, very simply, to be the attempt

---

58. Plantinga, *Warranted Christian Belief*, 210; cf. Cornelius Van Til, *The Defense of the Faith* (P&R, 1955), 92.

59. Plantinga, *Warranted Christian Belief*, 280–81.

60. Calvin, *Institutes*, 1.6.1.

61. Plantinga, *Warranted Christian Belief*, 280–81.

62. Plantinga, *Warranted Christian Belief*, 245–46.

63. Alvin Plantinga, "The Prospects for Natural Theology," *Philosophical Perspectives* 5 (1991): 287.

to provide proofs or arguments for the existence of God. More exactly, it is the project of producing proofs or arguments for *theism*, the view (roughly speaking) that there exists an all-powerful, all-knowing, wholly good person who has created the world."[64] This is classic NT2. What's missing is some acknowledgment that natural theology is more diverse than NT2.[65] This is also classic NT2. After defining natural theology as "producing proofs or arguments for *theism*," he then answers the second half of his question "What it is for?" with an introductory list of "things one might hope to accomplish by offering such arguments" before proceeding to discuss the matter in historical perspective. Cutting to the chase, the function of natural theology, according to Plantinga, has nothing to do with justification or warrant. As he explains:

> Natural theology is not needed for belief in God to have warrant; the natural view here, in fact, will be that many people *know* that there is such a person as God without believing on the basis of the arguments of natural theology. Of course it doesn't follow that natural theology has no role *at all* to play; there are lots of roles to play besides that of being the sole source of warrant.[66]

Arguments for God are not needed, but this does not mean that there are no good arguments. In fact, Plantinga has elaborated "Two Dozen (Or So) Theistic Arguments"[67] and confesses: "My intention had always been to write a small book based on these arguments, with perhaps a chapter on each of the main kinds. Time has never permitted, however, and now the chances

---

64. Plantinga, "Prospects for Natural Theology," 287.
65. I prefer definitions that acknowledge, even if only indirectly, the diversity of natural theologies, e.g., "Natural theology *in the sense of* arguments from evident features of the natural world to the existence of God." Swinburne, "Revival of Natural Theology," 303 (emphasis mine).
66. Plantinga, "Prospects for Natural Theology," 311.
67. Alvin Plantinga, "Two Dozen," 203–27. See also Plantinga, "Prospects for Natural Theology," 312: "There are good arguments from the nature of sets, of propositions, of numbers, of properties, of counterfactual propositions. There are good arguments from the nature of knowledge, from the nature of proper function, from the confluence of proper function with reliability, from simplicity and from induction. There are good moral arguments, good arguments from the nature of evil; from play, enjoyment, love, nostalgia; and perhaps from colors and flavors. There is no dearth of good theistic arguments; but this is not the place to explore them."

of my writing such a book are small and dwindling."[68] It would have been nice, but it wasn't necessary.

Assessment

Plantinga's claim to the Reformed tradition, as well as his understanding of the nature and function of the *sensus divinitatus*, have been questioned and criticized by fellow Reformed theologians. One such critic is John Beversluis. He calls Plantinga's exposition of Calvin on natural theology "rather selective and (sometimes) highly imaginative."[69] He argues:

> There is indeed a traditional Reformed objection to natural theology, but it is very different from—and, in fact, incompatible with—Plantinga's. Hence whatever the merits of his own position, he is quite mistaken in claiming that his objection is a clearer formulation of the "for the most part unclear, ill-focused, and unduly inexplicit" but essentially identical objection found in the writings of the Reformed theologians to whom he appeals and whose tradition he claims to represent.[70]

Specifically, Beversluis believes Plantinga misreads Calvin, overestimating the functioning capacity of the *sensus divinitatus* in fallen humanity. Beversluis writes that, according to Calvin:

> *Fallen* human beings lack both the direct and immediate knowledge of God with which they were originally created and the capacity to achieve it. In Plantinga's language, the 'innate tendency, or nisus, or disposition' to believe in God with which human beings were originally created is no longer operative in fallen humanity.[71]

Beversluis's criticism results from his understanding of Calvin as saying that

---

68. Plantinga, "Prospects for Natural Theology," 311. See Jerry L. Walls and Trent Dougherty, eds., *Two Dozen (Or So) Arguments for God: The Plantinga Project* (Oxford University Press, 2018).
69. John Beversluis, "Reforming the 'Reformed' Objection to Natural Theology," *Faith and Philosophy* 12 (1995): 190.
70. Beversluis, "'Reformed' Objection to Natural Theology," 190.
71. Beversluis, "'Reformed' Objection to Natural Theology," 193.

"in their present fallen condition, human beings have no eyes to discern the revelation of God in Nature."[72] While Beversluis accepts that the revelation of God in nature cannot be avoided, he argues that according to Calvin, human beings suppress, corrupt, and extinguish any tendency toward belief in God.

Paul Helm agrees with Beversluis that Calvin is primarily concerned with establishing culpability (i.e., knowledge that condemns) not rationality (i.e., knowledge that informs). He states:

> What Calvin emphasizes is not rationality but responsibility. His interest in knowledge is not an interest in the rational grounds for theistic belief, but in establishing that since all men and women in fact have some knowledge of God, they are culpable when they do not form their lives in a way that is appropriate to such knowledge.[73]

Helm goes on to discuss the possibility of using Calvin for other purposes, namely, whether or not one might rationally reconstruct Calvin to yield the distinctive tenets of "Reformed epistemology."[74] Apparently not, according to Helm, who concludes that Plantinga's argument is nowhere to be found in Calvin. Instead, Plantinga's argument has to do with "epistemic entitlement; but Calvin says nothing about this, and he may imply nothing about it either."[75]

I find this line of reasoning rather odd given that, for Calvin, the knowledge of God the Creator and its suppression are two simultaneous realities (i.e., one epistemic, one ethical). Recall C. Stephen Evans's two Pascalian principles (discussed in the introduction): wide accessibility and easy resistibility.[76] Calvin clearly states that even "in man's perverted and degenerate nature some sparks still gleam."

---

72. Beversluis, "'Reformed' Objection to Natural Theology," 194.
73. Paul Helm, "John Calvin, the *Sensus Divinitatus*, and the Noetic Effects of Sin," in *International Journal for Philosophy of Religion* 43 (1998): 104.
74. Helm, "John Calvin," 104.
75. Helm, "John Calvin," 105.
76. Calvin explains in *Institutes*, 2.2.12: "In these words both facts are clearly expressed. First, in man's perverted and degenerate nature some sparks still gleam. These show him to be a rational being, differing from brute beasts, because he is endowed with understanding. Yet, secondly, they show this light choked with dense ignorance, so that it cannot come forth effectively. Similarly the will, because it is inseparable from man's nature, did not perish, but was so bound to wicked desires

Elsewhere, he goes so far as to argue that "the signs of immortality which have been implanted in man cannot be effaced."[77] Thus Beversluis is not altogether correct when he argues that "Calvin advances the much stronger claim that this tendency has been '*extinguished* or *corrupted*' by ignorance and wickedness."[78] Calvin does say that "they show this light choked with dense ignorance,"[79] but he also comments that the presence of the divine majesty is inescapable, and though "it may sometimes seem to vanish for a moment, it returns at once and rushes in with new force."[80] For Calvin, this was not an either-or but rather a both-and. It is not that some sparks still gleam *but* the light is choked with "dense ignorance." Rather, it is that some sparks still gleam *and* the light is choked with "dense ignorance," but also that the presence of divine majesty "rushes in with new force." Thus human knowledge of God prior to regeneration is somewhat cyclical, a sort of ebb and flow that resembles "the sleep of drunken or frenzied persons, who do not rest peacefully even while sleeping because they are continually troubled with dire and dreadful dreams."[81] Calvin goes on to note:

> When we so condemn human understanding for its perpetual blindness as to leave it no perception of any object whatever, we not only go against God's Word, but also run counter to the experience of common sense. For we see implanted in human nature some sort of desire to search out the truth to which man would not at all aspire if he had not already savored it. . . . Yet this longing for truth, such as it is, languishes before it enters upon its race because it soon falls into vanity. Indeed, man's mind, because of dullness, cannot hold to the right path, but wanders through various

---

that it cannot strive after the right. This is, indeed, a complete definition, but one needing further explanation." Cf. Van Til, *Defense of the Faith*, 170.

77. Calvin, *Institutes*, 1.5.5.

78. Calvin, *Institutes*, 1.4.1 (my emphasis). See Beversluis, "'Reformed' Objection to Natural Theology," 194.

79. Elsewhere Calvin notes that "after we rashly grasp a conception of some sort of divinity, straightaway we fall back into the ravings or evil imaginings of our flesh, and corrupt by our vanity the pure truth of God." See Calvin, *Institutes*, 1.5.11.

80. Calvin, *Institutes*, 1.3.2.

81. Calvin, *Institutes*, 1.3.2.

errors and stumbles repeatedly, as if it were groping in darkness, until it strays away and finally disappears.[82]

Elsewhere, Calvin notes: "Men of sound judgment will always be sure that a sense of divinity which can never be effaced is engraved upon men's minds."[83] For Calvin, condemnation isn't the end of the story. The knowledge of God the Creator and its suppression are cyclical and perpetual. I see this as no different than Paul's language in Romans 7:15–25:

> I do not understand what I do. For what I want to do I do not do, but what I hate I do. And if I do what I do not want to do, I agree that the law is good. As it is, it is no longer I myself who do it, but it is sin living in me. For I know that good itself does not dwell in me, that is, in my sinful nature. For I have the desire to do what is good, but I cannot carry it out. For I do not do the good I want to do, but the evil I do not want to do—this I keep on doing. Now if I do what I do not want to do, it is no longer I who do it, but it is sin living in me that does it.
>
> So I find this law at work: Although I want to do good, evil is right there with me. For in my inner being I delight in God's law; but I see another law at work in me, waging war against the law of my mind and making me a prisoner of the law of sin at work within me. What a wretched man I am! Who will rescue me from this body that is subject to death? Thanks be to God, who delivers me through Jesus Christ our Lord!
>
> So then, I myself in my mind am a slave to God's law, but in my sinful nature a slave to the law of sin.

I take this to mean that even when the knowledge of God the Redeemer is in view, knowledge and suppression—"For what I want to do I do not do, but what I hate I do"—can be two simultaneous realities. I am aware of no one who has advanced the claim that because Paul sins, his knowledge of the law has been extinguished, rendering the knowledge of God the Redeemer ineffectual, and Paul is culpable—end of story. Whether the knowledge of God

---

82. Calvin, *Institutes*, 2.2.12. Plantinga discusses this passage from Calvin in *Warranted Christian Belief*, 172.
83. Calvin, *Institutes*, 1.3.3.

the Creator or Redeemer is in view, we find epistemic (and ethical) struggle. But recall Calvin's comment on the knowledge of God the Creator: "It may sometimes seem to vanish for a moment, it returns at once and rushes in with new force."[84] For this reason, I would again add a third principle to Evans's two: persistent possibility. Plantinga and his Reformed epistemology may well have faults, but contra Beversluis and Helm, his reading of Calvin is not among them.

His reading of Barth is a different story. Insofar as he acknowledges the capacity of human beings for the knowledge of God, Plantinga is more like Emil Brunner than Barth.[85] In his exchange with Barth on natural theology, Brunner writes:

> No one who agrees that only human subjects but not stocks [*sic*] and stones can receive the Word of God and the Holy Spirit can deny that there is such a thing as a point of contact for the divine grace of redemption. This point of contact is the formal *imago Dei*, which not even the sinner has lost, the fact that man is man, the *humanitas* in the two meanings defined above: capacity for words and responsibility. Not even sin has done away with the fact that man is receptive of words, that he and he alone is receptive of the Word of God. But this "receptivity" must not be understood in the material sense. This receptivity says nothing as to his acceptance or rejection of the Word of God. It is the purely formal possibility of his being addressed.[86]

I have resonated with Brunner's words since first reading them as a seminarian, and I still think Barth wrong, but more importantly Plantinga's claim to be developing a line of thinking implicit in Barth, while developing what Barth would have seen as natural theology, is worth noting. Plantinga is more Brunner than Barth. But this has little to do with the validity of Plantinga's work as such.

---

84. Calvin, *Institutes*, 1.3.2.
85. See Emil Brunner, "Nature and Grace," in Fraenkel, *Natural Theology*, 31–33.
86. Brunner, "Nature and Grace," 31.

PART 3

Signals

CHAPTER 5

Natural Theology as Signals of Transcendence

The possessors of alleged certitude have no need to go in search of signals of transcendence. The rest of us do, unless we are prepared to resign ourselves with stoic fortitude to the ultimate hopelessness of the world.[1]

—Peter Berger

Moving along from natural theology as proof/argument (NT2) to natural theology as signals of transcendence (NT3), it may well seem that we are signaling retreat, for these signs or pointers are a step away from deductive proofs and toward pointers and possibility or, to put it bluntly, a more chastened variety of argument. As I mentioned in the introduction, NT3 is in some ways a combination of the previous types. What I mean by this is that like NT1, NT3 takes experience seriously, but like NT2 it prefers argument. This third type highlights the "natural signs" or experiences that lie at the core of the traditional arguments for the existence of God. Drawing upon the Scottish philosopher Thomas Reid (1710–96), who developed a philosophy of common sense, C. Stephen Evans explains, "The natural signs that point to God's reality are signs that can be interpreted

---

1. Peter L. Berger, *Redeeming Laughter: The Comic Dimension of Human Experience* (De Gruyter, 1997), 214.

in more than one way and thus are sometimes misread and sometimes not even perceived as signs. They point to God but do not do so in a coercive manner."[2] From this, Evans draws two Pascalian principles: wide accessibility and easy resistibility. Regarding the former, Evans wants to say that the knowledge of God is not restricted but widely available, and regarding the latter that despite the knowledge of God being unrestricted, it is not forced on people. I will focus upon Evans's views in chapter 6, but in this chapter I widen the aperture with discussion of terms and distinctions relevant to the type, which is followed by a survey of proponents and then criticisms of the type. Just as one must understand the operative definition of nature and that to which it is opposed in order to understand some natural theology more generally, one must define signs and that to which they are opposed (or are related, but from which they are distinct) in order to understand a particular example of NT3. This leads us to signs, symbols, and sacraments.

Signs, Symbols, and Sacraments

While discussion of signs goes back to Aristotle,[3] the earliest Christian treatment is to be found in the writings of Augustine, who distinguishes between natural signs (*signa naturalia*) and given signs (*signa data*).[4] Smoke as a sign of fire is an example of the former, and words are an example of the latter. The bulk of Augustine's treatment has to do with given signs and the interpretation of Scripture, but he also discusses the distinction between the sign and the signified thing in relation to the sacraments. As one contemporary thinker explains, "Sacraments are the visible word of God to be received in

---

2. C. Stephen Evans, *Natural Signs and Knowledge of God: A New Look at Theistic Arguments* (Oxford University Press, 2010), 2.

3. That said, John Deely has argued "that there is no general concept of sign to be found in Greek philosophy," and that it was "Augustine . . . who, in an ignorant bliss, first began to speak of sign in general." John Deely, "The Role of Thomas Aquinas in the Development of Semiotic Conciseness," *Semiotica* 152 (2004): 95.

4. For a helpful overview and short bibliography, see Michael Cameron, "Sign," in *Augustine Through the Ages: An Encyclopedia*, ed. Allan D. Fitzgerald, OSA (Eerdmans, 1999), 793–98. The classic essay is R. A. Markus, "St. Augustine on Signs," *Phronesis* 2 (1957): 60–83.

faith."[5] The sacraments are sacred signs, material symbols, visible words (or signs) of invisible reality, but not every sign or symbol is a sacrament.

The study of signs and symbols is referred to as semiotics, and making one's way through the literature is no easy task, but if we are to understand natural theology and, more specifically, NT3 in relation to natural theologies of symbols and sacraments, we must learn to differentiate between signs, symbols, and sacraments. Going further, consideration of each of these distinct approaches problematizes an all too easy rejection of natural theology. For the sake of context, here are a few signposts. After Augustine, the most discussed figure is Charles Sanders Peirce (1839–1914), who argued that "every thought is a sign," and "every thought must be interpreted in another."[6] The innovation here is that, for Peirce, it is not simply a matter of the sign and the signified thing. As one contemporary historian explains, for Peirce "every thought is a sign without meaning until interpreted by a subsequent thought, an interpretant. Thus the meaning of every thought is established by a triadic relation, an *interpretation* of the thought as a *sign* of a determining *object*."[7] And so with Peirce, we have thoughts as signs, and the addition of the interpretant (that is, subsequent thought) to the standard relation of the sign and the signified thing (or object). Most, including Evans, would acknowledge that Peirce was influenced by Bishop George Berkeley (1685–1753),[8] an idealist for whom signs played an important role as part of his theory of perception,[9] and some philosophers have argued that Peirce's insight can be traced back to a series of Latin thinkers beginning with Aquinas and culminating in the Portuguese Dominican John Poinsot (1589–1644).[10] According to these philosophers, Peirce recovered and developed the Latin sense of

---

5. Emmanuel J. Cutrone, "Sacraments," in Fitzgerald, *Augustine Through the Ages*, 744. And as Cutrone points out, "A full understanding of Augustine's theological reflections on sacraments must begin with his treatment of signs" (741).

6. Charles Sanders Peirce, "Questions Concerning Certain Faculties Claimed for Man," in *Peirce on Signs*, ed. James Hoopes (University of North Carolina Press, 1991), 49.

7. James Hoopes, introduction to *Peirce on Signs*, 7.

8. For discussion, see James A. Moore, "The Semiotic of Bishop Berkley—A Prelude to Peirce?," *Transactions of the Charles S. Peirce Society* 20 (1984): 325–42.

9. See also Edward A. Sillem, *George Berkeley and the Proofs for the Existence of God* (Longmans, Green, 1957).

10. See, e.g., Deely, "Development of Semiotic Conciseness," 109.

signum (sign) that runs from Augustine up through Aquinas and Poinsot.[11] In any case, it should be clear from this extremely brief survey that speaking of signs is a complicated and contested affair with a long intellectual history. I have no interest in getting into the details, as it would take us down a rabbit hole from which we may never reemerge, but speaking of natural theology as natural signs means something, and what it means depends upon what is meant by *signs*.

Most theological discussions leave out this more complicated history and begin with the German-born American philosopher and theologian Paul Tillich (1886–1965), who distinguished between signs and symbols, arguing that while both "point beyond themselves to something else,"[12] the symbol "participates in that to which it points."[13] But as one recent commentator has noted, there is the difficulty of "understanding what Tillich means when he says of something that it *points to* something else, and what he means when he says of something that it *participates in* the reality of that to which it points."[14] This particular commentator "suggest[s] we interpret Tillich's notion of 'pointing to' as signifying,"[15] but concludes that Tillich "provide[s] no explanation of what is meant by the claim that symbols *participate* in that to which they point."[16] Perhaps symbols do participate in that to which they point, but saying this is so is not the same as explaining how it is so, and so we must look beyond Tillich to understand the relationship of signs and symbols.

Like Tillich, Ricoeur distinguishes between signs and symbols,[17] but he sees the difference as one between meaning and *meanings*. Whereas signs are "literal and manifest," "symbolic signs are opaque, because the first, literal, obvious meaning itself points analogically to a second meaning which

---

11. Deely, "Development of Semiotic Conciseness," 115. See also Umberto Eco and Costantino Marmo, eds., *On the Medieval Theory of Signs* (Benjamins, 1989).

12. Paul Tillich, *The Dynamics of Faith* (1957; repr., HarperOne, 2009), 47.

13. Tillich, *Dynamics of Faith*, 48. Louis Dupré (1925–2022) is a more recent example of someone who thinks signs and symbols distinct. Referencing "a field notorious for confusion," he argues that while signs "merely *point*" (i.e., univocally from sign to signified), symbols "*represent* . . . in the double sense of *making present* and *taking the place of*." See Louis Dupré, *Symbols of the Sacred* (Eerdmans, 2000), 1n1.

14. William L. Rowe, "Tillich's Theory of Signs and Symbols," *The Monist* 50 (1966), 593.

15. Rowe, "Tillich's Theory," 598.

16. Rowe, "Tillich's Theory," 604.

17. Paul Ricoeur, *The Symbolism of Evil*, trans. Emerson Buchanan (Harper & Row, 1967), 15: "Every sign aims at something beyond itself and stands for that something; but not every sign is a symbol."

is not given otherwise than in it. . . . This opacity constitutes the depth of the symbol, which it will be said, is inexhaustible."[18] From Ricoeur's perspective, the symbol moves us from literal sign to latent meaning. What is meant by the claim that symbols *participate* in that to which they point? Ricoeur answers: "The symbol is the movement of the primary meaning which makes us participate in the latent meaning and thus assimilates us to that which is symbolized."[19] According to Ricoeur, the participation is hermeneutical. We participate in meaning.

If not before, it should now be apparent that defining and distinguishing between signs, symbols, and sacraments is not always straightforward. While most would, in principle, distinguish between the three (with the acknowledgment that all sacraments are symbols, and all symbols signs, but not all signs symbols, nor all symbols sacraments), the terms are nevertheless in many cases used interchangeably with their nearest, more inclusive neighbor. Clearly related and sometimes overlapping, these three terms should nevertheless be seen as distinct. While a sign may simply be a communicative, physical gesture, it may also be a mark or some other indication or symbol. Consider the sacraments, which are, according to Augustine, outward and visible signs of an inward and invisible grace,[20] or as the *Oxford English Dictionary* has it, "the outward and visible aspect which symbolizes the inward and spiritual aspect."[21] Signs are, in other words, the most inclusive category. Symbols are more, but certainly not less, than signs. In some cases, the terms are conjoined (e.g., "sign symbol") to make the point. Like signs, symbols stand for or represent, but they suggest something more in the form of multivalent meaning. They don't simply stand for; they grant open-ended access to worlds of meaning. Sacraments are an even more particular,

---

18. Ricoeur, *Symbolism of Evil*, 15. David Brown puts it this way: "What gives symbols their power is their multivalency. That is, precisely because they open viewer or reader to a plurality of possibilities that helps explain why they retain their irreducibility or non-substitutionability for some more prosaic alternative." David Brown, *Divine Generosity and Human Creativity: Theology Through Symbol, Painting and Architecture*, ed. Christopher R. Brewer and Robert MacSwain (Routledge, 2017), 51. Brown thinks that "sacrament offers a layer beyond symbol in the promise of mediated divine presence or agency" (55).

19. Ricoeur, *Symbolism of Evil*, 16.

20. See also The Book of Common Prayer: sacraments as "outward and visible signs of inward and spiritual grace" (857).

21. *Oxford English Dictionary*, 2nd ed., s.v. "sign," 5.d.

religious variety of signs and symbols. They are for this reason sometimes called religious signs or religious symbols. It's easy to get lost while attempting to achieve clarity, but we must be mindful of the descriptive responsibility at every level. When Brown (NT1) advocates a natural theology of symbol, he means something different than Evans (NT3) who advocates a natural theology of signs. Even so, there are similarities. Neither, for instance, takes the deductive approach of NT2.[22] And while Berger speaks of "a sacramental universe,"[23] we should not assume that by this he means the same thing that Brown means when he speaks of sacramentality (by which he means transformed natural religion). Berger means analogously (i.e., signs functioning like sacraments) while Brown means expansively (i.e., a broader conception of sacramentality reaching beyond the traditional seven).

We must read carefully, for it is all too easy to mistake the meaning of words. The same goes for concepts. All too often, the reader will adopt (or react to) concepts from some thinker's work without taking account of the framework from which that concept springs. While accepting the concept need not mean accepting the framework, there are cases in which a concept cannot be extricated from its framework and so acceptance of the concept means accepting the framework. At the very least, understanding the framework gives context for the concept. It is for this reason that I take the time to explain the intellectual heritage of the words and concepts under discussion.

In the section that follows, I will introduce two proponents of NT3: Peter Berger and Aidan Nichols. In chapter 6, I will then focus on Evans. As the reader will see, each of these uses the language of natural theology as (natural) signs, but does so with reference to different theological and philosophical frameworks. Berger draws upon the German philosopher and theologian Friedrich Schleiermacher (1768–1834), Nichols upon the English theologian and philosopher John Henry Newman (1801–90), and Evans upon the Scottish philosopher Thomas Reid. The result is a wide variety of natural theologies even within this one type. A similar comment could be made with reference to the other types. In any case, I will defer to each

---

22. The approach of NT3, however, may well lead to NT2. That is to say, the signs lie at the core of the arguments.

23. Berger, *Redeeming Laughter*, 214.

thinker's usage of sign, symbol, or sacrament while detailing their respective frameworks. The section will conclude with a synthetic description of NT3.

Natural Theology as Signals of Transcendence (NT3)

The most well-known (and oft-cited) proponent of this type is Peter Berger.[24] For Berger, a sociologist whose early work dealt with secularization and the loss of religious interpretations of the world,[25] certain "prototypical human gestures"—such as ordering, playing, hoping, damning or condemning, and laughing[26]—could be described as signals, rumors, or intimations of transcendence.[27] Each of these is a moment when the transcendent breaks through or we break through. As Berger explains, these gestures and signals are "pointers towards a religious interpretation of the human situation."[28] To

---

24. Brown references Berger's book *A Rumor of Angels* as being "particularly good at forcing us to think more widely about how intimations of the supernatural are innate to our experience." See David Brown, *Invitation to Theology* (Blackwell, 1989), 131. See also Russell Re Manning, "A Perspective on Natural Theology from Continental Philosophy," in *The Oxford Handbook of Natural Theology*, ed. Russell Re Manning (Oxford University Press, 2013), 264–65.

25. See Peter L. Berger and Thomas Luckmann, *The Social Construction of Reality: A Treatise in the Sociology of Knowledge* (Anchor, 1967); and Peter L. Berger, *The Sacred Canopy: Elements of a Sociological Theory of Religion* (Anchor, 1969), 107–8 for a definition of secularization. Berger would later reject the idea that modernity necessarily leads to secularization. See Peter L. Berger, "The Desecularization of the World: A Global Overview," in *The Desecularization of the World: Resurgent Religion and World Politics*, ed. Peter L. Berger (Eerdmans, 1999), 2. While this last essay has been cited by Berger and others as the turning point, indications of this eventual rejection can be found much earlier in Berger's work. See, e.g., Peter L. Berger, *The Heretical Imperative: Contemporary Possibilities of Religious Affirmation* (Anchor, 1980), x–xi; and Peter L. Berger, *A Far Glory: The Quest for Faith in an Age of Credulity* (Free, 1992), 32–33, 37. In any case, after rejecting secularization theory, Berger then advocated a theory of pluralism. See Peter L. Berger, *The Many Altars of Modernity: Toward a Paradigm for Religion in a Pluralist Age* (De Gruyter, 2014). For Berger's intellectual autobiography, see Peter L. Berger, *Adventures of an Accidental Sociologist: How to Explain the World Without Becoming a Bore* (Prometheus, 2011).

26. Peter Berger, *A Rumor of Angels: Modern Society and the Rediscovery of the Supernatural* (Anchor, 1970), 53–72. To be clear, he writes: "This is by no means an exhaustive or exclusive list of human gestures that may be seen as signals of transcendence" (72). See also Berger, *Redeeming Laughter*, 214. More specifically, Berger suggests that we might also look to "yet other sources, such as those the artist and the poet draw from." See Berger, *Rumor of Angels*, 85. For a recent work inspired by Berger, see Os Guinness, *Signals of Transcendence: Listening to the Promptings of Life* (InterVarsity, 2023).

27. See Berger, *Rumor of Angels*, 52–53, 95; Berger, *Redeeming Laughter*, 214. In another book, he writes: "The human world in its entirety (including its various symbol systems) is itself a symbol—to wit, a symbol of the divine." See Berger, *Heretical Imperative*, 113. Elsewhere he mentions "transcendent points of reference." See Berger, "Desecularization of the World," 13.

28. Berger, *Rumor of Angels*, 62.

be clear, Berger differentiates between these signals and proofs for the existence of God.[29] Even so, he does speak of the signals as arguments, but these arguments are matters of interpretation. They lead us to interpret the world and our lives in a different way.

The signals are rooted in what Berger refers to as inductive faith, and this faith is informed significantly by Schleiermacher,[30] the German theologian and philosopher Rudolph Otto (1869–1937),[31] and the Romanian historian of religion Mircea Eliade (1907–86). Against Enlightenment rationalism and rational theology,[32] as well as the idea that religion can be equated with metaphysics or morality,[33] Schleiermacher argued that the essence of religion is the feeling of absolute dependence.[34] Following Schleiermacher's lead, Berger asks:

> What is the essence [*Wesen*] of religion? That essence is defined by Schleiermacher as the experience of the infinite or of God, also characterized as an experience of absolute dependence. *This* is what religion is all about—*not* theoretical speculation, *nor* moral preachings. Doctrines and moral maxims are the result of reflection about religious experience and of the practical application of such experience—that is, they are only the outer garb of religion. The underlying experience of all religion, its essence, is one of encountering the infinite within the finite phenomena of human life.[35]

---

29. Berger, *Redeeming Laughter*, 214.
30. See Berger, *Heretical Imperative*, xii, 116.
31. Discussed in chapter 2.
32. Friedrich Schleiermacher, *On Religion: Speeches to Its Cultured Despisers*, trans. and ed. Richard Crouter (Cambridge University Press, 1996), 19. For discussion, see Rudolph Otto, "Introduction," in Friedrich Schleiermacher, *On Religion: Speeches to Its Cultured Despisers*, trans. John Oman (Harper, 1958), xv–xvii. As Otto explains, the "cultured despisers" were not "the tired skeptics, the all-too-knowing ones who had fallen victim in the struggle between 'knowledge' and 'faith,' or the readers who despaired of the world, the spirit, and ideas", but "the disciples of Herder, Goethe, Kant, and especially Fichte" (xvi).
33. Schleiermacher, *On Religion*, 22.
34. Terrance Tice notes: "Although this concept appears very frequently in *Christian Faith* . . . it is among the most widely misunderstood. . . . that we feel ourselves to be absolutely [*schlechthin*] dependent . . . means the same thing as saying that we are 'conscious' that our existence utterly, purely, unexceptionally occurs 'in relation to God.'" Terrance Tice, *Schleiermacher* (Abingdon, 2006), 54–55.
35. Berger, *Heretical Imperative*, 118.

So Berger takes inspiration from Schleiermacher and sees religious experience as fundamental to religion. While some think this akin to Ludwig Feuerbach's reductive move, Berger sees Schleiermacher's method as a distinct alternative. From Berger's perspective, Feuerbach "sought to reduce infinity to finitude, to translate theology into anthropology."[36] Schleiermacher, on the other hand, as Berger explains, "uses an anthropological starting point in his theologizing, and he views the finite as being shot through with manifestations of the infinite."[37] This leads Berger to conclude (with reference to Schleiermacher): "The empirical universe is a symbol of the infinite, and it is 'miraculous' in that it is ongoingly permeated with signals of the latter's transcendent reality."[38] Berger moves from Schleiermacher to signals, extending his thinking with reference to Eliade.

Eliade was interested in "archaic ontology," which he describes as "the conceptions of being and reality that can be read from the behavior of the man of the premodern societies."[39] According to Eliade, there are two aspects of this archaic (or original) ontology. First, "reality is acquired solely through repetition or participation."[40] Archaic man seeks to move from chaos to cosmos through repetition of the cosmogony. Reality is thus conceived along Platonic lines as "a function of the imitation of a celestial archetype."[41] The second aspect highlighted by Eliade is that "he who reproduces the exemplary gesture . . . finds himself transported into the mythical epoch in which its revelation took place."[42] The key for Eliade is that "the archetypal gestures—finally reproduced in endless succession by man—were at the same time hierophanies or theophanies."[43] Theophany—"A manifestation or appearance of God or a god to man"[44]—is a familiar term. Hierophany—"The *act*

---

36. Berger, *Heretical Imperative*, 118–19.

37. Berger, *Heretical Imperative*, 119.

38. Berger, *Heretical Imperative*, 119.

39. Mircea Eliade, *The Myth of the Eternal Return*, 2nd ed., trans. Willard R. Trask (Princeton University Press, 2005), 3.

40. Eliade, *Myth of the Eternal Return*, 34.

41. Eliade, *Myth of the Eternal Return*, 5. It should be noted that Eliade is using *archetype* differently than Jung. Eliade explains: "I use the term 'archetype,' . . . as a synonym for 'exemplary model' or 'paradigm,' that is, in the last analysis, in the Augustinian sense" (xxix).

42. Eliade, *Myth of the Eternal Return*, 35.

43. Eliade, *Myth of the Eternal Return*, 105.

44. *Oxford English Dictionary*, 2nd ed., s.v. "theophany."

of manifestation of the sacred"[45]—is perhaps less so, but it is a key word for Eliade, and the point is that both theophanies and hierophanies can be revelatory. As Eliade explains: "When the sacred manifests itself in any hierophany, there is not only a break in the homogeneity of space; there is also revelation of an absolute reality, opposed to the nonreality of the vast surrounding expanse."[46] The hierophany is an interruption or irruption as well as an opening and a threshold.[47] Jacob's ladder is a classic example.[48] To be clear, the hierophany is a step beyond the sign, not merely indicating something more but also manifesting presence.

Returning now to Berger, remember that from his perspective the gestures are signals of transcendence.[49] They point beyond "our 'natural' reality."[50] As Berger explains (with reference to the argument from ordering): "In the observable human propensity to order reality there is an intrinsic impulse to give cosmic scope to this order, an impulse that implies not only that human order in some way corresponds to an order that transcends it, but that this transcendent order is of such a character that man can trust himself and his destiny to it."[51] The movement here is "from human experience to statements about God."[52] Moving beyond Eliade's "archaic ontology," Berger seeks to articulate a metaphysics of everyday experience that reignites theological conversation beyond the so-called death of God.[53] One might

---

45. Mircea Eliade, *The Sacred and the Profane: The Nature of Religion*, trans. Willard R. Trask (Harcourt, 1959), 11.

46. Eliade, *Sacred and the Profane*, 21.

47. See Eliade, *Sacred and the Profane*, 20–29. Interestingly, Eliade notes: "One might even say that all hierophanies are simply prefigurations of the miracle of the Incarnation, that every hierophany is an abortive attempt to reveal the mystery of the coming together of God and man." Mircea Eliade, *Patterns in Comparative Religion*, trans. Rosemary Sheed (1958; repr., University of Nebraska Press, 1996), 29.

48. For Eliade, Jacob's ladder is one of many cosmological images rooted in the symbolism of the Center of the World. See Eliade, *Sacred and the Profane*, 36–42. For additional discussion of Jacob's ladder (with reference to Berger), see Christopher R. Brewer, "'Surely the Lord Is in This Place': Jacob's Ladder in Painting, Contemporary Sculpture and Installation Art," in *The Moving Text: Interdisciplinary Perspectives on David Brown and the Bible*, ed. Garrick V. Allen, Christopher R. Brewer, and Dennis F. Kinlaw III (SCM, 2018), 107–21.

49. Clearly influenced by Eliade's archaic ontology, it is worth remembering that Berger is articulating a theological anthropology in a nutshell.

50. Berger, *Rumor of Angels*, 53.

51. Berger, *Rumor of Angels*, 56.

52. Berger, *Rumor of Angels*, 57.

53. Berger was responding to the radical theology of the 1960s. See Berger, *Rumor of Angels*, 76–93.

describe Berger's signals as flies in the ointment of a purely secular reading of the world. They problematize what Desmond refers to as "postulatory finitism,"[54] or what Taylor calls "the immanent frame."[55] The signals point toward something more. These are not deductive proofs. The signals are everyday experiences that require religious interpretation. They are in this sense like Ricoeur's symbols. The sign (or symbol) is hermeneutical.

English theologian Aidan Nichols argues similarly but again takes a different route. Drawing upon Newman's erudite discussion of assent, Nichols helps us understand how Berger's signals of transcendence might lead to belief in God. Generally speaking, Newman was opposed to the idea that in order to be considered rational, faith must be demonstrated via proofs. Newman distinguished between implicit and explicit reasoning and thought the former no less rational than the latter. One need not argue explicitly for implicitly held beliefs. As one commentator explains, "Newman wants to show that the scope, range, and modalities of human cognition cover more territory than an ideal version of rationality (e.g. a formal kind of reasoning). . . . Newman's approach, then, is to explore how the mind actually works, not how we think it ought to work."[56] This leads him to consider the ways we consider and judge evidence and, more specifically, to what he refers to as "the Illative Sense."[57] The basic idea is that the illative sense gathers up discrete bits of experience and evidence into a cumulative case. As Nichols explains:

> Newman . . . highlighted the proper form that an argument for God's existence should take. This is neither deductive, nor in any strict, formal sense, inferential, as theological rationalists would hold; nor is it couched purely in terms of religious experience straitly so called, as many of their extreme opponents would allege. It is, rather, a cumulation of experiential

---

54. William Desmond, *Is There a Sabbath for Thought? Between Religion and Philosophy* (Fordham University Press, 2005), 14.

55. Charles Taylor, *A Secular Age* (Belknap, 2007), 539–93. See also p. 5 (where Taylor references Berger).

56. Frederick D. Aquino, "Epistemology," in *The Oxford Handbook of John Henry Newman*, ed. Frederick D. Aquino and Benjamin J. King (Oxford University Press, 2018), 382.

57. John Henry Cardinal Newman, *An Essay in Aid of a Grammar of Assent* (University of Notre Dame Press, 1979), 270–99.

cues (many of them apparently secular in character) that indicates the reasonableness of assent to the proposition, "God exists," although, in the nature of things, these cues cannot compel that assent.[58]

In the same paragraph Nichols speaks of "the experiential indicators of God," and then "these various pointers to a transcendence implicit in experience, yet going beyond it."[59] Like Berger and Ricoeur, Nichols thinks interpretation and, more specifically, interpretive contexts are significant,[60] and drawing upon Newman he argues that these interpretative contexts (or patterns) are what take us beyond isolated signals. And while this is person-relative, we have not only our own experience but also "the tradition of reflection upon these matters."[61] But what might this look like applied to art? According to Jeremy Begbie:

> Art can point to what is true of all our engagement with the world—the world always exceeds our grasp of it. There is a "generative excess" in reality that calls forth and provokes all human inquiry. . . . Again, this does not amount to a knock-down proof of a Creator, but it is highly consonant with belief in a God who himself is generative excess, who lives as generous, excessive love, and who both creates and envelops his creation with this same love.[62]

Here, generative excess and excessive love serve as signs and, alongside Evans's signs, participate in something like Nichols's grammar of consent.[63]

And so with Berger we have a Schleiermacher-inspired concept, and with Nichols we have a more robust, Newman-inflected articulation. NT3 is a conceptually rich type, but with each proponent drawing upon

58. Aidan Nichols, *A Grammar of Consent: The Existence of God in Christian Tradition* (University of Notre Dame Press, 1991), 1.

59. Nichols, *Grammar of Consent*, 1.

60. Nichols, *Grammar of Consent*, 6–7.

61. Nichols, *Grammar of Consent*, 36. In addition to Newman, Nichols discusses Gregory of Nyssa, Augustine, Anselm, Aquinas, John of the Cross, Blaise Pascal, Immanuel Kant, Søren Kierkegaard, Gabriel Marcel, and G. K. Chesterton as being helpful in this regard.

62. Jeremy Begbie, "The Future: Looking to the Future: A Hopeful Subversion," in *For the Beauty of the Church: Casting a Vision for the Arts*, ed. W. David O. Taylor (Baker, 2010), 173–74.

63. Nichols, *Grammar of Consent*.

distinct traditions of thought it can be difficult to keep up. The Descriptive Responsibility never lets up. In chapter 6, I will focus on Evans, who draws upon Reid's concept of a natural sign to get behind (or beyond) the traditional arguments for the existence of God.[64] At this stage, however, it would be useful to review the key considerations with reference to Berger and Nichols.

In *The Social Construction of Reality*, Berger and his coauthor understand nature sociologically, preferring to speak of "the reality of everyday life."[65] While they speak of "the nature and scope of the sociology of knowledge,"[66] "the nature . . . of ideas,"[67] "the nature of social reality,"[68] "the nature of philosophical prolegomena,"[69] and so forth, they rarely speak of nature as such, but when they do it is most often "human nature" (i.e., Begbie's second sense) that is being discussed.[70] Coming now to that to which nature is opposed, Berger and his coauthor see the reality of everyday life (i.e., "paramount reality") as being opposed to "non-everyday experiences" and speak of "a dialectic between nature and society."[71] They explain: "In the dialectic between nature and the socially constructed world the human organism itself is transformed. In this same dialectic man produces reality and there

---

64. Yet another example of this type can be found in William Desmond's articulation of the hyperboles of being. William Desmond, *Godsends: From Default Atheism to the Surprise of Revelation* (University of Notre Dame Press, 2021), 94: "Between finitude and infinity there is a movement of being carried beyond every whole. This comes home to us when we attend to the signs of the over determinate in immanence. As happenings in immanence that are not determined by immanence alone, the hyperboles of being are neither merely determinate, nor merely indeterminate, nor yet self-determining. They communicate the over determinate and so cause us to rethink the threshold between finitude and infinity." See also William Desmond, *God and the Between*, Illuminations: Theory and Religion (Blackwell, 2008).

65. Berger and Luckmann, *Social Construction of Reality*, 19. The authors explain: "This wide-awake state of existing in and apprehending the reality of everyday life is taken by me to be normal and self-evident, that is, it constitutes my natural attitude" (21).

66. Berger and Luckmann, *Social Construction of Reality*, 16.

67. Berger and Luckmann, *Social Construction of Reality*, 20.

68. Berger and Luckmann, *Social Construction of Reality*, 28.

69. Berger and Luckmann, *Social Construction of Reality*, 34.

70. Berger and Luckmann, *Social Construction of Reality*, 67: "There is no human nature in the sense of a biologically fixed substratum determining the variability of socio-cultural formations. There is only human nature in the sense of anthropological constants (for example, world-openness and plasticity of instinctual structures) that delimit and permit man's socio-cultural formations. . . . While it is possible to say that man has a nature, it is more significant to say that man constructs his own nature, or more simply, that man produces himself." See also 209, 220n7.

71. Berger and Luckmann, *Social Construction of Reality*, 21, 26, 201.

produces himself."[72] In *The Sacred Canopy*, Berger speaks of culture as "second nature" (i.e., Cicero's second sense),[73] "nature" (i.e., Cicero's first sense),[74] and "human nature" (i.e., Begbie's second sense).[75] The function of natural theology from Berger's perspective is, at the most fundamental level, the construction of reality (i.e., sacred reality as opposed to merely profane).

Nichols spends little to no time in *A Grammar of Consent* discussing his views of nature or that to which it is opposed. Instead, he defers to each figure considered as is evident when he says:

> First, I am not suggesting that the reader should attempt to adopt simultaneously all the metaphysical systems espoused by the various figures described in this book. To do so would indeed be intellectual suicide and perhaps a very good way to send oneself to Bedlam. All I am proposing is that we should attend as carefully as possible to what they have to say about particular aspects of human experience that for them were crucial in the approach to God. Their illumination of these is partially, though not perhaps wholly, distinguishable from their wider speculative systems (where they had such).[76]

What this means is that we must look to the individuals discussed in Nichols's book if we are to drill down on definitions of nature and that to which it is opposed. We do, however, catch a glimpse of the function of natural theology in Nichols when he quotes Régis Jolivet (1891–1966), noting that "he goes on to say that the question is more a matter of 'uncovering' God than of 'proving' God."[77]

Shifting now from these three thinkers and the key considerations to more general observations, it is important to keep several things in mind. For proponents of NT3, the function of natural theology is to gesture or point, perhaps even to interrupt or probe, but not to prove. Deductive proof is, from their perspective, disconnected from everyday life, and arguments

---

72. Berger and Luckmann, *Social Construction of Reality*, 204. See also 233n44.
73. Berger, *Sacred Canopy*, 6.
74. Berger, *Sacred Canopy*, 6–8.
75. Berger, *Sacred Canopy*, 7, 25.
76. Nichols, *Grammar of Consent*, 15.
77. Nichols, *Grammar of Consent*, 10.

are secondary to that which lies at the core. NT3 has to do with attending to the signs of transcendence found in immanence. The proofs and arguments (NT2) can wait. But not everyone agrees with this approach.

Pushing for Proof

While Berger, Nichols, and Evans have argued that we should at the very least begin with signs rather than proof, Matthew Levering thinks that "this effort to avoid the term 'proof' is mistaken," for, as he goes on to say, "the word 'prove' reminds us that we are not here dealing with an experiential intuition, a gesture toward infinite mystery, or an opinion based on personal sensibility."[78] According to Levering, "It is urgent that Christians today reclaim the two-millennia-old Christian tradition of demonstrating God's existence."[79] Edward Feser concurs, writing:

> Natural theology, historically, was a confident discipline. A long line of thinkers from the beginnings of Western thought down to the present day—Aristotelians, Neo-Platonists, Thomists, and other Scholastics, early modern rationalists, and philosophers of some other schools too, whether pagans, Jews, Christians, Muslims, or philosophical theists—have affirmed that God's existence can be rationally demonstrated by purely philosophical arguments. The aim of this book is to show that they were right, that what long was the mainstream position in Western thought ought to be the mainstream position again.[80]

For Levering and Feser, there is no reason to retreat from proof and argument to the more modest claims of NT3, but as Desmond observes:

> This is not simply a matter of reasserting old "proofs" of God or devising new. It calls for an exploration of what is prior to determinate "proof." This is not to deny that in trying to situate "proofs" in light of the primal

---

78. Matthew Levering, *Proofs of God: Classical Arguments from Tertullian to Barth* (Baker Academic, 2016), 5.

79. Levering, *Proofs of God*, 7.

80. Edward Feser, *Five Proofs of the Existence of God* (Ignatius, 2017), 15.

ethos, it might well happen that something of their slumbering promise is refreshed. It is not a matter of slighting them, but of stepping back, so to say, from the foreground of certain arguments, to try to discern some of the enabling metaphysical conditions that fund their intelligibility and potential persuasiveness.[81]

Stepping back need not mean retreat, and if Desmond is right, we may well need to "rock backwards to get out of a rut and budge the jam and then roll with release into the future."[82] Rocking back is, in the context of this chapter, digging deeper into the signs before (or at the core of) the arguments. In many ways, NT3 is the most exciting (and difficult) variety of natural theology, for it draws upon the fundamental components of meaning, blurring the lines between nature and culture (for all signs are ideas, be they natural or otherwise).[83] Having surveyed the depth and breadth of NT3, I will now examine one particular advocate: Evans.

---

81. Desmond, *God and the Between*, 3.

82. Desmond, *Desire, Dialectic, and Otherness*, xxvii.

83. See Nathan Lyons, *Signs in the Dust: A Theory of Natural Culture and Cultural Nature* (Oxford University Press, 2019).

CHAPTER 6

The Signs at the Core:
C. Stephen Evans

Many of the classical arguments for God's existence, such as the cosmological, teleological, and moral arguments, are grounded in what I shall call "natural signs" that point to God's reality. These theistic arguments derive their force and enjoy whatever plausibility they possess from the signs that lie at their core. The nature of a sign, as I shall develop the notion, is to be a "pointer," something that directs our attention to some reality or fact and makes knowledge of that reality or fact possible, and this feature is what explains the continuing appeal of the arguments.[1]

—C. Stephen Evans

Christians should welcome natural theology so long as the goals of natural theology are modest.[2]

—C. Stephen Evans

---

1. C. Stephen Evans, *Natural Signs and Knowledge of God: A New Look at Theistic Arguments* (Oxford University Press, 2010), 2.
2. C. Stephen Evans, *Why Christian Faith Still Makes Sense: A Response to Contemporary Challenges* (Baker Academic, 2015), 75.

In chapter 5, I described natural theology as signals of transcendence (NT3), and in this chapter I will discuss an important, contemporary proponent of this type. American philosopher C. Stephen Evans references Berger's signals of transcendence, but rather than following Schleiermacher via Berger he instead draws upon the philosophers Thomas Reid (1710–96) and Søren Kierkegaard (1813–55) to develop a natural theology of natural signs. Evans suggests that we take a step back from the proofs of NT2 and consider the signs that lie at the core of the various theistic arguments: the experience of cosmic wonder, the experience of purposive (elsewhere beneficial) order, the sense of being morally accountable, the sense of human dignity and worth (elsewhere the intrinsic worth of human beings), and the longing for transcendent joy.[3] Evans speaks of these signs as *pointing* and not *participating*, as with David Brown's NT1, or *proving*, as with some versions of NT2. But as with any type or expression of natural theology, there are intellectual currents flowing beneath the surface. To understand what Evans is up to, we need to understand these currents.

C. Stephen Evans in Context

At the most basic level, Evans is a philosopher of religion responding to the evidentialist objection to religious belief.[4] According to the evidentialist, the justification of religious belief requires evidence, and according to those who advance the evidentialist objection to religious belief, there is insufficient evidence. As Evans explains, there are two possible responses to this objection: (1) to meet the objection by providing evidence or (2) to question the role of evidence.[5] Alvin Plantinga took the latter route, arguing that there are all sorts of things for which we don't have evidence but nevertheless take to be the case (e.g., the existence of other minds). If we don't need evidence for other minds, he reasons, perhaps we don't need evidence for God. After critiquing

---

3. See C. Stephen Evans, *Natural Signs*; and Evans, *Christian Faith*, 39. Evans lists the first four of these signs in the former and all five in the latter.

4. See C. Stephen Evans and R. Zachary Manis, *Philosophy of Religion: Thinking About Faith*, 2nd ed. (InterVarsity, 2009), 188–91. On the relation of signs and evidence, see James Allen, *Inference from Signs: Ancient Debates About the Nature of Evidence* (Clarendon, 2001).

5. Evans and Manis, *Philosophy of Religion*, 191–95. See also C. Stephen Evans, *Faith Beyond Reason: A Kierkegaardian Account* (Eerdmans, 1998), 39.

evidentialism, Plantinga (and his colleagues, including Wolterstorff and others) then provides an alternative: Reformed epistemology. Evans is an advocate of Reformed epistemology and, like Plantinga, thinks that while one need not provide evidence, this does not mean that evidence cannot be provided.[6] But whereas Plantinga spent his time questioning the role of evidence, Evans assumes this background but nevertheless spends most of his time providing evidence for the existence of God in the form of clues or signs. While acknowledging that the objection may be flawed, he still thinks meeting it worthwhile and possible via a cumulative case. But Evans is no classical foundationalist. Drawing upon Kierkegaard, he argues against the supposed objectivity of foundationalism and for the subjective nature of knowledge.[7] Evans explains:

> Many writers think the problem of knowing religious truth is primarily an evidential problem. For them the question is whether we have enough good evidence. For Kierkegaard (and I agree with him here) the main problem lies not in the evidence but in the knower. How do we become the kinds of people who are capable of understanding and grasping the truth?[8]

Against this backdrop, natural theology is deemed worthwhile, but in the end Evans thinks it accomplishes very little. He thinks NT2 fails in terms of proof but thinks the arguments and even more so, the signs at their core (formulated as NT3) are valuable as part of a cumulative case that points to the possibility of theistic faith and perhaps even God. Even so, he does not see natural theology "as providing us with an adequate, positive knowledge of God but as supporting . . . 'anti-naturalism.'"[9] In fact, Evans suggests "that we reconceive natural theology as a defense of anti-naturalism."[10] This is essential context for understanding Evans's approach. Evans's signs point in the form of a question,[11] and the signified lies beyond the reach of natural theology. As Evans

6. Evans, *Christian Faith*, 16.
7. See C. Stephen Evans, *Subjectivity and Religious Belief: An Historical Critical Study* (Eerdmans, 1978).
8. Paul Pardi, "Interview with C. Stephen Evans: Kierkegaard, Natural Signs and Knowledge of God," *Philosophy News*, March 2, 2011, https://philosophynews.com/interview-with-c-stephen--evans-kierkegaard-natural-signs-and-knowledge-of-god/.
9. Evans, *Christian Faith*, 20.
10. Evans, *Christian Faith*, 20.
11. See Evans, *Christian Faith*, 20–21.

explains, "Natural theology does not replace a full, special self-revelation of God; it makes us open to the possibility of such a revelation."[12] But I then wonder: Why must natural theology either be nothing or everything? Why must it deliver "an adequate, positive knowledge of God,"[13] and if it fails to do so, be judged a failure with respect to a function not its own? Does not its function differ from that of so-called revealed theology, and to the extent that it does, should it not be judged by its own function or standard?

Turning now to the key considerations, Evans defines nature (with reference to signs) as "nature which is outside of ourselves," on the one hand, and "human nature," on the other.[14] Nature, so defined, is opposed to "religious authority," "divine revelation," and "special revelation."[15] The function of natural theology has to do with the rationality of religious belief. Signs are formulated as arguments, and "these arguments can be viewed as attempts to test the Christian conception at particular points where it makes contact with human experience."[16] It is clear that Evans thinks natural theology, which is a particular variety of evidentialist apologetics, is valuable even if nonessential. It can, as just noted, test the Christian conception defensively, but it can also go on the offensive, "play[ing] a useful if limited role by challenging the dogmatic assumption that we live in a closed universe and thereby opening people to the possibility of a God who might reveal Himself in more special, personal terms."[17] It can, in other words, have a preparatory effect, and this in spite of sin. For Evans, these natural signs, formulated as arguments, form "a cumulative case for the reasonableness of believing in God."[18]

A Natural Theology of Theistic Natural Signs

In Evans's earlier work,[19] he speaks of "evidence" and "clues." These clues include the mystery of cosmic wonder, the mystery of purposive order, and

---

12. Evans, *Christian Faith*, 27.
13. Evans, *Christian Faith*, 20.
14. Evans, "Apologetics in a New Key," 73.
15. Evans, "Apologetics in a New Key," 65, 67–68.
16. Evans, "Apologetics in a New Key," 71.
17. Evans, "Apologetics in a New Key," 75.
18. Evans, "Apologetics in a New Key," 75.
19. C. Stephen Evans, *The Quest for Faith: Reason and Mystery as Pointers to God* (InterVarsity, 1986);

the mystery of a moral order.[20] According to Evans, "These mysteries are what Peter Berger calls '*signals of transcendence* within the . . . human condition.'"[21] As I said in chapter 5, Berger is the most well-known proponent of NT3, and many others reference his work as a sort of touchstone. But while Berger was primarily concerned with the social construction of reality and inductive faith, Evans is concerned with evidence for the rationality of religious belief as well as the subjective nature of faith and reason.[22] These mysteries or clues may or may not be convincing to the unbeliever, that is to say, they can be discounted or reinterpreted.

The Influence of Thomas Reid

While Evans wrote about pointers, clues, and mysteries in earlier books, it wasn't until *Natural Signs and Knowledge of God* (2010) that he "express[ed] them . . . in a more developed and intellectually rigorous form."[23] In that book, Evans draws upon Thomas Reid's concept of natural signs,[24] and as he points out, "Reid himself probably took the term 'sign' from George Berkeley."[25] For Berkeley and Reid, signs have to do with perception, and perceptual awareness has to do with sensations, which are natural signs. As Evans explains (following Reid), while some natural signs do not need to be taught, others are learned, and the natural signs for God are an example of the latter.[26] Here, Evans sounds like Nichols (discussed in chapter 5), who argues that "if we are to stand any decent chance of discerning the presence of God

revised and republished as C. Stephen Evans, *Why Believe? Reason and Mystery as Pointers to God* (InterVarsity, 1996).

20. Evans, *Quest for Faith*, 37–43, and 44ff. See also 49.

21. Evans, *Quest for Faith*, 49 (with a quotation from Peter Berger, *Rumor of Angels*, 52).

22. Put differently, Berger is, as I explained in chapter 5, drawing upon Schleiermacher, while Evans is drawing upon Kierkegaard (who critiqued Schleiermacher's approach), and so while Evans references Berger's signals, his theistic natural signs are genealogically (and so theologically) distinct.

23. Evans, *Natural Signs*, viii. That said, the best introduction to his mature reflections (in my opinion) can be found in Evans, *Christian Faith*.

24. Even so, Evans is quick to clarify: "I am not merely putting the concept of natural signs to use in an area where Reid did not imply it, but modifying the concept in significant ways. I do not claim, therefore, that my concept of a natural sign is the same as Reid's, even if his work provides the inspiration for my concept" (Evans, *Christian Faith*, 27, see also 30).

25. Evans, *Christian Faith*, 26. See Manuel Faso and Peter West, eds., *Berkeley's Doctrine of Signs* (De Gruyter, 2024).

26. Evans, *Christian Faith*, 31.

in the most basic facts of our human experience we cannot afford to be individualists in splendid isolation."[27] By saying this, Nichols means to emphasize the ways we learn from "the living past" and "the communion of saints."[28]

In the 1990 essay "Apologetics in a New Key," Evans defines natural theology as "the enterprise of attempting to prove or show the reasonableness of belief in God apart from acceptance of any religious authority."[29] In that same sentence, he goes on to define evidentialist apologetics as "the larger enterprise of attempting to show the reasonableness of Christian faith, of which natural theology might naturally be seen as a significant component."[30] Evans is, in other words, still very much concerned with evidence. In fact, he sees natural theology as part of the larger project of evidentialist apologetics. After elaborating and responding to five objections to natural theology, Evans articulates what he calls "Natural Theology in a New Key," and by this he means "to think of the evidence that God has provided for His reality as consisting of *natural signs*."[31] He explains:

> On this view the traditional philosophical arguments for God's existence can be seen as attempts to articulate these natural signs and formulate them as rigorous arguments. I see nothing wrong with the attempt to do this. But it is a mistake to regard them as *proofs*. And it is a mistake to think that they are without value if they fail as conclusive proofs. The natural signs which the arguments are attempting to articulate retain their value as God's calling cards, even if a particular attempt to articulate the sign fails, when judged by a certain standard of proof.[32]

From this, it is clear that for Evans signs inform the arguments for the

---

27. Nichols, *Grammar of Consent*, xi.

28. Nichols, *Grammar of Consent*, xii and xi, respectively.

29. C. Stephen Evans, "Apologetics in a New Key: Relieving Protestant Anxieties Over Natural Theology," in *The Logic of Rational Theism: Exploratory Essays*, ed. William Lane Craig and Mark S. McLeod (Mellon, 1990), 65. But natural theology need not be—and as Wolterstorff has argued, has not always been—a variety of evidentialist apologetics. Here again, see Nicholas Wolterstorff, "The Migration of the Theistic Arguments: From Natural Theology to Evidentialist Apologetics," in *Rationality, Religious Belief, and Moral Commitment: New Essays in the Philosophy of Religion*, ed. Robert Audi and William J. Wainwright (Cornell University Press, 1986), 39.

30. Evans, "Apologetics in a New Key," 65.

31. Evans, "Apologetics in a New Key," 73ff.

32. Evans, "Apologetics in a New Key," 73.

existence of God, but these arguments are not, and need not be, conclusive proofs. While the signs are widely available, they are *"resistible* or *discountable."*[33] These claims—later expressed as the wide accessibility principle and the easy resistibility principle—are similar to Brown's twin commitment to divine generosity and human freedom. But whereas Brown's solution was to explore the role of symbols in an effort to preserve human freedom with respect to divine dialogue, Evans argues that "there is evidence to which faith can respond. But the evidence is ineffective for the individual who lacks the proper kind of 'subjectivity.'"[34] But "for the person who is seeking God and willing to serve Him,"[35] "they provide a cumulative case for the reasonableness of believing in God."[36] Evans concludes:

> None of this implies that natural theology is essential for faith, and it certainly does not imply that natural theology has much value by itself. But it does imply that in a secular culture such as our own, natural theology might sometimes play a useful if limited role by challenging the dogmatic assumption that we live in a closed universe and thereby opening people to the possibility of a God who might reveal Himself in more special, personal terms.[37]

I confess that I find this conclusion strange and will have more to say (in response) in this chapter's final assessment.

In the second edition of *Philosophy of Religion* (2009), Evans (along with his coauthor) defines natural theology as the "attempt to determine the truth of theism without assuming the standpoint of a particular religion. . . . The natural theologian attempts to see what can be known about God independently of any special religious authority."[38] Worth noting here again is that Evans thinks that "the distinction between natural theology and

---

33. Evans, "Apologetics in a New Key," 71–72. See also Evans, *Natural Signs*, 2.
34. Evans, "Apologetics in a New Key," 72.
35. Evans, "Apologetics in a New Key," 72.
36. Evans, "Apologetics in a New Key," 75.
37. Evans, "Apologetics in a New Key," 75.
38. C. Stephen Evans and R. Zachary Manis, *Philosophy of Religion: Thinking About Faith*, 2nd ed. (InterVarsity, 2009), 55.

revealed theology is not so easy to make as one might think."[39] He explains that "the concept of natural theology is not all that clear and that no sharp line can be drawn between natural theology and other kinds of theology."[40] Even so, he thinks "that there is an important initial distinction to be drawn between believing in God on the basis of arguments, which take as their starting point general features of nature or human experience, and believing in God on the basis of highly specific experiences or events."[41] For Evans, the line between natural theology and revealed theology is blurry but still useful as an abstract concept. Natural theology is, again, closely related to apologetics,[42] and it isn't necessarily the best way to acquire knowledge of God,[43] nor is its success "crucial to religious belief."[44]

With these caveats out of the way, Evans goes on to discuss NT2, pointing out that it is only "one way the project of natural theology has been formulated."[45] The truth is that Evans doesn't think proof necessary for justified true belief. Even so, he thinks arguments may well be worthwhile even if they fail as proofs.[46] Like Sudduth (discussed in the introduction), Evans distinguishes between a model-specific objection and a project objection, though he doesn't use those terms. He explains (rightly in my view):

> It is important to recognize that there is no such thing as *the* cosmological argument or *the* teleological argument, although some philosophers have mistakenly assumed this to be the case. Many different versions of each of these arguments have been proposed, and some differ radically from others

---

39. Evans and Manis, *Philosophy of Religion*, 56.
40. Evans and Manis, *Philosophy of Religion*, 57. Perhaps this is why he confuses the function of natural theology with the function of revealed theology, but if no sharp line can be drawn between so-called natural theology and so-called revealed theology, then it must be admitted that the functions of the distinct parts do not apply without modification to the new whole. My argument stands whether natural and revealed theology are two distinct parts of a larger whole or two nondistinct parts of a larger whole.
41. Evans and Manis, *Philosophy of Religion*, 57.
42. Evans continues (in the sentence after those just quoted), noting: "The potential value of natural theology for religious apologetics is evident, since it will be far easier to argue that some individual or book is a revelation from God if it is antecedently known (or probable) that there is a God." See Evans and Manis, *Philosophy of Religion*, 57.
43. Evans and Manis, *Philosophy of Religion*, 57.
44. Evans and Manis, *Philosophy of Religion*, 56.
45. Evans and Manis, *Philosophy of Religion*, 57.
46. Evans and Manis, *Philosophy of Religion*, 61.

in the same category. For this reason alone one should be wary of claims to have given a final refutation of one of these types of arguments. It would be difficult to show that an objection applies to *all forms* of an argument and even more difficult to show that no one will ever invent a version of the argument to which the objection does not apply.[47]

I mentioned in the introduction that there is, in an important sense, no such thing as natural theology but rather only natural theologies. This applies not only to the five types but also to versions within (or even beyond) these types. As I have said repeatedly, one cannot simply say "No!" to natural theology, for saying "No!" to the project would require careful consideration and then refutation of each and every model. Some might respond that these types and versions share some fundamental organizing principle to which one can in fact object, but even if this were so, such an argument would require ignoring human experience and reason and so fail as a comprehensive theological approach. One may well caricature and reject natural theology by treating one part of the conversation as the whole, but doing so betrays ignorance, obstinance, or both. My argument in this book is for a more careful, empirical approach. Patience is a virtue, and (contra Barth) we need not fear natural theology as if it were a Medusa stare.

The Influence of Søren Kierkegaard

In *Faith Beyond Reason: A Kierkegaardian Account* (1998), Evans elaborates "two Kierkegaardian themes: 1. Faith is a trait of the whole person that is essential to gaining true religious knowledge; and 2. Human reason has its limits and it is reasonable to recognise those limits."[48] In dialogue with Kierkegaard, Evans defends a "responsible fideism,"[49] which, to be clear, has everything to do with "Christian claims about sin and the effects of sin on human reason."[50] Fideism functions as a sort of governor on Evans's natural theology, limiting its operations to the faithful. As he explains:

---

47. Evans and Manis, *Philosophy of Religion*, 62.
48. Evans, *Faith Beyond Reason*, vii.
49. Evans, *Faith Beyond Reason*, 52.
50. Evans, *Faith Beyond Reason*, 13.

What I wish to argue is that a fideist does not have to deny that there is any such thing as a natural knowledge of God. What the fideist must deny is that there is any knowledge of God, or at least any worthwhile knowledge, that can be had independently of faith. Such a claim is consistent, however, with affirming the possibility of real knowledge that is dependent on faith.[51]

But what about the widely available, sign-informed arguments? If they are widely available and can be easily resisted, that would suggest that natural theology extends beyond the faithful to everyone, even those who resist the evidence. But according to Evans, recognition of the signs comes with faith. He explains:

A Kierkegaardian may therefore see some arguments for God's existence as attempts to articulate and make clearer what I would call signs or pointers to God's presence. Without the heightened sensitivities that faith provides one cannot properly recognize and appreciate those divine signs and pointers. Nevertheless, the signs and pointers thus recognised might be quite real and could function as reliable indicators of God's reality.[52]

Not all proponents of NT3 make this move, but NT3 is a sort of hinge between NT1 and NT2, on the one hand, which in most, if not all, cases function antecedently (i.e., before faith), and NT4 and NT5, on the other, which in most, if not all cases, function consequently (i.e., after faith).

Evans unpacks this further in his essay "Kierkegaard, Natural Theology, and the Existence of God." He explains: "Far from denying that humans have a natural knowledge of God, Kierkegaard—it would be closer to the truth to say—simply takes for granted that humans can know that God exists through their awareness of God's claim on their lives. He takes this for granted, but it never becomes a major or central theme in his works."[53] With this in mind,

---

51. Evans, *Faith Beyond Reason*, 116.
52. Evans, *Faith Beyond Reason*, 121. Evans revisits this point in the book's concluding paragraph; see p. 153.
53. C. Stephen Evans, "Kierkegaard, Natural Theology, and the Existence of God," in *Kierkegaard and Christian Faith*, ed. Paul Martens and C. Stephen Evans (Baylor University Press, 2016), 35.

Evans highlights two points made by Kierkegaard: first, that "mere propositional knowledge that there is a God, even if it is accurate, has little value," and second, "that this knowledge is highly unreliable, shot through with mistakes."[54] This does not mean, however, that it has no value.[55] According to Evans, "Natural religious knowledge, when it is motivated by a passionate desire to know and please God, can then have genuine value as a preparation for the gospel."[56] But where does this passionate desire to know and please God come from? Plantinga speaks of the internal instigation of the Holy Spirit, but unless I've missed it, Evans gives no explicit answer.

Assessment

While some critique of NT3 has come from proponents of NT2 such as Levering and Feser (both mentioned in chapter 5), it comes equally from proponents of NT5, such as the British New Testament scholar N. T. Wright. According to Wright, "The resurrection opens up . . . a new public world in which the questions raised by humans within the present creation can be seen as provisional signposts to God," but "they are . . . 'broken signposts' . . . none will lead us to Utopia, let alone to God."[57] Like Evans, Wright thinks natural theology's signs point in the form of a question, but the signified lies beyond the reach of natural theology. Speaking of signs is well and good so long as we don't expect them to lead us anywhere. But then what is the value of a sign pointing like a bridge to nowhere?

In the end, Evans thinks natural theology is of limited use given that the knowledge it delivers is vague (or "meager") and "highly theoretical."[58] I confess that I have never understood this concern and critique. Evans concludes that natural theology is deficient for the reasons just stated, but this is an error that results from trading the declared function of natural theology for the caricature rejected. Why argue that natural theology has a different function but then critique it from the perspective of the function rejected?

---

54. Evans, "Kierkegaard," 35.
55. Evans, "Kierkegaard," 36.
56. Evans, "Kierkegaard," 36.
57. N. T. Wright, *History and Eschatology: Jesus and the Promise of Natural Theology* (Baylor University Press, 2019), xvii.
58. Evans and Manis, *Philosophy of Religion*, 97.

This is a category error all too common in the literature critiquing natural theology. It is, and I realize there may well be issues with the analogy, like saying that eighth grade is deficient because it doesn't result in graduation from high school, or that friendship (in general) is deficient because it is not in all cases romantic (i.e., particular) friendship or, taking it a step further, the consummation of a particular romantic relationship in sexual love. But this is absurd. Part of the conversation need not be the whole, whether we are speaking of schooling, friendship and intimacy, or varieties of natural theology and progression toward faith.

I often find myself beginning conversations with a word on conversation. As a human being, I can only say one thing at a time. My mouth, physically, can only say one thing at a time. So, any time we have a conversation, implicit in this is the fact that we are making a choice of one conversation from among many. We choose to speak about one thing instead of another, this rather than that. Part of that acknowledgment is that we have made a choice not only to have one part of the conversation from among many but also to have the other parts of the conversation in turn. I think that communication breakdown happens when we mistake (or intentionally substitute) one part of the conversation for another, or a part of the conversation for the whole conversation, and we see this all the time. Take political debates, for example. Someone asks a question from one conversation, and they get an answer to a different conversation. These are sly ways of shifting conversation, and not all of us mean to do this, but we find ourselves doing it all the time. There is a sort of injustice when someone raises a conversation to not have that part of the conversation, and so, again, I often find myself saying things like, "This is an important conversation. It's just not the one we're having. So if we can just finish the one we are having, then we can move on to another (part of the) conversation."

Returning now to Evans's conclusion (which, I confessed, I found strange), when he says that "none of this implies that natural theology . . . has much value by itself," he seems to be judging the worth of natural theology with reference to the standard (or function) of revealed theology (i.e., substituting one part of the conversation for another). To the extent that natural theology is distinct from revealed theology, it has its own purpose(s), and its success can only be judged relative to that purpose and not some other.

If, as Evans suggests, the purpose of natural theology is to "challenge the dogmatic assumption that we live in a closed universe," then it is successful, perhaps valuable, and maybe even essential to the extent that it achieves this purpose, which is distinct from the purpose(s) of so-called revealed theology. To suggest that natural theology is nonessential or lacking in value because it is not the revelation of God "in more special, personal terms" is to make a category error that betrays a particularly Protestant anxiety. It exchanges one part of the conversation for another, and this category error is rampant in the literature of natural theology. Having said all of this, there is at least one place Evans recognizes natural theology's value in relation to its function. He writes:

> Whether something has value or is to be judged a failure without value depends on the purposes to which it is being put. If one wanted to cross an ocean, a canoe would be of no use, but no one would say that this means that canoes are failures as modes of water transportation. They work quite well on rivers and small lakes. Similarly, an estimate of the value of theistic arguments, or natural theology in general, depends on what one is trying to accomplish via natural theology.[59]

But that's the question, isn't it? What is Evans trying to accomplish with his valuable but nonessential version of NT3? The shift from proofs to signs is indeed promising, but his ultimate evaluation of these signs is less so from my perspective. Pushing even further toward restrictive views of natural theology, I now turn to NT4: natural theology as *Christian* natural theology.

---

59. Evans, *Natural Signs*, 10. See also Catherine Z. Elgin, *True Enough* (MIT Press, 2017). I need to give this more thought, but following Elgin one could argue that we should accept felicitous falsehoods (as epistemic responsibilists) and that, as a result, natural theology may well be *true enough*.

PART 4

Christian Natural Theology

Natural Theology as *Christian* Natural Theology

I believe there is . . . reason to renew the enterprise of natural theology for the sake of faith itself.[1]

—John Cobb Jr.

A fourth type of natural theology—natural theology as *Christian* natu-ral theology (NT4)—adjusts the fader from antecedent to consequent, from anyone and everyone to the faithful. The arguments of natural the-ology, in this case, are retrospective for those who already believe. As I said in the introduction, proponents of NT4 typically read Barth through T. F. Torrance (1913–2007) who argued that, according to Barth, "natural the-ology is included *within* revealed theology, where we have to do with actual knowledge of God as it is grounded in the intelligible relations in God him-self."[2] Torrance argued that Barth's primary objection to the traditional type of natural theology was its independent character.[3] It was, in other words, a model-specific rather than a project objection. This reading has rightly been

---

1. John Cobb Jr., *A Christian Natural Theology: Based on the Thought of Alfred North Whitehead*, 2nd ed. (Westminster John Knox, 2007), xvi.
2. T. F. Torrance, *The Ground and Grammar of Theology: Consonance Between Theology and Science* (T&T Clark, 2001), 91. For his use of "*Christian natural theology*," see p. 107.
3. Torrance, *Ground and Grammar of Theology*, 92. See also T. F. Torrance, "The Problem of Natural Theology in the Thought of Karl Barth," *Religious Studies* 6 (1970): 121–35.

contested by the theologian Paul Molnar,[4] and for this reason I have distinguished between NT4 and NT5. Contemporary proponents of NT4 include Alister E. McGrath, whose "scientific theology" takes Torrance as its prolegomena,[5] and also Anthony Monti (d. 2004), who explores natural theology with reference to the arts.[6] But these Torrance-inspired readings of Barth are, as Fergusson has rightly noted, a "revision of Barth"[7] and, as such, are distinct from NT5. According to Torrance's reading of Barth, the problem with natural theology traditionally conceived is that it seeks a foundation independent of God's revelation in Jesus Christ. The problem is not with natural theology *per se* but with any natural theology that seeks to stand on its own two feet.

In addition to Torrance-inspired readings of Barth, NT4 includes Christian natural theology influenced by Alfred North Whitehead (1861–1947), the father of process philosophy. As the American theologian and philosopher John B. Cobb Jr. explains (with reference to the first edition of Whitehead's book): "The book reflected the dominance of Neo-orthodox and Bultmannian existentialism that was brewing at the time I was writing."[8] Both Torrance-inspired and Whitehead-inspired versions of NT4 have been influenced by Barth but are, at the same time, distinct from NT5. Describing his approach, Cobb writes:

> I tried to show that even those theologies which explicitly repudiate natural theology have had assumptions or developed implications that should, in fact, be recognized as belonging to the sphere of natural theology. In the case of those theologies which affirm natural theology, I argued that the natural theology in question has specifically Christian character. If

---

4. Paul D. Molnar, "Natural Theology Revisited: A Comparison of T. F. Torrance and Karl Barth," *Zeitschrift für Dialektische Theologie* 21, no.1 (2005): 53–83.

5. For discussion of the connection with Torrance, see Benjamin Myers, "Alister McGrath's Scientific Theology," in Alister E. McGrath, *The Order of Things: Explorations in Scientific Theology* (Blackwell, 2006), 2–3.

6. See Jeremy S. Begbie, "Incarnation, Creation, and New Creation: T. F. Torrance and a Theological Re-Visioning of the Arts," *Participation* 11 (2023): 61–79; Anthony Monti, "'Types and Symbols of Eternity': How Art Points to Divinity," *Theology* 105 (2002): 118–26; and Anthony Monti, *A Natural Theology of the Arts: Imprint of the Spirit* (Ashgate, 2003).

7. David Fergusson, "Types of Natural Theology," in *The Evolution of Rationality: Interdisciplinary Essays in Honor of J. Wentzel van Huyssteen*, ed. F. LeRon Shults (Eerdmans, 2006), 393n27.

8. Cobb, *Christian Natural Theology*, xi.

this is the case, it is reasonable to propose that we take the problem of constructing a natural theology with utmost seriousness, while not supposing that in doing so we are employing a rationality itself unaffected by our Christian commitments.[9]

But what does it mean to say that "natural theology is included *within* revealed theology," or "that the natural theology in question has specifically Christian character"?[10] In an effort to answer this (or these) question(s), I turn now to the conversation of antecedent, consequent, and anatheist construals of natural theology (or faith).

Antecedent, Consequent, and Anatheist

Arguments over the place of natural theology in Christian theology inevitably come down to the relationship of natural theology to Christian faith and, more specifically, to their relationship in time. This is especially the case for NT4. Is natural theology a legitimate antecedent to Christian faith or only a consequent? Proponents of NT1, as well as some versions of NT2, would answer "antecedent and consequent." Proponents of NT3 differ. Proponents of NT4 would answer "consequent." Natural theology, in this case, is for the faithful.

According to the German theologian Jürgen Moltmann (1926–2024), "The place given theologically to *theologia naturalis* has always been determined by salvation history: the natural knowledge of God which is now given and possible is a 'remainder' left over from the knowledge of God that existed in paradise."[11] Moltmann suggests that natural theology has three functions: an educative (or preparatory) function, a hermeneutical function, and an eschatological function. That said, Moltmann seems to minimize the relevance of natural theology when he refers to "pure *theologia naturalis*" as "theology under the conditions of the pristine creation," for this theology

---

9. Cobb, *Christian Natural Theology*, xv.

10. Torrance, *Ground and Grammar of Theology*, 91; Cobb, *Christian Natural Theology*, xv.

11. Jürgen Moltmann, *God in Creation: A New Theology of Creation and the Spirit of God* (Fortress, 1993), 57.

is no longer accessible to us.[12] The mode of the presence of God in our time is revealed theology. As Moltmann explains: "Revealed theology is natural theology in the conditions of history, just as theology in paradise was revealed theology in the conditions of the pristine creation. The theology of glory is then true natural theology and perfected revealed theology in the condition of a consummated creation and history."[13] For Moltmann, natural theology is a remainder and recollection (with reference to God's good creation) as well as an anticipation and prereflection (with reference to God's kingdom).[14] It is, in other words, a former mode of the presence of God transposed. The theology of the moment is revealed.[15] This is the kind of thinking that leads to NT4, and though Moltmann speaks of an educative function, one may well wonder what role natural theology, neither given nor possible at this time, has to play.[16] If "the messianic understanding of the world is the true natural theology,"[17] as Moltmann claims, then natural theology is, at best, consequent, that is, seen from the perspective of faith. This stands in contrast to earlier types rooted in natural religion and reason. For those types, natural theology functions beyond the bounds of faith.

But rather than speaking of natural theology with reference to salvation history à la Moltmann (where natural theology is an objectively outmoded mode of the presence of God) or one's personal faith journey (where natural theology is a mode of human reflection, as well as the contents of that collective reflection, possible and/or accessible before and/or after faith), must we not also speak of natural theology after the death of faith not only subjectively (with reference to one's personal faith journey) but also objectively (with reference to our secular or postsecular society)?

In the conclusion to his book *The Symbolism of Evil*, Ricoeur argues for the re-creation of language via symbol. Hermeneutics (i.e., "criticism") demythologizes, but hermeneutics can also, via the symbol, lead us beyond

---

12. Moltmann, *God in Creation*, 59.
13. Moltmann, *God in Creation*, 60.
14. Moltmann, *God in Creation*, 57 (remainder), 57 (recollection), 58 (anticipation), and 59 (prereflection).
15. See Moltmann, *God in Creation*, 60.
16. As Moltmann explains: "We have defined the theology which is given and possible at the present time as revealed theology" (*God in Creation*, 60). By logical extension, natural theology is neither given nor possible at this time.
17. Moltmann, *God in Creation*, 60.

criticism. "Beyond the desert of criticism," he says, "we wish to be called again."[18] There is, according to Ricoeur, a precritical "primitive naïveté" (i.e., received beliefs) and a postcritical "second naïveté" (i.e., "second immediacy"). The movement from "primitive naïveté" to "criticism" is one from faith to understanding, and the movement from "criticism" to "second naïveté" is a movement from understanding to faith.[19] In his 1966 Columbia University Bampton Lectures, "Religion, Atheism, and Faith,"[20] Ricoeur argues "that atheism does not exhaust itself in the negation and destruction of religion; rather, that atheism clears the ground for a new faith, a faith for a postreligious age."[21]

The Irish philosopher Richard Kearney has developed Ricoeur's postreligious option, advocating for "the possibility of a third way beyond the extremes of dogmatic theism or militant atheism."[22] This third way, "anatheism," is, according to Kearney, a wager: To believe or not to believe? That is the question. It is a question repeatedly asked and answered. The strength of Kearney's work, from my perspective, is this emphasis upon faith not as a once and for all decision.[23] He writes: "The choice of faith is never taken once and for all. It needs to be repeated again and again—every time we speak in the name of God or ask God why he has abandoned us."[24] Less ideal from my perspective is the postmetaphysical stance that accompanies this perpetual,

---

18. Paul Ricoeur, *The Symbolism of Evil*, trans. Emerson Buchanan (Beacon, 1967), 349. See also Richard Kearney, "Ricoeur and Biblical Hermeneutics: On Post-Religious Faith," in *Ricoeur Across the Disciplines*, ed. Scott Davidson (Continuum, 2010), 30–43.

19. See also William Desmond, *Is There a Sabbath for Thought? Between Religion and Philosophy*, Perspectives in Continental Philosophy (Fordham University Press, 2005), 19; Russell Re Manning, "A Perspective on Natural Theology from Continental Philosophy," in *The Oxford Handbook of Natural Theology*, ed. Russell Re Manning (Oxford University Press, 2013), 266–68. For Desmond's discussion of the proofs, see *Hegel's God: A Counterfeit Double?* (Ashgate, 2003), 97–98.

20. Paul Ricoeur, "Religion, Atheism, and Faith," in Alasdair MacIntyre and Paul Ricoeur, *The Religious Significance of Atheism*, Bampton Lectures in America 18 (Columbia University Press, 1969), 57–98.

21. Ricoeur, "Religion, Atheism, and Faith," 59. He later refers to this as "a faith beyond accusation and consolation" (60).

22. Richard Kearney, *Anatheism: Returning to God After God* (Columbia University Press, 2010), 3.

23. Particularly when expressed as it is in his "Hermeneutics of the Possible God," in *Givenness and God: Questions of Jean-Luc Marion*, ed. Ian Leask and Eoin Cassidy (Fordham University Press, 2005), 242; cf. Richard Kearney, "Ana-Theism: God After God," in *Phenomenology and the Theological Turn. The Twenty-Seventh Annual Symposium of The Simon Silverman Phenomenology Center*, ed. Jeffrey McCurry and Angelle Pryor (Simon Silverman Phenomenology Center, 2012), 23.

24. Kearney, *Anatheism*, 16.

new beginning. Advocating a "God of possibility" (i.e., "the eschatological *posse*, from a postmetaphysical poetical perspective"[25]), Kearney prioritizes possibility over actuality, and this results in an eschatological orientation.

The archeological and metaphysical alternative to Kearney's eschatological and postmetaphysical approach is to be found in Desmond, who begins with astonishment (i.e., an "original wonder before the givenness of being").[26] Being is, for Desmond, overdetermined. There is a "too muchness" to being. Like a generous gift, it astonishes us. But this first movement—more properly called "first astonishment"—is followed by a second, what Desmond calls "first perplexity." In this second modality of wonder, we feel a lack and seek to overcome this lack. In so doing, we move from intimacy to strangeness, fullness to lack, overdeterminacy to indeterminacy. Curiosity follows as the third modality. But this determinate curiosity is all too often thought to be wonder, and so it replaces wonder. Wonder becomes determinate curiosity, determinate science. We seek to move beyond first astonishment and first perplexity and, in the process, unwittingly supplant the source of our astonishment. We become the all-knowing scientist and proclaim the death of God, metaphysics, faith, and so forth. Against this tendency, Desmond wants to return to the primal modality (i.e., "first astonishment"). But how, if it is even possible, does one move from the so-called death of metaphysics to its resurrection? For Desmond, it comes down to a simple fact: "We cannot escape metaphysics, twist and turn as we will."[27] Why is this? Because metaphysical perplexity persists. This "second perplexity," itself a kind of purgatory, is the fourth modality of wonder, and it leads to the fifth one, the resurrection of astonishment, a "second astonishment." For Desmond, then, the question of faith has less to do with what comes "after" than it does with what comes "before."[28] We are, so far as Desmond is concerned, *returned* to awareness, and here art has a special role to play. As Desmond notes: "Art and the great artist can have a significant role in renewing our rapport with creation, recharging our responsiveness to being as mystery, and hence mediately

25. Kearney, "Hermeneutics of the Possible God," 237. See also Richard Kearney, "God Who May Be: A Phenomenological Study," *Modern Theology* 18 (2002): 75–85; cf. Kearney, "Ana-Theism," 8.
26. William Desmond, *The Intimate Strangeness of Being: Metaphysics After Dialectic* (Catholic University of America Press, 2012), 5.
27. William Desmond, *God and the Between*, Illuminations: Theory and Religion (Blackwell, 2008), 18.
28. Desmond, *Intimate Strangeness of Being*, 132.

to its ultimate origin. In this light, there is always a religious dimension to art, just in its power to precipitate astonishment and perplexity."[29] Art, from Desmond's perspective, can kick-start desire's drive through the modalities of wonder, reinvigorating not only metaphysics but also faith.

But what does all of this have to do with natural theology? Rather than speaking of antecedent and consequent, as if those were the only two options, we must recognize the need for natural theology beyond *before and after*. Natural theology is necessary throughout, from my perspective, including not only before and after the moment of faith but also *after and before*, that is to say, after the death of faith and before its (possible) return. To this point, natural theology has been concerned with the transition from before belief to belief. That is the point of which we speak when we speak of *before and after*, antecedent and consequent. But what about devotional doubt, the death of faith and its possible return? What about *after and before*? What might natural theology mean when faith is not seen as a once and for all decision? Before and after, antecedent and consequent begin to lose their meaning, do they not? Which before? Which after? And with what knowledge? If one comes to faith (not in a once and for all manner, as I believe all do) but then doubts and so questions, are they not in a manner of speaking *after and before* faith? The issue from my perspective has less to do with whether natural theology is antecedent or consequent than it does with the possibility of faith beyond the death of faith, and this whether we are speaking of individuals or entire societies. This is where natural theology works. This is where we begin again. But not according to proponents of NT4.

Natural Theology as *Christian* Natural Theology (NT4)

Generally speaking, McGrath's project follows in the footsteps of Torrance, that is to say, McGrath has worked out a "scientific theology" that takes Torrance as its prolegomena.[30] More recently, McGrath has turned his attention to natural theology. In *The Open Secret*, he suggests the following

---

29. Desmond, *God and the Between*, 38.
30. Myers, "Alister McGrath's Scientific Theology," 2–3. See also Alister E. McGrath, *A Scientific Theology*, vol. 1, *Nature* (T&T Clark, 2002); McGrath, *A Scientific Theology*, vol. 2, *Reality* (T&T Clark, 2002); McGrath, *A Scientific Theology*, vol. 3, *Theory* (T&T Clark, 2003).

preliminary definition: "Natural theology can broadly be understood as the systematic exploration of a proposed link between the everyday world of our experience and another asserted transcendent reality."[31] That said, McGrath's approach might be characterized as follows: (1) Over against Enlightenment notions of natural theology, McGrath argues that the meaning of *nature* is not self-evident but is instead a fluid, indeterminate, and constructed concept.[32] Furthermore, nature is stratified and is thus experienced and encountered from a number of perspectives and at a number of levels (e.g., the level of the observable world, of human interaction with this world, and of human culture and society).[33] (2) As a critical realist, McGrath points out that we are embodied and situated as opposed to detached and objective. That is to say, we are not passive spectators but active interpreters.[34] (3) Drawing upon the work of the Scottish-American philosopher Alasdair MacIntyre, McGrath argues for a natural theology of tradition-mediated rationality as opposed to universal rationality.[35] He prefers the designation natural Christian theology to natural theology and sees the project as being concerned with "retrospective validation of belief in God" (i.e., resonance, abduction, or retroduction) as opposed to proofs for God's existence.[36] That is not to say that it does not appeal to those outside the church, but instead that it presupposes the Christian view of the world.[37] According to McGrath, "Nature is here interpreted as an 'open

---

31. Alister E. McGrath, *The Open Secret: A New Vision for Natural Theology* (Blackwell, 2008), 2. See also John Macquarrie, *Principles of Christian Theology*, rev. ed. (SCM, 1966), 57. Elaborating a "new style natural theology," Macquarie writes: "It will provide a bridge between our everyday thinking and experience and the matters about which the theologian talks: it will relate religious discourse to all the other areas of discourse. It will do this by setting out from ordinary situations that can be described in secular language, and will seek to move from them into the situations of the life of faith."

32. McGrath, *Scientific Theology*, 1:81–133. See also McGrath, *Open Secret*, 7–10. Likewise, "The Enlightenment is more variegated and heterogeneous than an earlier generation of scholars believed, making it problematic to speak of 'an Enlightenment natural theology,' as if this designated a single, well-defined entity" (8). See also McGrath, "Thomas F. Torrance and the Search for a Viable Natural Theology: Some Personal Reflections," *Participatio* 1 (2009): 77–78.

33. McGrath, *Scientific Theology*, 1:249–57; McGrath, *Open Secret*, 126ff.

34. McGrath, *Open Secret*, 11; cf. 80–111. Here, McGrath is influenced by T. F. Torrance; cf. N. T. Wright, *The New Testament and the People of God*, vol. 1 of *Christian Origins and the Question of God* (Fortress, 1992), 32–46; Andrew Collier, *Critical Realism: An Introduction to Roy Bhaskar's Philosophy* (Verso, 1994); José López and Gary Potter, eds., *After Postmodernism: An Introduction to Critical Realism* (Athlone, 2001).

35. McGrath, *Open Secret*, 165–70.

36. McGrath, *Order of Things*, 68; McGrath, *Open Secret*, 233–38.

37. McGrath, *Order of Things*, 68.

secret'—a publicly accessible entity, whose true meaning is known only from the standpoint of the Christian faith."[38] (4) Finally, McGrath is concerned to extend the reach of natural theology. Beyond the Enlightenment's "enterprise of sense-making," McGrath wants natural theology's imaginative potential to be realized. He explains: "Natural theology is to be understood to include the totality of the human engagement with the natural world, embracing the human quest for truth, beauty, and goodness."[39] This emphasis upon the imaginative potential of natural theology runs throughout McGrath's works,[40] and yet while calling for dialogue with literature and the arts (i.e., imagination), he does not, so far as I can tell, pursue the dialogue himself. In any case, a number of attempts have been made in this general direction, and it is to these efforts that we now turn.[41]

In *Real Presences*, the Franco-American literary critic George Steiner (1929–2020) argues "that the experience of aesthetic meaning . . . infers the necessary possibility of this [i.e., God's] 'real presence.'"[42] More recently, Monti doubled down on Steiner's "wager on transcendence."[43] He notes:

> It [i.e., the present book] will attempt to set out the epistemological, metaphysical and theological grounds for maintaining that artistic creativity can most adequately be understood as an expression of the "real presence" of God, and that this is the ultimate meaning and truth of such activity. In so doing, it will go on to argue (in disagreement with Steiner) that the God who is present in works of art can best be understood in a Trinitarian way.[44]

Monti begins by reading Barth via Colin Gunton (1941–2003), who suggests

---

38. McGrath, *Open Secret*, 16.
39. McGrath, *Open Secret*, 19. See also 18.
40. McGrath, *Order of Things*, 65, see also 18–20; Alister E. McGrath, "The Natural Sciences and Apologetics," in *Imaginative Apologetics: Theology, Philosophy and the Catholic Tradition*, ed. Andrew Davison (Baker Academic, 2012), 156.
41. Anthony Monti mentions several such attempts in *Natural Theology of the Arts*, 3, 34. These include John Ruskin, Jacques Maritain, Brian Hebblethwaite, George Steiner, Timothy Gorringe, and George Pattison.
42. George Steiner, *Real Presences* (Faber & Faber, 1989), 3. See also Nathan A. Scott and Ronald A. Sharp, eds., *Reading George Steiner* (John Hopkins University Press, 1994).
43. Steiner, *Real Presences*, 4, see also 214–15.
44. Monti, *Natural Theology of the Arts*, 6.

the possibility of redefining natural theology as a theology of nature.[45] From there, Monti moves on to reading Barth through Torrance, who, according to Monti, argues that "natural theology, as Barth later understands it, can no longer be understood as independent of or *logically* prior to 'theological science,' that is, the study of actual knowledge of God."[46] Monti summarizes: "Thus we find that the possibility merely hinted at in Gunton of a 'transformed' post-Barthian natural theology becomes in Torrance a fully worked-out reinterpretation which takes full account of Barth's criticisms yet which also works out the development implicit in the master's later thought."[47] But how exactly does this work?

Monti, like McGrath, begins with critical realism à la Torrance, suggesting that it opens "out onto an ontology that finds its completion in the existence of God."[48] Regarding this ontology, Monti begins with John Polkinghorne's (1930–2021) notion of flexible openness but bolsters it by appropriating and situating Gunton's metaphysic within Polkinghorne's more comprehensive scheme. He further nuances Polkinghorne by way of Michael Polanyi's (1891–1976) stratified ontology (again, via Torrance), and Moltmann's notion of creation as an open system.

Having made explicit his epistemological and metaphysical underpinnings, Monti moves on to the concept of metaphor. According to Monti, "metaphor is what constitutes art as a form of natural theology."[49] Here, Monti leans on Moltmann who states: "All knowledge of the world 'as' creation is hence a *metaphorical* knowledge of the world as parable of the world to come."[50] In an effort to understand metaphor, then, Monti appropriates Janet Martin Soskice and N. T. Wright. He notes:

> [For Soskice] "metaphor is that figure of speech whereby we speak about one thing in terms which are seen to be suggestive of another." As a gloss to

---

45. Monti comments: "Although Gunton's argument is directed against the tradition of natural theology as he defines it, his proposal for a 'theology of nature' suggests the possibility of redefinition." Monti, *Natural Theology of the Arts*, 31.

46. Monti, *Natural Theology of the Arts*, 32.

47. Monti, *Natural Theology of the Arts*, 32.

48. Monti, *Natural Theology of the Arts*, 26.

49. Monti, *Natural Theology of the Arts*, 57.

50. Moltmann, *God in Creation*, 59, quoted in Monti, *Natural Theology of the Arts*, 57.

this definition, N. T. Wright observes, "Metaphor consists in bringing two sets of ideas close together, close enough for a spark to jump, but not too close, so that the spark, in jumping, illuminates for a moment the whole area around, changing perceptions as it does so."[51]

With this working definition in hand, Monti returns to Polanyi's distinction between focal awareness and subsidiary awareness with regard to three types of integration: indication, symbol, and metaphor.[52] With indication, the focal object has intrinsic interest. With symbol, on the other hand, the subsidiary particulars have intrinsic interest (e.g., a flag). With metaphor, then, both the focal object and the subsidiary particulars may be of intrinsic interest. What is important, however, is Wright's spark. Turning to Begbie (who is reading Polanyi and Soskice), Monti argues that metaphors are irreducible and then goes on to argue that "art may be considered to be a kind of vastly extended, complex metaphor."[53]

Having considered metaphor, Monti considers Steiner's project by examining "actual reports of such knowledge" (i.e., "knowledge and/or experience of God").[54] Before doing so, however, Monti is concerned to define the relationship between natural theology and revelation. He wonders: "In experiencing a work of art, are we experiencing God himself, as in a revelation, or are we coming to know him indirectly by subsequent reflection on the character of our experience, the more usual definition of natural theology?"[55] Monti answers by way of Soskice and Polkinghorne, suggesting that we understand "pointed" and "diffuse" experiences as the two poles of a continuum with "our experience of art [being] both a natural theology and a revelation . . . with specific experiences of particular art works sometimes closer to the one pole, sometimes to the other."[56] The remainder of the chapter deals with aesthetic experience, generally and then specifically, and concludes with a question: "do these reported aesthetic experiences 'fit in' with the best story we can tell about reality, so that these experiences lend

---

51. Monti, *Natural Theology of the Arts*, 58.

52. Monti, *Natural Theology of the Arts*, 59ff.

53. Monti, *Natural Theology of the Arts*, 63–65; quote from 65.

54. Monti, *Natural Theology of the Arts*, 91.

55. Monti, *Natural Theology of the Arts*, 91.

56. Monti, *Natural Theology of the Arts*, 92.

support to the story even as the story makes sense of these experiences (the hermeneutic circle)?"[57]

In his final chapter, Monti seeks to answer this question in dialogue with Steiner. More specifically, he argues against Steiner's notion of "counter-creation" and for the notion of "responsive creation." For Monti, art does not imitate nature, but creation. Creation, then, is ongoing, anticipating the new creation (i.e., it is eschatological). From this perspective, art anticipates the new creation as a sort of parable of the world to come, and "may be said to be, in the broadest sense of the term, 'sacramental,' that is, 'suffused [like the New Jerusalem] with the divine presence.'"[58] Monti concludes, then, that art has the potential to suggest, point to, and reveal the Trinitarian God.[59]

Paul Molnar and the Question of Christian Natural Theology

Both McGrath and Monti read Barth through Torrance, who argues that Barth's primary objection to natural theology was its independent character.[60] Molnar has, however, called Torrance's reading into question. He argues:

57. Monti, *Natural Theology of the Arts*, 130.

58. Monti, *Natural Theology of the Arts*, 142. Monti backs this up with an ecumenical survey of supporters including Moltmann, Polkinghorne, Richard Bauckham and Trevor Hart, Vladimir Solovyov and Nicholas Berdyaev as well as Sergius Bulgakov (via Patrick Sherry), Etienne Gilson, Hans Urs von Balthasar, Abraham Kuyper, Nicholas Wolterstorff, Timothy Gorringe, and Jeremy Begbie (142–44). It should be noted, however, that Monti qualifies these experiences. He states: "This does not mean, of course, that each individual must himself or herself have fully subscribed to revelation before recognizing (however imperfectly) the signs of creation in nature; rather, it means that individuals could never have been brought to such a recognition in the first place, except, penultimately (however far back in the historical chain of events), by those to whom God *revealed* his world as creation, and therefore ultimately by God himself revealing his world as creation" (163).

59. While this may sound like NT3 (with the mention of suggesting and pointing), Monti's natural theology is rooted in the doctrine of creation, which is classic NT4. Monti explains: "According to this account, through highly complex metaphors manifesting the three transcendentals of perichoresis, particularity and relationality, art imitates creation and anticipates the new creation, thereby fulfilling the educative, hermeneutical and eschatological functions of a genuine natural theology consistent with an epistemology of critical realism and a metaphysic of flexible openness. In so doing, art may be said by its very nature as art to refer beyond itself—ultimately suggesting, pointing to, at times even 'revealing' [in the loose sense defined in chapter 5] the Trinitarian God, whose 'real presence' is at once so keenly felt and so inadequately understood by Steiner." See Monti, *Natural Theology of the Arts*, 169.

60. Torrance, "Problem of Natural Theology," 121–35.

Torrance cannot have it both ways. A choice is required here. . . . Either natural theology functions *solely* within revelation (in which case of course it is no longer natural theology but becomes instead a revelation based theology leading to a theology of nature) or it may function prior to and/or apart from revelation, perhaps with its silent cry or perhaps with its search for intelligibility. But one cannot say that natural theology must function within revelation as Torrance does and then claim, even as an exceptional circumstance, that we can achieve clarity by bracketing the material content of theology as Torrance also does at another point in his thinking. Part of the difficulty here is that Torrance really thinks natural theology will keep to the limit he sets for it, i.e., natural theology will recognize that the intelligibility of creation points beyond itself to an answer it cannot give. But it is in this very way that, from Barth's point of view, Torrance has conceded too much to nature and has in fact idealized nature by not taking proper account of its sinful status in and through which we are always prone to control revelation itself.[61]

For what it's worth, Torrance's nephew, Alan Torrance,[62] agrees with Molnar: "I think that Molnar's argument is correct in that Torrance's enthusiasms did take him further in the direction of natural theology than was consistent with his fundamental conviction that knowledge of God requires to be conceived in irreducibly Trinitarian terms."[63] With Molnar (and Alan

---

61. See Molnar, "Natural Theology Revisited," 79–80; cf. W. Travis McMaken, "The Impossibility of Natural Knowledge of God in T. F. Torrance's Reformulated Natural Theology," *International Journal of Systematic Theology* 12 (2010): 319–40. McMaken argues that Molnar has misunderstood Torrance, and that there is "fundamental agreement between Torrance and Barth" (337). That said, even if Torrance reads Barth correctly (i.e., following McMaken, contra Molnar), my argument stands: Torrance either falls with Barth or, if we stick with Molnar's reading, abuses Barth. Either way, we can move beyond the reformulations of Torrance and his disciples as neither using nor abusing Barth leads to a viable natural theology.

62. Alan Torrance is the son of T. F.'s brother James. On a personal note, the first paper that I presented while a PhD student at St. Andrews—"Exploring the Possibility of an Imaginative Natural Theology"—was in Alan Torrance's theology research seminar.

63. Alan Torrance, "Assessing T. F. Torrance in Dialogue with Paul Molnar," *Journal for the Theology of Culture* 8 (2012): 78. It should be noted that Alan Torrance does go on to acknowledge that "[a] defense of [T. F.] Torrance could be mounted" (78). In any case, Alan Torrance thinks that "Molnar is surely correct in suggesting that [T. F.] Torrance would not have been happy with the direction in which Alister McGrath has sought to go, in which seeking he has commandeered Torrance to develop his own particular natural theological agenda" (78).

Torrance), I would argue that a choice is required. One is either with Barth and against natural theology, or one is against Barth and for natural theology. One cannot have it both ways.[64] That said, I am not with Barth, so from my perspective Molnar's argument simply points out a (potential) problem with Torrance's NT4 and, by extension, McGrath's use of Torrance. It should be noted that not everyone agrees with Molnar and Alan Torrance. W. Travis McMaken, for instance, thinks that Molnar has "failed to do [T. F.] Torrance justice on this point."[65] From McMaken's perspective, "traditional natural theology has been destroyed and reformulated," and "it is a very different thing."[66] McMaken thinks that Molnar "fails to distinguish adequately here between Torrance's reformulated natural theology and natural theology in the traditional sense."[67] Either way, I don't think using or abusing Barth helpful to the natural theologian.

---

64. See Paul D. Molnar, introduction to *Space, Time and Resurrection*, by Thomas F. Torrance, 2nd ed. (T&T Clark, 2019), xxviii: "So, in a changed form, what was an effort of natural theology can only be a theology, that is, a proper use of human reason in knowing God from within revelation and by faith through grace. That, however, is no longer natural theology."

65. McMaken, "Impossibility of Natural Knowledge," 319. McMaken argues that Molnar has misunderstood Torrance and that there is "fundamental agreement between Torrance and Barth" (337).

66. McMaken, "Impossibility of Natural Knowledge," 330.

67. McMaken, "Impossibility of Natural Knowledge," 338.

CHAPTER 8

The Transformation of Natural Theology: Thomas F. Torrance

If there is this deep natural connection between theology and science, such that they share basic ideas that are natural to science and natural to theology, that common basis must surely be the proper ground for a natural theology. But if these basic ideas have a definitely Christian source, and are grounded ultimately on divine revelation, in what sense may we speak here of a "natural theology"?[1]

—Thomas F. Torrance

What we are concerned with is some form of Christian natural theology, particularly as those basic ideas were derived through thinking out the interrelations of the incarnation and the creation.[2]

—Thomas F. Torrance

While the types previously discussed begin with reason and religious experience as potentially revelatory, the Scottish Protestant theologian Thomas F. Torrance (1913–2007) begins emphatically with the revelation of

---

1. Thomas F. Torrance, *The Ground and Grammar of Theology* (T&T Clark, 1980), 76.
2. Torrance, *Ground and Grammar of Theology*, 107.

God in Jesus Christ, or as he puts it, "the actual knowledge of God given in and with concrete happening in space and time."[3] For this reason, he writes: "We do not therefore begin with ourselves or our questions, nor indeed can we choose where to begin; we can only begin with the facts prescribed for us by the actuality of the object positively known."[4] For Torrance, the object of theological knowledge is always in control, and here the influence of Barth is obvious. But as McGrath argues, "Torrance is no uncritical disciple of Barth, and has expressed reservations concerning aspects of Barth's theology."[5] Even so, Torrance is generally identified as a Barthian theologian, and with good reason. Torrance studied with Barth in Basel (1937–38), completed his doctorate with Barth in 1946, and served as one of two editors on Barth's *Church Dogmatics* translation project.[6] But Torrance goes further than Barth with his Einstein-influenced transformation of natural theology. As Torrance recounts (a conversation with Barth in 1968),

> I put it this way. With relativity theory Einstein rejected the Newtonian dualism between absolute mathematical space and time and bodies in motion. He argued, therefore, that instead of idealizing geometry by detaching it from experience, and making it an independent conceptual system which was then used as a rigid framework within which physical knowledge is to be pursued and organized, geometry must be brought into the midst of physics where it changes and becomes a kind of natural science (four dimensional geometry) indissolubly united to physics. Instead of being swallowed up by physics and disappearing, however, geometry becomes the epistemological structure in the heart of physics, although it is incomplete without physics. It is in a similar way, I argued, that Karl Barth treats natural theology when he rejects its status as a *preambula*

---

3. Thomas F. Torrance, *Theological Science* (T&T Clark, 1969), 26.
4. Torrance, *Theological Science*, 26–27. See also Thomas F. Torrance, *Space, Time and Incarnation* (T&T Clark, 1969), 54–55.
5. Alister E. McGrath, *T. F. Torrance: An Intellectual Biography* (T&T Clark, 1999), 196. Where Torrance is critical of Barth, McGrath sees the influence of Torrance's University of Edinburgh professor Hugh Ross Mackintosh (1870–1936) and suggests "that Torrance saw himself as continuing and representing a distinctively 'Scottish voice' in modern theology" (139). See also pp. 29–30, 139, 197n6.
6. This was perhaps the greatest contribution to the English-language world's reception of Barth. See McGrath, *T. F. Torrance*, 113–45, 125–33 in particular.

fidei, that is, as a preamble of faith, or an independent conceptual system antecedent to actual knowledge of God, which is then used as an epistemological framework within which to interpret and formulate actual empirical knowledge of God, thereby subordinating it to distorting forms of thought. To set aside an *independent* natural theology in that way is demanded by rigorous scientific method, according to which we must allow all our presuppositions and every preconceived framework to be called in question by what is actually disclosed in the process of inquiry. However, instead of rejecting natural theology *tout court*, Barth has transposed it into the material content of theology where in a changed form it constitutes the epistemological structure of our knowledge of God. As such, however, it cannot stand on its own as an independent logical structure detached from the actual subject matter of our knowledge of God. . . . Karl Barth expressed full agreement with my interpretation of his thought, and said, rather characteristically, of the relation of geometry to physics, "I must have been a blind hen not to have seen that analogy before."[7]

Several things are worth noting here. First, Torrance was clearly going beyond Barth, developing his insights in dialogue with the natural sciences. Second, while Barth apparently expressed full agreement (in 1968, the year of his death) with Torrance's development of his position, this position was never articulated by Barth himself. This was Torrance's distinctive contribution. Third, Torrance's transformed natural theology goes beyond the idiosyncratic, so much so that it is fair to ask: Is this natural theology any longer, or has natural theology been swallowed up by the doctrines of creation and incarnation?[8] In an effort to understand Torrance's transformed natural theology, I turn now to the more general features of his work.

Thomas F. Torrance in Context

Following Barth, Torrance begins with (1) theology as a distinctive science, and (2) the rejection of dualist modes of thought.[9] In relation to theology

---

7. Thomas F. Torrance, *Space, Time and Resurrection* (Bloomsbury, 1976), ix–x.
8. Torrance, *Ground and Grammar of Theology*, 77.
9. For discussion, see Torrance, *Ground and Grammar of Theology*, 140–41. Torrance elsewhere speaks

being a distinctive science, Torrance means simply that "the method of knowledge must correspond to the nature of the object," which in the case of theology means that "we have to cast ourselves on the Grace of God and allow Him to determine the form our knowledge will take, and the kind of verification appropriate to Him."[10] For Torrance, our knowledge of God begins with the Word of God,[11] and the possibility of theological knowledge is grounded in the actual, historical reality of the person of Jesus Christ.[12] Going further, Torrance argues: "If God is triune in his nature, then really to know God means that we must know him in accordance with his triune nature from the start."[13] There is no antecedent but, instead, only actual knowledge of God. With Torrance, it can easily feel as though we must know everything before we can know anything.

In relation to the rejection of dualist modes of thought, it should be noted that by dualist modes of thought, Torrance means everything from the dualisms of Plato and Aristotle up through (and beyond) Immanuel Kant's distinction between the phenomenal (i.e., empirical or knowable) and noumenal (i.e., theoretical or unknowable) realms.[14] According to Torrance, these dualist modes of thought (and Kantian dualism in particular) "severed the connection between science and faith, depriving faith of any objective or ontological reference and emptying it of any real cognitive content."[15] Torrance advocates the acceptance of a unitary (or integrated) understanding of reality as creation based upon the doctrine of the incarnation.[16] Whereas

in a more qualified sense of "the rejection of radical dualism," by which he means "the rejection of a deistic disjunction." This leads him to conclude: "God's interaction with the world He has made maintains a proper dualism between them." Torrance, *Space, Time and Incarnation*, 71.

10. Torrance, *Theological Science*, 38. See also McGrath, *T. F. Torrance*, 205–6.

11. Torrance, *Theological Science*, 39. According to Torrance, "We cannot truly know God without being reconciled and renewed in Jesus Christ. Thus the objectivity of our theological knowledge is immutably soteriological in nature" (41). See also 43: "It will be through ruthless and relentless Christological criticism of all our knowledge of God that we will be able to distinguish, as far as possible, between genuine and false objectivity."

12. Torrance, *Theological Science*, 43–44.

13. Torrance, *Ground and Grammar of Theology*, 148.

14. Torrance, *Ground and Grammar of Theology*, 15ff.; cf. H. E. Root, "Beginning All over Again," in *Soundings: Essays Concerning Christian Understanding*, ed. A. R. Vidler (Cambridge University Press, 1962), 7–19. For discussion of Kant's distinction, see Nicholas F. Stang, "Kant's Transcendental Idealism," *The Stanford Encyclopedia of Philosophy*, last updated March 4, 2016, https://plato.stanford.edu/archives/spr2024/entries/kant-transcendental-idealism/.

15. Torrance, *Ground and Grammar of Theology*, 27.

16. Torrance, *Ground and Grammar of Theology*, ix, 39–40.

dualism detaches Jesus Christ from God,[17] the Christian doctrine of the incarnation gives us "knowledge of God in his internal relations as Father, Son and Holy Spirit."[18] For Torrance, "Jesus Christ is the one place in space and time where we may really know the Father,"[19] and this is why, as Torrance explains with reference to Barth's objection to traditional natural theology and his own reconstruction of natural theology, "natural theology is included *within* revealed theology."[20] But what does this mean?

According to Torrance:

> What Barth objects to in traditional natural theology is not any invalidity in its argumentation, nor even its rational structure, as such, but its *independent* character—i.e., the autonomous rational structure that natural theology develops on the ground of "nature alone," in abstraction from the active self-disclosure of the living and triune God—for that can only split the knowledge of God into two parts, natural knowledge of the One God and revealed knowledge of the triune God, which is scientifically as well as theologically intolerable.[21]

He continues:

> This is not to reject the place of a proper rational structure in knowledge of God, such as natural theology strives for, but to insist that unless that rational structure is intrinsically bound up with the actual content of knowledge of God, it is a distorting abstraction. That is why Barth claims that, properly understood, natural theology is included *within* revealed theology, where we have to do with actual knowledge of God as it is grounded in the intelligible relations in God himself, for it is there under the compulsion of God's self-disclosure in Being and Act that the rational structure that can be abstracted from the actual knowledge of God with which it is integrated, and made to stand on its own as an independent

---

17. Torrance, *Ground and Grammar of Theology*, 37.
18. Torrance, *Ground and Grammar of Theology*, 40.
19. Torrance, *Ground and Grammar of Theology*, 40.
20. Torrance, *Ground and Grammar of Theology*, 91.
21. Torrance, *Ground and Grammar of Theology*, 90–91.

or autonomous system of thought, for then it would be meaningless, like something that is complete and consistent in itself but without any ontological reference beyond itself: it becomes merely a game to be enjoyed like chess—which Barth is as ready to enjoy as much as anyone else, although he cannot take it seriously.[22]

So what Torrance (claims that Barth) objects to is not natural theology *per se* but antecedent or independent natural theology, and by this he means an "autonomous rational structure that natural theology develops on the ground of 'nature alone.'"[23] To be clear, this is a natural consequence of Torrance's rejection of dualism. There is nothing actual about our knowledge of God derived from nature abstracted from creation and incarnation. And there is nothing opposed to nature or natural theology, for there is no separation between natural and revealed theology, properly construed.[24]

From this perspective, natural theology is always after (or intrinsic) and never before (or extrinsic),[25] for anything before is an abstraction detached from the reality of the true God revealed in and through Jesus Christ. As a distinctive science, theology is determined by its object. Its object is the one God, and for Torrance, "theological knowledge is immutably soteriological."[26] The function of natural theology is structural, but it cannot stand on its own. We can only speak of natural theology from the perspective of positive theology, or as Torrance put it, "transposed . . . into the material content of theology where in a changed form it constitutes the epistemological structure of our knowledge of God."[27] For Torrance, natural theology has work to do, but it does its work with the benefit of hindsight, that is, in a transformed, intrinsic state. Contrast this with someone like Plantinga (NT2), for whom natural theology is nice but not necessary, or Evans (NT3), for whom natural theology is worthwhile but accomplishes very little. But, again, is Torrance's NT4 *natural* theology, or has he defused natural theology, transforming it into something else entirely?

---

22. Torrance, *Ground and Grammar of Theology*, 91.
23. Torrance, *Ground and Grammar of Theology*, 90–91.
24. Torrance, *Space, Time and Incarnation*, 69.
25. Torrance, *Space, Time and Incarnation*, 70.
26. Torrance, *Theological Science*, 41.
27. Torrance, *Space, Time and Resurrection*, x.

Natural Theology Transformed

According to Torrance, "It is within the compass of that integrated theological understanding of creation and incarnation that we have embedded the argumentation that some would regard as 'natural theology.'"[28] This is no small thing. Embedding natural theology (in scare quotes) within creation and incarnation, as Torrance does, means understanding natural theology from a confessional perspective.[29] Nature can only be understood in Christ and, more specifically, through the reality of the *homousion*.[30] Remember, this is *Christian* natural theology (NT4). For Torrance, natural theology is legitimate *if and only if* it has been stripped of its association with "nature," as if the rational structure of our knowledge of God could precede—or live outside—the actual knowledge of God given in and through Jesus Christ.

It seems to me that what Torrance wants to affirm is the impulse, or as he says, "the place of a proper rational structure in knowledge of God, such as natural theology strives for,"[31] rather than the investigation, and this because the approach is fundamentally dualist. As Torrance argues: "If natural theology is to have a viable reconstruction even in something like its traditional form, it can be only on the basis of a restored ontology in which our thought operates with a fundamental unity of concept and experience, or of form and being, within a contingent but inherently unintelligible and open-structured universe."[32] But again I ask, is this natural theology a distinction without a difference, or perhaps something else altogether, such as an epistemology of theology?

While it should by now be clear that natural theology comes in a wide variety of types and versions, it is worth asking if natural theology, in order to be called natural theology, must satisfy some minimum requirement. Is there some characteristic that separates natural theology from theology generally or other specific types of theology? Are there defining features of natural theology that span the types elaborated in this book? To be clear, one need

---

28. Torrance, *Ground and Grammar of Theology*, 77.
29. See Keith Ward, *Religion and Revelation* (Oxford University Press, 1994), 36–42, 40 in particular. Ward identifies and discusses two types of theology: confessional and comparative.
30. See McGrath, *T. F. Torrance*, 151–58.
31. Torrance, *Ground and Grammar of Theology*, 91.
32. Torrance, *Ground and Grammar of Theology*, 86–87.

not embrace essentialism for the want of clarity or distinction.[33] Nor need one give up (and give in) to the equivocal state of affairs, as if no more can be said. But what can be said? I have thus far resisted going beyond the types to offer something like a general definition, but given the moves that Torrance is making it seems necessary at this intermediate stage to reflect back on the four types discussed thus far in an effort to answer that question with which the book began: What is natural theology?

Natural theology is a tradition, a fundamental impulse, a way of thinking and being that attends to (and in many cases privileges) reason and religious experience. Natural theology along these lines seeks to nurture a quotidian piety, an awareness of everyday life. It is, in any case, a theology informed by nature and the natural. For some this means acknowledging givenness and (sacramental) presence or seeking to preserve porosity. For others, it means looking for pointers or developing proofs or arguments for the existence of God. What all of these approaches—presence, pointers, and proofs—have in common, so far as I can tell, is the acknowledgment of a fundamental, metaphysical perplexity and a resulting metaphysical mindfulness that moves beyond the buffered self of postulatory finitism to the porous self, the question of ultimacy, and transcendent possibility.[34] I am here again referencing Taylor and Desmond, but I might just as easily reference Calvin's *sensus divinitatus*, the capacity that, in tandem with grounds, can result in a persistent knowledge of God that precedes and exceeds faith.[35] It goes beyond, in the

---

33. As Alister E. McGrath explains, "It is simply not possible to offer an essentialist definition of 'natural theology,' as if there exists or existed some correct or normative understanding of the notion which is necessary to its identity and function, and grounded in its intrinsic nature." Alister E. McGrath, *Re-Imagining Nature: The Promise of a Christian Natural Theology* (Wiley-Blackwell, 2017), 17.

34. See William Desmond, *Perplexity and Ultimacy* (State University of New York Press, 1995), ix: "Perplexity is in another dimension to determinate cognition. One might say it flanks our determinate cognition on the extremes. At one extreme, perplexity is prior to definite curiosity about this and that thing, as an indeterminate opening to being as other to us, and as arousing as yet undetermined thought. At the other extreme, perplexity succeeds definite cognition as the disquieted mindfulness that being in its otherness has not been conceptually mastered by this cognition. Perplexity precedes determinate curiosity and exceeds determinate cognition."

35. See Calvin, *Institutes*, 1.3.2. And while I am well aware of the chapter that follows this section of Calvin's *Institutes* (chapter 4: "This Knowledge Is Either Smothered or Corrupted, Partly by Ignorance, Partly by Malice"), I would draw the reader's attention to that chapter's final paragraph, and the last sentence in particular (see 1.4.4): "From this it is clear that they have not been utterly ignorant of God, but that what should have come forth sooner was held back by stubbornness." The problem, according to Calvin, is ethical, not epistemological. This is the point of Rom 1:32

sense of after, which can just as easily be another before. It is in many ways akin to a critical apparatus. It stands in relation and not only in time. It is inseparable from the main text that it, in a very real sense, precedes as well as accompanies, mediates, and follows. Natural theology grapples. It develops and it changes. And it need not be abstract.

For Torrance, NT4 is a correction—a correction of "natural theology of the traditional kind."[36] As a result, it could be said that, for Torrance, natural theology is opposed to itself or, more accurately, a transformed natural theology is opposed to natural theology of the traditional kind. The natural theology I have in mind is by no means traditional, but then, which natural theology is (given the ever-present dynamic of change and the previously discussed interplay of ethos and ways)? I find sweeping dismissals (or affirmations) unhelpful, and in any case they can never be once and for all, entire-project objections. They can only (and must) be model specific. With this in mind, I turn now to the assessment of Torrance's NT4.

Assessment

Torrance was no doubt a significant figure, and his NT4 is a rigorous attempt to put natural theology to rights. There is clearly a logic at work. But as I made clear at the end of chapter 7, not everyone thinks his attempt was successful. Intramural interpretive debates aside, I believe that Torrance underestimates the cognitive significance of vagueness. And what do I mean by that? Might natural theology, the arts, and natural theology through the arts in particular not only be valuable or significant but perhaps also in some ways more engaging, with understanding being a matter of engagement,[37] than so-called

---

(with respect to the knowledge of God the Creator). I would argue that we see a similar dynamic at work in Rom 7:15–20 (with respect to the knowledge of God the Redeemer), but I have not yet seen someone raise a project objection in relation to revealed theology as a result. My point: if we are to reject natural theology because it is sufficient but not efficient with respect to saving knowledge, then we might just as well reject revealed theology, because it is sufficient but not efficient with respect to achieving moral perfection (i.e. perfecting knowledge) in this life. But to do so would be to miss the point. The knowledge of God—as both Creator and Redeemer—is persistent, and the divide between natural and revealed, less significant than one might think (in terms of finding and holding onto faith). Here again, see Kearney, *Anatheism*.

36. Torrance, *Ground and Grammar of Theology*, 89.
37. Andrew Louth, *Discerning the Mystery: An Essay on the Nature of Theology* (Clarendon, 1983), 68.

revealed theology, despite its lack of specificity? Could an implied or indirect meaning be more appealing or more cognitively significant than literal or direct meaning? The problem of vagueness has been discussed by philosophers of religion and (philosophical) theologians along the following lines: Does the vagueness of an experience (or belief) mean that such an experience (or belief) is not reliable? In this context, vagueness is related to knowledge, and its deficiency measured against the standard of true belief. But what if vagueness serves a different purpose? Rather than judging natural theology, the arts, and natural theology through the arts solely on what might be called the x-axis of true belief, I would argue that we must also take account of the y-axis of engagement (i.e., degree of engagement).

The neuroscientist V. S. Ramachandran and the philosopher William Hirstein have suggested that our brains are hardwired for perceptual problem solving. If that is indeed the case, then theology should take natural theology, the arts, and natural theology through the arts seriously, and this means judging them with reference to not only true information delivered but also their (perhaps) more primary purpose of engagement. There may well be some things that natural theology, the arts, and natural theology through the arts do better than so-called revealed theology. Perhaps there is a cognitive significance to vagueness, but this would need to be tested, and before it can be tested empirically or experimentally, it needs to be properly contextualized and conceptualized. If our brains are indeed hardwired to prefer unfinished works (e.g., puzzle pictures), then it might be the case that our brains are also hardwired to prefer incomplete theistic information by design. There may well be some things that natural theology does better than so-called revealed theology, but suggesting that we must know everything before we can know anything neglects this potential.

PART 5

Theology of Nature

CHAPTER 9

Natural Theology as Theology of Nature

Although both a theology of nature and natural revelation are biblical, natural theology is not.[1]

—Stephen R. Spencer

When it comes to natural theology as theology of nature (NT5), the outlook is decidedly theological (i.e., christological). Christians have something to say about nature in terms of creation. The Bible, Barth, and Barthians dominate the space with discussion of (secular) parables, the Word and words, the Light and lights, frequent and prolonged.[2] The basic idea is that while truth may well be found out there in the world, it can only be seen and understood from a Christian perspective. Following Barth, the English Anglican priest and theologian T. J. Gorringe argues that "great art can function as a kind of parable—to be precise, a secular parable."[3] More specifically,

---

1. Stephen R. Spencer, "Is Natural Theology Biblical?," in *Grace Theological Journal* 9 (1988): 72.
2. See Barth, *Church Dogmatics* IV/3.1. For discussion, see George Hunsinger, *How to Read Karl Barth: The Shape of His Theology* (Oxford University Press, 1991), 234–80.
3. T. J. Gorringe, *Earthly Visions: Theology and the Challenges of Art* (Yale University Press, 2011), 14. In an earlier work, Gorringe argued that art is "the one valid form of natural theology." See T. J. Gorringe, *Discerning Spirit: A Theology of Revelation* (SCM, 1990), 12. He elaborates: "Great art faces the reality of evil and suffering and yet continues to affirm goodness and love as ultimate. As the true form of natural theology it leads us to Christ whose life, death and resurrection have exactly this function. It is if not the only, then at least the most sure and most profound, propaedeutic to the gospel" (121).

Gorringe wants to suggest that paintings function as parables of the kingdom (this by way of their eschatological reality), contributing to the greater good (i.e., *shalom*) and teaching us to see things differently (i.e., cultivating attention).[4] According to Barth, however, these parables should direct us to Scripture.[5] As Barth explains, "They can only be words which will lead the community more truly and profoundly than ever before to Scripture."[6] In light of this, one might then wonder if the Bible itself says anything about (what we now refer to as) natural theology, either for or against it.

The Bible and Natural Theology

Most discussions of natural theology and the Bible begin with Psalm 19; Acts 17:16–34; or Romans 1:18–32.[7] With reference to these texts, Barth argued that "the Bible intends to speak from no other source than a particular revelation of God as distinct from a general revelation—or from revelation itself as distinct from the knowledge of man in the cosmos as such."[8] That said, Benjamin D. Sommer has rightly called Barth's exegetical strategy with respect to Psalm 19 into question.[9] According to Sommer, "The strongest reading sees revelation as supplementing natural theology in valuable ways."[10] Barth was wrong about Psalm 19, and he was wrong about Acts 17 as well. As Martin Dibelius has argued, "The Areopagus speech is a Hellenistic speech with a Christian ending; its theme is knowledge of God, to which every human being can attain, since man's own position in the world and the affinity of his nature with God's inevitably leads him there. Nothing is said of the claim of the Christian message that true knowledge of God can

---

4. Gorringe, *Earthly Visions*, 21–22.

5. Barth, *Church Dogmatics* IV/3.1, 115.

6. Barth, *Church Dogmatics* IV/3.1, 115.

7. For discussion of these and other related texts, see James Barr, *Biblical Faith and Natural Theology* (Clarendon, 1993), 21–101; John J. Collins, *Encounters with Biblical Theology* (Fortress, 2005), 91–104, 117–26; Christopher Rowland, "Natural Theology and the Christian Bible," in *The Oxford Handbook of Natural Theology*, ed. Russell Re Manning (Oxford University Press, 2013), 23–37.

8. Barth, *Church Dogmatics*, II/1, 102. For discussion of Acts 17, see 121–22.

9. Benjamin D. Sommer, "Nature, Revelation, and Grace in Psalm 19: Towards a Theological Reading of Scripture," *Harvard Theological Review* 108 (2015): 390–99.

10. Sommer, "Psalm 19," 400.

be possessed and imparted only through revelation."[11] But what of Romans 1? Channeling Barth, Douglas A. Campbell has argued for an alternative reading of Romans 1:19–20, in which "the principles of general revelation enunciated in 1.19–20 (as well as in 2.14–15) . . . belong to the gospel of Paul's opponents."[12] For this reason, Campbell sees this passage as "a critique, not Paul's systematic deployment."[13] On this reading, Romans ironically subverts rather than straightforwardly supports natural theology. This is a classic strategy for reading texts against the grain, but I am not convinced. In any case, conversations limited to these texts imply that an argument against one or more of these texts supporting natural theology is an argument against the biblical basis for natural theology *in toto*.

While I do not think biblical support for natural (or historical or systematic or philosophical) theology are necessary,[14] nor that contortionist readings against the probability of biblical support are helpful, I wish to draw attention to a less frequently explored pairing of texts: the book of Ecclesiastes and Matthew 2:1–2. As John J. Collins has argued: "There are certain fundamental aspects of the sages' approach to reality that are common to natural theology in all ages. Specifically, the sages attempted to discern the religious dimension of common, universal human experience without appeal to special revelation or the unique experience of one people."[15] James Barr quoted these lines approvingly and after making two brief remarks writes: "However, the book I wish to speak about in particular is the work of later Wisdom, Ecclesiastes or Qoheleth, for it is particularly significant in relation to our study."[16] According to Barr, "Qoheleth seems, at least at first sight, to be the

---

11. Martin Dibelius, *Studies in the Acts of the Apostles*, ed. Heinrich Green, trans. Mary Ling (SCM, 1956), 58. See also See Joshua W. Jipp, "Paul's Areopagus Speech of Acts 17:16–34 as *Both* Critique *and* Propaganda," *Journal of Biblical Literature* 131 (2012): 567–88.

12. Douglas A. Campbell, "Natural Theology in Paul? Reading Rom. 1.19–20," *International Journal of Systematic Theology* 1 (1999): 252.

13. Campbell, "Natural Theology in Paul?," 252.

14. As Casserley explains, "The question of whether a natural theology exists is primarily a question of fact; do we discover points of convergence, not by reading the Bible, but by reading all sorts of other books? And surely the answer to that, by any honest mind that does read other books, can only be that in some sense we do." J. V. Langmead Casserley, *Graceful Reason: The Contribution of Reason to Theology* (Seabury, 1954), 9.

15. Collins, *Encounters with Biblical Theology*, 104. See also David Brown, *The Divine Trinity* (Open Court, 1985), 60–61.

16. Barr, *Biblical Faith and Natural Theology*, 93. Brown has argued similarly, noting "that one particular genre of Old Testament literature can best be understood as early attempts at natural theology,

most akin to Barthianism,"[17] but in fact "stands closer to the standpoint of natural theology."[18] However, little has been done since Collins and Barr to develop this line of thought. Like Collins and Barr, I think Ecclesiastes significant with reference to natural theology, and this because Qoheleth provides precedence not only for natural theology but also for the cultivation of *new* wisdom through observation. Michael V. Fox has pointed out: "He pursues knowledge not merely by absorbing existing wisdom and elaborating on it or applying it intelligently, but by pushing back the frontiers of wisdom, creating knowledge that did not exist before his investigation."[19] Qoheleth was in this sense unique, employing an empirical methodology to gain and validate new wisdom. For some, this makes Ecclesiastes a prooftext. I think it is more valuable as a performance-inviting text. The point of my argument is that Qoheleth should not merely be read and his discoveries used, but his methodology should also be mimicked.[20]

But we need not limit ourselves to the Old Testament, for the New Testament includes another text, infrequently cited, that seems particularly significant. Matthew 2:1–2 reads: "After Jesus was born in Bethlehem in Judea, during the time of King Herod, Magi from the east came to Jerusalem and asked, 'Where is the one who has been born king of the Jews? We saw his star when it rose and have come to worship him.'" Commenting upon this text, David Brown writes:

> Matthew in effect accepts here a form of natural theology since, to pro-
> vide a proper parallel, prediction through the stars must be no less true

---

as attempts to read the character of God and his purposes for mankind from the natural order. Here one has in mind such books as Proverbs, Ecclesiastes and Job, books that have come to be known as the 'Wisdom literature.'" See David Brown, *Invitation to Theology* (Blackwell, 1989), 57.

17. Barr, *Biblical Faith and Natural Theology*, 93.

18. Barr, *Biblical Faith and Natural Theology*, 94.

19. Michael V. Fox, "Qohelet's Epistemology," *Hebrew Union College Annual* 58 (1987): 148. See also Fox, *A Time to Tear Down and a Time to Build Up: A Rereading of Ecclesiastes* (Eerdmans, 1999), 71–86; Fox, *Ecclesiastes: The Traditional Hebrew Text with the New JPS Translation/Commentary*, JPS Bible Commentary (Jewish Publication Society, 2004), xi–xii; cf. Choon-Leong Seow, *Ecclesiastes: A New Translation with Introduction and Commentary*, Anchor Bible 18C (Doubleday, 1997), 54–60.

20. Rather than opening with an appeal to data/revelation or testimony, Qoheleth begins with commonly observable, shared experience, more specifically, a poem (1:3–11). He then goes on to share his testimony in 1:12 and following, and "after all has been heard" (12:13a) presents the data/ revelation (12:13b–14).

than through Jewish prophecy. To the modern mind accustomed to the nonsense of contemporary astrology that may seem unlikely; but it should be remembered that even as late as the sixteenth century Christian society (and its theologians) continued to assume some sort of connection between the stars and the human condition (e.g. *King Lear*, IV, iii, 34).[21]

This example is particularly relevant, for in this case natural theology quite literally led to Christ. Even Calvin admits: "The heavenly Father chose to appoint the star and the Magi as our guides, to lead directly to his Son."[22] Now, Calvin goes on to question the connection with natural theology, arguing that "since astrology is undoubtedly confined within the limits of nature, its guidance alone could not have conducted the *Magi* to Christ; so that they must have been aided by a secret revelation of the Spirit." He continues: "I do not go so far as to say, that they derived no assistance whatever from the art: but I affirm, that this would have been of no practical advantage, if they had not been aided by a new and extraordinary revelation."[23] This is, however, an argument from silence. We are told of no "new and extraordinary revelation," at least not in Matthew 2:2. What we are told is that it was the star which led the magi to Christ, a point reinforced in verses 7, 9, and 10.[24] The "new and extraordinary revelation" comes in verse 12 with the warning "in a dream not to go back to Herod." But this verse should not be conflated with the earlier verses, as if they were one and the same. Calvin's explanation is rooted in conflation and speculation rather than a plain reading of the text. Ironically, just before this section he has just spent two pages criticizing "the Papists" for going further than the evangelist. Surely the charge of *tu quoque* applies here to Calvin. One cannot accuse their opponents of rank speculation only then

21. David Brown, *God in a Single Vision: Integrating Philosophy and Theology*, ed. Christopher R. Brewer and Robert MacSwain (Routledge, 2016), 84n19. See also David Brown, *Tradition and Imagination: Revelation and Change* (Oxford University Press, 1999), 86–92, 341.

22. John Calvin, *Commentary on a Harmony of the Evangelists, Matthew, Mark, and Luke*, trans. William Pringle (Baker, 2005), 1:128.

23. Calvin, *Harmony of the Evangelists*, 1:130.

24. Craig S. Keener makes much of the fact that the star only took the magi so far (i.e., to the city), and that "for more specific direction they must ask the leaders in Jerusalem where the king is to be born (2:2)." He thus concludes that "their celestial revelation was only partial; they must finally submit to God's revelation in the Scriptures, preserved by the Jewish people." See Craig S. Keener, *The Gospel of Matthew: A Socio-Rhetorical Commentary* (Eerdmans, 2009), 100. But what of verses 9–10 where, after the magi speak with the leaders in Jerusalem, the star once again "went ahead of them"?

to argue from silence for the explanation that best conforms to one's own prior (and in this text unsupported) theological commitments.

In his discussion of Matthew's account, G. W. H. Lampe points out that the magi "represent a shady and unsavoury aspect of paganism,"[25] and that patristic commentaries "handle the story very uneasily."[26] Lampe then surveys a variety of attempts to deal with (i.e., "tone down") Matthew's narrative,[27] concluding:

> We need not doubt that his story of the appearance of the star has its roots in the Old Testament—in Balaam's oracle, "I see him, but not now: I behold him, but not nigh: a star should come forth out of Jacob, and a sceptre shall rise out of Israel" (Num. 24:17), linked with the prophecy of Isa. 60:3, "And nations shall come to your light, and kings to the brightness of your rising." Nor is it improbable that Matthew was acquainted with Jewish traditions, reproduced later by the Christian Fathers, which connected the magi of Chaldaea and Persia with Balaam, the Gentile whom God had made, against his own will, a channel of prophetic revelation. He gives no hint, however, that he expects his readers to be familiar with such traditions and to realize that through the link with Balaam magi from the East might be regarded almost as honorary prophets of Israel rather than as heathen astrologers. Nor is there any ground for supposing that Matthew thought that this star was a unique creation, perhaps not a physical object at all, and therefore no part of the subject-matter of astrology. Neither Matthew himself nor his Old Testament background offer any support for the idea that the gifts offered by the magi represent the surrender of the tools of their wicked trade and their conversion from "belief in astrology and faith in horoscopes." There is no parallel here to the collection and burning (not the presentation as acceptable gifts to the Lord) of their books by the magicians of Ephesus who were converted by Paul. On the contrary, taken at its face value,

---

25. G. W. H. Lampe, "Athens and Jerusalem: Joint Witnesses to Christ?," in *The Philosophical Frontiers of Christian Theology: Essays Presented to D. M. Mackinnon*, ed. Brian Hebblethwaite and Stewart Sutherland (Cambridge University Press, 1982), 26.

26. Lampe, "Athens and Jerusalem," 27.

27. Lampe, "Athens and Jerusalem," 28–33.

Matthew's story tells us uncompromisingly that the birth of the King of the Jews was revealed, like that of Alexander, by a star which was observed by magi in the regular practice of astrology, and that, after they had communicated this revelation to the people of Jerusalem, these heathens were led to the Messiah by the joint guidance of their star and the scriptural prophecy of Micah, worshipped him, presented him with their treasures, and were favoured with a special divine revelation to enable them to return safely to their own country.[28]

Put simply, the magi give us a biblical example of natural theology practiced by nonbelievers. A provocative example with a fascinating interpretive history, this text deserves further reflection. Discussions of natural theology and the Bible need not be limited to Psalm 19; Acts 17:16–34; and Romans 1:18–32, for as Barr suggests, "the Bible is *full* of natural theology."[29] Turning now from the Bible and natural theology, I will describe this final type in detail.

Natural Theology as Theology of Nature (NT5)

At the outset of an oft-cited section of the *Church Dogmatics*, Barth declares: "We begin with Jesus Christ."[30] Few would object, in principle, to beginning with Jesus Christ (depending on the subject of conversation), but there is more to Barth's beginning than meets the eye. When Barth speaks of the Word and words, Jesus Christ is the one Word of God, and "the words of the Bible" are only "witnesses to Jesus Christ."[31] Barth unpacks this later in the same section, writing:

---

28. Lampe, "Athens and Jerusalem," 33.

29. Barr, *Biblical Faith and Natural Theology*, 136.

30. Barth, *Church Dogmatics* IV/3.1, 38; cf. Sherry, "Religious Roots of Natural Theology, 302: "In the order of being God precedes the world, for without Him there could not be anything. But in the order of knowledge we proceed in the opposite direction, from something we already know, like the world or (for Descartes) one's own self, and proceed from there to God." Sherry is here introducing, in plain words, the distinction between the *analogia entis* (the analogy of being) and the *analogia fidei* (the analogy of faith). I will return to this subject in chapter 10.

31. Barth, *Church Dogmatics* IV/3.1, 110. Barth later identifies the Old and New Testaments, as well as the utterances of the Christian community, as "two secondary forms of the Word of God which derive from the primary and are subjected to it in this order" (113).

It will help to an appreciation of the various elements in this general answer if we pause for a moment to discuss the problem of the parables of Jesus as handed down in the Gospels. [παραβολαί] are little stories which it seems anyone might tell of ordinary human happenings. But they are called [παραβολαί] of the [βασιλεία], and it is often said expressly that the [βασιλεία] is "likened unto" [ὡμοιώθη] these events, or, with an obvious view to this equation, that the events themselves, or the leading characters in them, are "like the [βασιλεία]." It is also said that the kingdom in its likeness to these events, or these events in their likeness to the kingdom, can and will be heard by those who have ears to hear, i.e., by those to whom it is given to hear (Mk. 4:9f.). That is to say, they will hear and receive the equations or likenesses as such, whereas those who are "without" will not perceive and understand what is at issue, namely, the "mystery" of the kingdom.[32]

For Barth, the knowledge of God available in nature (words) is only able to be understood in relation to Jesus Christ (the Word), and in this sense the words are analogous to parables, which are only seen and understood by the faithful (i.e., in light of the Word, the Light). According to Barth, these words are to be received "as a commentary on Holy Scripture."[33] That said, "they certainly cannot be collected, and assembled as words of universal authority, and as such laid alongside Scripture as a kind of second Bible."[34] The point here is that these lesser lights, which are by no means "natural theology," are in many ways like the book of nature previously discussed. From this perspective, the second volume is of little use without the first. In fact, one may well wonder: Who needs the second volume if we have the first? These lesser lights are, again, simply commentary.

N. T. Wright argues similarly, describing "the task summarized in the phrase 'natural theology'" as "a Christian account, 'reading backwards,' like Jesus retelling Israel's story on the road, to show how the 'natural' world had in fact been pointing, however brokenly, to the truth."[35] This is why, despite

---

32. Barth, *Church Dogmatics* IV/3.1, 112.
33. Barth, *Church Dogmatics* IV/3.1, 130.
34. Barth, *Church Dogmatics* IV/3.1, 133.
35. Wright, *History and Eschatology*, 218.

Wright's use of "signposts,"[36] I see him as belonging to this type. For Wright, the great evil is "a modern variation of ancient Epicureanism,"[37] and history is the solution. Jesus was a historical figure and *ipso facto* part and parcel of the so-called natural world.[38] A "refreshed 'natural theology'" includes Jesus.[39] As Wright says, "Jesus himself [is] the starting-point and clue to the questions that concern 'natural theology.'"[40] This is, more or less, a version of Richard Bauckham's argument that "a theology of nature cannot simply presuppose a distinction between humanity and the rest of nature."[41]

For Colin Gunton, creation is central. Gunton, who defines a theology of nature as "an account of what things naturally are, by virtue of their createdness,"[42] argues "that there is an immense difference between a theology of nature and a natural theology."[43] Natural theology is, from his perspective, "the knowledge of God that is obtainable independently of revelation."[44] Operating with the standard definition as a foil, Gunton dismantles this one model as if it were the project. The problem, from Gunton's perspective, is that "a doctrine of creation mediated by revelation" has been replaced "with one directly or indirectly discovered by the human mind."[45] While Gunton

---

36. Wright identifies and describes seven "vocational signposts" (Wright, *History and Eschatology*, 224–34) that, while broken, can be validated retrospectively (225). Wright explains: "By themselves, they do not point to God; or, if they seem to, they might simply be building a new Tower of Babel. They can be deconstructed, interpreted otherwise. And yet. *At the very moment of their failure, they point to the ultimate broken signpost, which turns out to be the place in real life, in concrete history, where the living God is truly revealed, known and loved.* Each of the signposts lead to the same place" (237). And later: "The trail of broken signposts leads to the broken God on the cross" (244).

37. Wright, *History and Eschatology*, 155.

38. While history is regularly included among the sources of general revelation, it typically stands alongside—rather than being embedded within—nature and conscience.

39. Wright, *History and Eschatology*, 127.

40. Wright, *History and Eschatology*, 152; cf. David Brown, *Gospel as Work of Art: Imaginative Truth and the Open Text* (Eerdmans, 2024). From Brown's perspective, an obsession with history as the only form of truth is part of the problem.

41. Richard Bauckham, "First Steps to a Theology of Nature," *Evangelical Quarterly* 58 (1986): 231.

42. Colin Gunton, "The Trinity, Natural Theology, and a Theology of Nature," in *The Trinity in a Pluralistic Age: Theological Essays on Culture and Religion*, ed. Kevin J. Vanhoozer (Eerdmans, 1997), 98.

43. Gunton, "Trinity," 100–101: "A theology of nature is the gift of biblical revelation, for it teaches us that the unity of things is upheld neither by the formal causality of the Greeks nor by the supposed omnipotence of human reason, but by the incarnate Lord whose power was exercised in the power of the Spirit and in weakness. It is because we have a theology of revelation that we can look for the glory of God in the things that have been made."

44. Gunton, "Trinity," 89.

45. Gunton, "Trinity," 94.

may well be right with respect to the standard definition, my argument throughout has been that the standard definition does not apply to each and every case, and in fact neither Brown (NT1) nor Plantinga (NT2), Evans (NT3), or Torrance (NT4) would define the natural theology they espouse as knowledge of God obtainable independent of revelation. We must not allow deism's definition of natural theology to be extended to all models. To do so is a misleading, faulty generalization. In any case, it should be noted that Gunton thinks that while Barth "has a doctrine of creation, there is reason to suppose that he does not have much of a theology of nature, and this suggests that he, too, failed adequately to distinguish between natural theology and a theology of nature."[46]

In the published version of his 2001 Gifford Lectures,[47] Stanley Hauerwas argues that "Karl Barth is the great natural theologian of the Gifford Lectures—at least he is so if you remember that natural theology is the attempt to witness to the nongodforsakenness of the world even under the conditions of sin."[48] Hauerwas wants to redefine natural theology as a theology of nature, but rather than abandoning the term, he continues to use it. As he explains, "Natural theology cannot be abstracted from a full doctrine of God. . . . Once that claim is accepted, 'natural theology' should be considered a legitimate and necessary theological task to help us see that we do not live in a God-forsaken world. Accordingly natural theology can be understood as the ongoing attempt to help us locate our lives in God's life."[49] So we have Barth and Gorringe discussing secular parables, Wright reminding us that history is part of nature, Bauckham pointing out that humans are part of nature, Gunton seeking to reestablish creation as foundational, and Hauerwas defending Barth as a natural theologian par excellence. But what can be said of this type more generally?

Proponents of NT5 understand nature theologically, that is, as creation. In a sense, nature is opposed to (or distinguished from) creation, and natural

---

46. Gunton, "Trinity," 90.

47. For an introduction to and discussion of the Gifford Lectures, see Christopher R. Brewer, ed., *The Gifford Lectures: Advancing Natural Theology in the Twenty-First Century* (Edinburgh University Press, forthcoming).

48. Stanley Hauerwas, *With the Grain of the Universe: The Church's Witness and Natural Theology*, 2nd ed. (Baker Academic, 2013), 20.

49. Hauerwas, *Grain of the Universe*, 243.

theology is, quite literally, opposed to Jesus Christ. Natural theology (standard definition) has no function, and according to Barth it does not exist, for it has no basis in reality. This is why he was willing to deliver the Gifford Lectures at the University of Aberdeen in 1937–1938, for, as he puts it, "I certainly see—with astonishment—that such a science as Lord Gifford had in mind does exist, but I do not see how it is possible for it to exist. I am convinced that so far as it has existed and still exists, it owes its existence to a radical error."[50]

Assessment

Responding to Barth and his ilk, the British philosopher Brian A. Davies has argued that "the current theological rejection of natural theology revolves around three main claims: 1. Natural theology, especially in the sense of proof, is incompatible with love of God and free acceptance of him. 2. Natural theology and belief or faith are unconnected. 3. Natural theology is alien to the Bible."[51] The second claim is most relevant here. Davies addresses the claim that natural theology and belief or faith are unconnected with reference to Tillich and Barth and more specifically challenges "Barth's assertion that God is immeasurably distant from man, that, as Barth is better known for putting it, God is 'wholly other.'"[52] Accepting Barth's claim would, according to Davies, mean abandoning not only natural theology but theology *in toto*. As he explains:

> Taken at its face value, one might suppose that the description of God as "wholly other" entails that God is absolutely different from everything besides himself. But in so far as one can make sense of such an entailment it seems to commit its exponent to abandoning theology. For however different God may be he must be spoken of through the use of terms applicable to what is not God. Yet if this is the case God cannot be absolutely

---

50. Karl Barth, *The Knowledge of God and the Service of God According to the Teaching of the Reformation: Recalling the Scottish Confession of 1560; The Gifford Lectures Delivered in the University of Aberdeen in 1937 and 1938*, trans. J. L. M. Haire and Ian Henderson (Hodder & Stoughton, 1938), 5.
51. Brian A. Davies, "Theology and Natural Theology," *New Blackfriars* 58 (1977): 258.
52. Davies, "Theology and Natural Theology," 260.

different from everything besides himself. If a theologian denies this he may be extricated from the position of saying that God might be reasoned to by natural theology, but only at the cost of admitting that nothing can be said of God.[53]

Davies proceeds, suggesting that while Barthians may well accept the soundness of these arguments "on a human level," they would no doubt argue that this "level is corrupted by sin."[54] Davies finds this unconvincing and responds:

> Certainly a Christian theologian is treading on thin ice if he claims to produce all the truths of Christianity out of some logical box in some way that bypasses the idea of the gift of revelation. But if reason is so clouded that it cannot make a true statement about God by its own powers then it cannot even say that God is "beyond" reason, for there is only human reason to make such a claim.[55]

Moving on, Davies mentions yet another potential objection from the Barthians, something like Torrance's claim for theology as a distinctive science.[56] Davies responds along four lines, but it is here sufficient to note that, from his perspective, making the argument against natural theology is slightly more complicated than demanding objectivity or shouting, "Christ!"[57] Suffice to say that, for Davies, "the contemporary theological critique of natural theology is not unanswerable."[58] Even so, Barth had his reasons,[59] and it is to Barth that we now turn.

---

53. Davies, "Theology and Natural Theology," 261.
54. Davies, "Theology and Natural Theology," 261.
55. Davies, "Theology and Natural Theology," 262.
56. He summarizes the objection as follows: "Recent philosophical and scientific development stresses the importance of approaching any field of inquiry with the methods appropriate to it. If one forgets one's field of research and applies oneself to it using the methods appropriate to some other one will ask the wrong questions, and one's tools, though valuable enough in the right research, will be unable to deliver whatever goods there might be to lay hold of." Davies, "Theology and Natural Theology," 262.
57. See Davies, "Theology and Natural Theology," 262–64 for his detailed response.
58. Davies, "Theology and Natural Theology," 267.
59. For discussion, see Christine Tietz, Karl Barth: A Life in Conflict (Oxford University Press, 2021), 69–73, 199–267.

CHAPTER 10

The Key to the Secret of Creation: Karl Barth

We have established that from every angle Jesus Christ is the key to the secret of creation. It is thus clear that the knowledge of creation, of the Creator and of the creature, is a knowledge of faith, and that here too the Christian doctrine is a doctrine of faith.[1]

—Karl Barth

We recognise that the fact that Jesus Christ is the one Word of God does not mean that in the Bible, the Church and the world there are not other words which are quite notable in their way, other lights which are quite clear and other revelations which are quite real. . . . Our statement is simply to the effect that Jesus Christ is the one and only Word of God, that He alone is the light of God and the revelation of God.[2]

—Karl Barth

I would gladly concede that nature does objectively offer a proof of God, though man overlooks or misunderstands it.[3]

—Karl Barth

---

1. Barth, *Church Dogmatics* III/1, 28.
2. Barth, *Church Dogmatics* IV/3.1, 97.
3. Karl Barth, "Letter to Carl Zuckmayer (May 7, 1968)," in *A Late Friendship: The Letters of Karl Barth and Carl Zuckmayer*, trans. Geoffrey W. Bromiley (Eerdmans, 1982), 42.

In chapter 9, I described natural theology as theology of nature (NT5), and in this final chapter I turn to Karl Barth, who would have no doubt preferred that we speak of the doctrine of creation rather than a theology of nature.[4] Why then is he located here as this type's featured proponent? Just as Brown's NT1 is a *transformed* natural religion and Plantinga's NT2 a natural theology of *nice but not necessary*, Barth's NT5 is idiosyncratic. As I have argued throughout, there are not only a diversity of types but also diversity within each type. In some cases, the type is merely nuanced. In others, the type is subverted or transformed. What Barth's NT5 shares with every other version of NT5 is a decidedly theological outlook. That said, I begin with the acknowledgment that reading Barth can be tricky, if for no other reason than that it is difficult to know where to begin. I began with part 1 of volume 2 of *Church Dogmatics* followed by part 1 of volume 4 and then the dialogue with Emil Brunner, after which I read *Homiletics* and *Anselm* as well as a number of additional primary and secondary texts.

When I arrived in St. Andrews to write a PhD on natural theology and the arts, I was sometimes asked by theologically aware individuals: "Have you read Karl Barth?"[5] It was as if the question was itself a sufficient response to my project. I normally responded, "Yes, I have, though of course not everything." More times than not, my befuddled interlocutors would then suggest one or another text I'd not yet read as the key to understanding Barth, the idea being that if I understood Barth, I wouldn't be writing a thesis on natural theology.

As I have said, reading Barth can be tricky, not only because of the sheer volume and style of his work,[6] but also because of the difficulty of finding a

---

4. As Andrew K. Gabriel observes, "Barth does not develop a theology of nature." See Gabriel, *Barth's Doctrine of Creation: Creation, Nature, and the Trinity* (Cascade, 2014), 63.
5. This was my introduction to Barth as a "thought-terminating cliché." First used by Robert Jay Lifton, *Thought Reform and the Psychology of Totalism: A Study of "Brainwashing" in China*, 2nd ed. (University of North Carolina Press, 1989), 429: "The language of the totalist environment is characterized by the thought-terminating cliché. The most far-reaching and complex of human problems are compressed into brief, highly reductive, definitive-sounding phrases, easily memorized and easily expressed. These become the start and finish of any ideological analysis." See also Amanda Montell, *Cultish: The Language of Fanaticism* (HarperCollins, 2021), 83ff.
6. As John Macquarrie has observed, "One of the major difficulties in the way of understanding, expounding and criticizing Barth's thought is just the fact that one can never take an isolated sentence or paragraph at face value without seeking to discover whether its assertion is not modified or corrected elsewhere by another sentence or paragraph of a seemingly contrary sense." John

reliable, authoritative guide. Barth published more than six hundred works. His first book, a commentary on the book of Romans, was published in 1919 (with five subsequent editions and an English translation of the sixth and final edition in 1933)[7] and a book on Anselm in 1931 (with a second edition in 1958 and an English translation in 1960).[8] His major work, the multivolume *Church Dogmatics*, was published 1932–67 (with English translations appearing 1936–69),[9] and a number of additional books and articles were also published along the way. While it might seem reasonable to begin at the beginning with the early work (e.g., *Romans*) and read straight through, even if selectively, some commentators think it best to begin with the later work (e.g., *Church Dogmatics*), and others think it best to begin with particular works (e.g., *Anselm*) that function as keys to reading Barth. In cases such as these, it is almost always best to begin with a good introduction,[10] but when the novice picks up and reads an introduction, they must remember that they have entered the conversation from a side: traditionalist, revisionist, of whatever the case may be. This is precisely why C. S. Lewis recommended that ordinary readers—if forced to choose between reading "only the new or only the old"—"Read the old."[11] For as he says:

> A new book is still on trial and the amateur is not in a position to judge it. It has to be tested against the great body of Christian thought down the ages, and all its hidden implications (often unsuspected by the author himself) have to be brought to light. Often it cannot be fully understood without the knowledge of a good many other modern books. If you join at eleven o'clock a conversation which began at eight you will often not see the real bearing of what is said. Remarks which seem to you very ordinary will produce laughter or irritation and you will not see why—the reason,

Macquarrie, *God-Talk: An Examination of the Language and Logic of Theology* (SCM, 1967), 47.

7. Karl Barth, *The Epistle to the Romans*, 6th ed., trans. Edwin C. Hoskyns (Oxford University Press, 1933).

8. Karl Barth, *Anselm: Fides quarens intellectum; Anselm's Proof of the Existence of God in the Context of His Theological Scheme*, trans. Ian W. Robinson (SCM, 1960).

9. For a helpful introduction and overview, see Christine Tietz, *Karl Barth: A Life in Conflict* (Oxford University Press, 2021), 362–82.

10. E.g., Paul T. Nimmo, *Barth: A Guide for the Perplexed* (Bloomsbury T&T Clark, 2017).

11. C. S. Lewis, introduction to *On the Incarnation*, by St. Athanasius (St Vladimir's Seminary Press, 1944), 4.

of course, being that the earlier stages of the conversation have given them a special point. In the same way sentences in a modern book which look quite ordinary may be directed "at" some other book; in this way you may be led to accept what you would have indignantly rejected if you knew its real significance. . . . It is a good rule, after reading a new book, never to allow yourself another new one till you have read an old one in between. If that is too much for you, you should at least read one old one to every three new ones.[12]

While Lewis is speaking of old and new books, the same point could be made with reference to primary and secondary literature in this context: After reading a book about Barth, never allow yourself to read another book about Barth till you have read a book by Barth in between. But that is an awful lot of Barth. Too much, some might say. In any case, more context is required before getting into the details of Barth's NT5 expressed in terms of the doctrine of creation.

Karl Barth in Context

A significant engagement with Barth's theology was published in 1951 by Hans Urs von Balthasar (1905–88),[13] and this is the book "at" which many subsequent books on Barth are aimed. According to Balthasar, Barth "underwent two conversions. . . . The first, his turn from liberalism to radical Christianity, occurred during the First World War and found expression in *The Epistle to the Romans*. The second was his final emancipation from the shackles of philosophy, enabling him finally to arrive at a genuine, self-authenticating theology."[14] From Balthasar's perspective, there was a development in Barth's thought leading from liberalism to dialectical theology to the concept of analogy.[15] The second conversion is particularly

---

12. C. S. Lewis, introduction to *On the Incarnation*, 4.
13. Hans Urs von Balthasar, *The Theology of Karl Barth*, trans. Edward T. Oakes, SJ (Ignatius, 1992). A second edition was published in 1961 and an English translation in 1971.
14. Balthasar, *Theology of Karl Barth*, 93. For an excellent overview of the German context from which Barth emerged, see Tuska Benes, *The Rebirth of Revelation: German Theology in an Age of Reason and History, 1750–1850* (University of Toronto Press, 2022).
15. Balthasar's two conversions reading has, however, been called into question. See Bruce L.

significant here. On this reading, the key to understanding Barth's thought in relation to Roman Catholic theology was to recognize his rejection of the *analogia entis* (the analogy of being) in favor of the *analogia fidei* (the analogy of faith).[16] As George Hunsinger explains, "The celebrated work of *The Theology of Karl Barth*, by the Roman Catholic theological Hans Urs von Balthasar, is dominated by a quest for the *Denkform* [thought form]. . . . As is turn out, Barth is seen to have both a thought form and a material foundation (*Grundlegung*). . . . The thought form is the *analogia fidei*, and the material foundation is christology."[17] According to Hunsinger, however, Balthasar's effort to find an overarching principle through which the *Church Dogmatics* could be read and understood was misguided. As Hunsinger suggests, "A number of attempts have been made in the past to discover a single overriding conception that would serve as a key to reading Barth. Such a conception, if it could be found, would have a number of advantages."[18] But according

---

McCormack, *Karl Barth's Critically Realistic Dialectical Theology: Its Genesis and Development 1909-1936* (Clarendon, 1995), 1: "For over forty years now, interpretations of Karl Barth's theological development has stood beneath the massive shadow cast by Hans Urs von Balthasar's 1951 book, *Karl Barth: Darstellung und Deutung seiner Theologie.*" For further discussion, see pp. 16–23. For a counter to McCormack, see D. Stephen Long, *Saving Karl Barth: Hans Urs von Balthasar's Preoccupation* (Fortress, 2014).

16. Barth famously said: "I regard the *analogia entis* as the invention of Antichrist, and think that because of it one can not become Catholic." See Barth, *Church Dogmatics* I/1, x. See also Erich Przywara, *Analogia Entis: Metaphysics. Original Structure and Universal Rhythm*, trans. John R. Betz and David Bentley Hart (Eerdmans, 2014). According to Rowan Williams, Przywara "outlines a model of analogy which, so far from being the idolatrous construction Barth imagines, in fact settles most of Barth's own concerns within the framework of a theologically informed ontology not at all alien to what Barth himself sketches in CD, III.1." See Williams, "Dialectic and Analogy: A Theological Legacy," in *Religion*, ed. Nicholas Boyle, Liz Disley, and Nicholas Adams, vol. 4 of *The Impact of Idealism: The Legacy of Post-Kantian German Thought* (Cambridge University Press, 2013), 285. Williams goes on to note: "As for Barth, it is uncomfortably clear that he had read little or nothing of Przywara's monograph on analogy and continues to speak of the *analogia entis* in complete disregard of the way in which it is explained by Przywara and others. . . . But whether or not Barth adequately digested Przywara's argument, or even the critique to which he responds briefly in CD, I.1 of the *Dogmatics*, Przywara's own theological integrity and intelligence led him to a position not at all radically different from the argument that the *Dogmatics* developed. Przywara would not, I suspect, have used the language of 'covenant' as does Barth to reintroduce an analogical principle; but insofar as this notion carries with it just the sense of a radical, *ex nihilo* bestowal of relationship that Przywara insists upon, there are connections to be traced" (289). Cf. Keith L. Johnson, *Karl Barth and the Analogia Entis* (T&T Clark, 2010).

17. George Hunsinger, *How to Read Karl Barth: The Shape of His Theology* (Oxford University Press, 1991), 6.

18. Hunsinger, *How to Read Karl Barth*, 3.

to Hunsinger, "Such a conception is unlikely to be found."[19] Rather than seeking to identify *the key* to reading Barth, Hunsinger identifies a handful of motifs (i.e., thought forms or patterns) that can help us navigate the works of Barth.[20]

Bruce McCormack takes a different route, questioning the idea that Barth left dialectic behind by situating both the dialectical method and analogy within "the *Realdialektik* of the divine movement in revelation."[21] According to McCormack, "Karl Barth remained—even in the *Church Dogmatics*!—a *dialectical theologian*."[22] Stepping back from the intramural debates over which books are the key to reading Barth, his development and periodization, and so forth—not to mention the debates between traditionalists and so-called revisionists over election, the Trinity, and more—it seems necessary to describe the dialectical in more detail before turning to significant influences and concepts. As McCormack explains (with reference to the work of Michael Beintker), there are various dialectics at work early on, including a noetic dialectic (preceded by and grounded in *Realdialektik*, that is, "a dialectic in objectively real relations"),[23] the two principal forms of *Realdialektik*, and the dialectic of life. In seeking to understand Barth's dialectical approach, we are confronted with a Matryoshka doll of dialectics, and this is the relevant point. As McCormack argues, "It will no longer be possible to speak simply of a 'turn from dialectic to analogy' without at least making clear which dialectic is thought to be left behind and which—if any—continue to make themselves felt at later stages."[24] The same applies to any discussion of Barth as a dialectical theologian. In what sense dialectical? And to return to the theme of this book, what does this have to do with understanding natural theology?

---

19. Hunsinger, *How to Read Karl Barth*, 3.
20. These motifs include actualism, particularism, objectivism, personalism, realism, as well as rationalism, and, as Hunsinger makes clear, "Jesus Christ is the center of the motifs." Hunsinger, *How to Read Karl Barth*, 229.
21. McCormack, *Karl Barth's Critically Realistic Dialectical Theology*, 18.
22. McCormack, *Karl Barth's Critically Realistic Dialectical Theology*, 18.
23. McCormack, *Karl Barth's Critically Realistic Dialectical Theology*, 11. For discussion of the noetic dialectic, McCormack refers the reader to Karl Barth, "The Word of God as the Task of Theology, 1922," in *The Word of God and Theology*, trans. Amy Marga (T&T Clark, 2011), 171–98 (including an introduction, 171–73). See pp. 190–95 in particular.
24. McCormack, *Karl Barth's Critically Realistic Dialectical Theology*, 12.

Dialectical theology—"The see-saw of 'Yes' and 'No'"[25]—is a theology of Yes and No, of No and Yes, a theology always speaking "on the other hand." Everything is qualified by its opposite and never final. God is revealed. God is concealed. He is concealed in his revealing, and revealed in his concealing. But what is the point? Barth answers:

> I have done all I could to alert you to the fact that my affirmation, like my negation, does not claim to be the truth of God. It only claims to be a *witness* to the truth of God who stands in the center, on the other side of every "Yes" and "No." For this very reason, I have never affirmed without negating, never negated without affirming, because the one, like the other, is not the ultimate thing.[26]

The dialectical method is a protective mechanism that prevents Barth, or anyone else, from anthropomorphically laying claim to God's truth. As Barth makes clear, "Only *God* can speak of God. The task of theology is the Word of God. This means the certain *defeat of all* theology and *of every* theologian."[27] Natural theology, as Barth sees it, suggests that we can say more, and that we can say this more on our own terms. As he explains in the dialogue with Brunner, "By 'natural theology' I mean every (positive *or* negative) *formulation of a system* which claims to be theological, *i.e.* to interpret divine revelation, whose *subject*, however, differs fundamentally from the revelation in Jesus Christ and whose *method* therefore differs equally from the exposition of Holy Scripture."[28] To speak of God on our own terms means speaking of something other than God because he is not the object of, or subject to, human words. As Christoph Schwöbel explains: "To attempt to know God apart from God's revelation is to deny God, because God *is* his revelation. Natural theology, therefore, is for Barth the futile attempt to erect a Tower of Babel through which humans might aspire to knowledge of God alongside

---

25. Barth, *Epistle to the Romans*, 204.
26. Barth, "Word of God," 193.
27. Barth, "Word of God," 197.
28. Karl Barth, "No! Answer to Emil Brunner," in *Natural Theology: Comprising "Nature and Grace" by Professor Dr. Emil Brunner and the Reply "No!" by Dr. Karl Barth*, trans. Peter Fraenkel (Centenary, 1946), 74–75.

the Jacob's Ladder on which God comes to meet us in his revelation."[29] Again, "only *God* can speak of God,"[30] and this is why the first two-part volume of the *Church Dogmatics* has to do with the doctrine of the Word of God.[31] The doctrine of creation (III/1–4) follows the doctrine of the Word of God (I/1–2) and the doctrine of God (II/1–2), and this because "Barth views the doctrine of creation as an article of the Christian faith."[32] To understand Barth's rejection of natural theology, as well as the potential for a Barthian theology of nature, we now turn to Barth's doctrine of creation.

The Doctrine of Creation

While natural theology begins with nature, Barth begins with creation as a doctrine of faith. He elaborates:

> Our first emphasis is on this final point that the doctrine of the creation no less than the whole remaining content of Christian confession is an article of faith, i.e., the rendering of a knowledge which no man has procured for himself or ever will; which is neither native to him nor accessible by way of observation and logical thinking; for which he has no organ and no ability; which he can in fact achieve only in faith; but which is actually consummated in faith, i.e., in the reception of and response to the divine witness, so that he is made to be strong in his weakness, to see in his blindness and to hear in his deafness by the One who, according to the Easter story, goes through closed doors. It is a faith and doctrine of this kind which is

---

29. Christoph Schwöbel, "Theology," in *The Cambridge Companion to Karl Barth*, ed. John Webster (Cambridge University Press, 2000), 32. Schwöbel continues: "This is the reason why Barth consistently and annoyingly connects natural theology with the failure of the church in Germany to perceive the true character of Hitler's totalitarian regime, to recognize it for what it was and to act upon such a recognition. The denial of the God who can only be known through his revelation in Christ and not in the 'national revolution' is, for Barth, the common denominator of natural theology, the theology of the *Deutsche Christen* and the ideology of the National Socialist regime" (33).

30. Barth, "Word of God," 197.

31. This is followed by a two-part volume on the doctrine of God, a four-part volume on the doctrine of creation, and a four-part volume on the doctrine of reconciliation. Barth planned to write a fifth volume on the doctrine of redemption, but he died before writing it. For discussion of the completed volumes and their corresponding doctrines, see Nimmo, *Barth*, 19–48 (on the doctrine of the Word of God), 49–74 (on the doctrine of God), 75–106 (on the doctrine of creation), and 107–65 (on the doctrine of reconciliation).

32. Gabriel, *Barth's Doctrine of Creation*, 17.

expressed when in and with the whole of Christendom we confess that God is the Creator of heaven and earth.[33]

This doctrine is not native, nor is it accessible, for we have no organ nor ability. Here, Barth pushes the light of reason (found in Aristotle and Aquinas) and the point of contact (found in Brunner), as well as the *sensus divinitatus* (found in Calvin) to the side. The doctrine of creation is a matter of faith, and as Andrew K. Gabriel explains, "Creation does not lead a person to faith; rather, faith leads a person to confess (and understand) creation."[34] Here again, there is no such thing as natural theology, for there is no such thing as natural knowledge of God. The doctrine of creation entails a doctrine of the Creator, and knowledge of this Creator is the result of God's revelation in Jesus Christ.

Barth goes on to describe creation as the external basis of the covenant, and the covenant as the internal basis of creation. According to Barth, while creation comes first, the purpose and meaning of creation is God's covenant.[35] As Gabriel explains, "When Barth argues that creation is the external basis of the covenant, he means the creation allows for the actualization of the covenant. . . . The goal of creation is the covenant and thus creation is, to some extent, a means to an end."[36] The challenge is that this arrangement privileges covenant over creation, or as David Fergusson puts it: "Barth's theological ontology suffers much of the time from an inherent anthropocentric leaning with an attendant ecological deficit."[37] For this reason, Fergusson calls for "a more robust re-thinking" beyond—even if through and with all due respect to—Barth.[38] As Fergusson writes elsewhere:

---

33. Barth, *Church Dogmatics* III/1, 4.
34. Gabriel, *Barth's Doctrine of Creation*, 11.
35. See Barth, *Church Dogmatics* III/1, 42.
36. Gabriel, *Barth's Doctrine of Creation*, 32.
37. David Fergusson, "Karl Barth's Doctrine of Creation: Church Bells Beyond the Stars," *International Journal of Systematic Theology* 18 (2016): 430.
38. Fergusson, "Karl Barth's Doctrine of Creation," 431. More fully: "Our own context is characterised by a rather different set of problems and a more collaborative mode of engagement. The most pressing of these is a cluster of environmental issues concerning the degradation of the natural world whether through depletion of resources, pollution, climate change and extinction of species. A theology that undergirds a positive appreciation of the natural world as valuable, apart from its human utility, is now required" (415). Fergusson here echoes Jürgen Moltmann, who in the preface to the published version of his Gifford Lectures wrote: "In the 1930s, the problem of the

Natural theology has many functions, not all of which are vulnerable to Barth's charge of establishing the truth claims of faith on false ground. We can usefully distinguish between a natural theology and a theology of nature as two different projects, the latter proceeding from within the faith community and seeking to understand nature as God's good creation of which we are an integral part. Earlier fears around natural theology should not prevent us from developing a strong theology of nature as an expression of faith in God the Creator.[39]

From the perspective of NT5, this is best case scenario, for nature can only be understood in relation to God, and as such it is better understood as creation, and this in relation to covenant. Given that there is no such thing as natural theology, there is nothing to which it is opposed, and it has no positive function. From Barth's perspective, "Only the theology and the church of the antichrist can profit from it."[40] Apparently, natural theology isn't nice after all.

Assessment

In chapter 2, I detailed Barth's critiques of Brown's NT1, and so it seems appropriate to begin this section with Brown's critique of Barth's NT5. While noting multiple positive aspects of Barth's approach, Brown suggests that Barth's "stress on revelation is . . . not without its difficulties."[41] He explains:

> An obvious problem is that, the more one exalts the contribution revelation makes, the greater is the temptation to demote the human contributions, which then reinforces the reasons why we need the divine contributions

---

doctrine of creation was knowledge of God. Today the problem of the doctrine of God is knowledge of creation. The theological adversary then was the religious and political ideology of 'blood and soil,' 'race and nation.' Today the theological adversary is the nihilism practised in our dealings with nature. Both perversions have been evoked by the unnatural will to power, and the inhumane struggle for domination on earth." Jürgen Moltmann, *God in Creation: A New Theology of Creation and the Spirit of God*, trans. Margaret Kohl (Fortress, 1993), xiii.

39. David Fergusson, *Creation* (Eerdmans, 2014), 78.
40. Barth, "No!," 128.
41. David Brown, *Invitation to Theology* (Blackwell, 1989), 133.

so much. But not only does this demean the dignity of human beings, it demeans God himself as the creator of our capacity to reflect on our experience of his activity in the world. This was certainly a fault at the Reformation and one from which Barth himself was not entirely free.[42]

Brown repeats this criticism in a subsequent book, but only after elaborating yet another objection.

First, it is hard to see how we could recognize "father" as an appropriate term, unless we had first discovered its positive character elsewhere. In other words, language cannot function as a bolt out of the blue. Revelation could modify our understandings of the correct way in which a word is to be used; it could not simply create it. If this linguistic point is difficult to understand, essentially the same argument can be expressed non-linguistically. For it is impossible to see how man could respond to revelation unless there was something there first that enabled him to see such revelation positively as answering his questions. Otherwise it would simply appear as an irrelevance. So a total lack of previous contact is equally ruled out in this way. But, secondly, the Calvinist view of man's prior condition is not just derogatory of man, it is also demeaning of God. For it suggests that, rather than being seen as their ultimate author, God is indifferent to all those splendid outpourings of human creativity that do not explicitly bear his name.[43]

---

42. Brown, *Invitation to Theology*, 133–34.

43. David Brown, *Continental Philosophy and Modern Theology: An Engagement* (Blackwell, 1987), 13. For some additional discussion of the linguistic point, see Brown, *God in a Single Vision: Integrating Philosophy and Theology*, ed. Christopher R. Brewer and Robert MacSwain (Routledge, 2016), 5n3: "In *Credo* the meaning of Father is virtually identified with power. . . . So it comes as no surprise that in the *Church Dogmatics* creation and fatherhood are seen as a single revelation. . . . But what such footwork ignores is that both terms have a range of antecedent meanings. Thus, so far from escaping natural theology, all Barth is in effect doing is accepting one cultural understanding of 'father' to which questions of power are central over against other meanings that in more recent times have assumed greater prominence, for example love." Brown repeats the nonlinguistic argument in *Divine Generosity and Human Creativity*: "Unless God in his revelation builds on the way human beings are actually situated, it is hard to see why its message should be relevant to socially conditioned beings like ourselves." See *Divine Generosity and Human Creativity: Theology Through Symbol, Painting and Architecture*, ed. Christopher R. Brewer and Robert MacSwain (Routledge, 2017), 30.

Brown thinks Barth's stress on revelation overlooks the way language works, as well as the relevance of our questions and contributions, while also demeaning God who created us with a capacity to know him.[44] Brown advances one additional criticism elsewhere, noting: "Barth's great strength is his insistence that God as the transcendent Other should never be seen as subject to human manipulation, but his weakness in my view is his failure to engage adequately with the messiness of the world." Here (with numerous examples given) Brown wants to emphasize "God in the everyday," and "the transcendent Other . . . constantly there in the messiness, awaiting human response."[45] And while some think Barth changed his mind, Brown disagrees: "Although Barth's later theology is undoubtedly much more positive about the work of God outside the biblical revelation, the extent of the change seems to me often exaggerated and his earlier negative comments on 'religion' in effect largely stand."[46]

In addition to these various critiques from Brown, I would advance one more (though I do not have the space here to develop it fully)—namely, Desmond's fourfold logic as a more comprehensive critique of what might be called Barth's threefold logic, which, from Desmond's metaxological perspective, comes up short. Desmond began his doctoral dissertation—later published as *Desire, Dialectic, and Otherness*—with the problem of otherness and more specifically, "the contemporary concern with finitude."[47] Seeking to explicate what he calls a "more generous hermeneutic,"[48] Desmond proposes four fundamental possibilities or "relations between man and what is other."[49] These relations recur throughout Desmond's *oeuvre* and include the univocal, the equivocal, the dialectical, and the metaxological. Put simply, the univocal stresses sameness, and the equivocal stresses difference. The dialectical is, according to Desmond, self-mediating, stressing as it does the self.[50] What then of the metaxological? He answers: "The metaxological relation

---

44. In advancing these two lines of criticism, Brown echoes Avery Dulles, *Models of Revelation* (Orbis, 1983), 96–97.
45. Brown, *Divine Generosity and Human Creativity*, 16.
46. David Brown, *God and Enchantment of Place: Reclaiming Human Experience* (Oxford University Press, 2004), 7.
47. William Desmond, *Desire, Dialectic, and Otherness: An Essay on Origins*, 2nd ed. (Cascade, 2014), 3.
48. Desmond, *Desire, Dialectic, and Otherness*, 7.
49. Desmond, *Desire, Dialectic, and Otherness*, 8.
50. Desmond, *Desire, Dialectic, and Otherness*, 9.

has to do with a *logos* of the *metaxu*, a discourse concerning the middle, of the middle, and in the middle. Thus it has a close affinity with the dialectical relation. . . . But, unlike the dialectical, it does not confine the mediation of external difference to the side of the self. It asserts, rather, that external difference can be mediated from the side of the *other*, as well as from that of the self."[51] This, says Desmond, "is not only *self*-mediation but also *inter*mediation."[52] But what does this have to do with Barth?

In "The Word of God as the Task of Theology," Barth speaks of three ways: dogmatism, self-criticism, and dialectic. These more or less correspond to the univocal, equivocal, and dialectical. Speaking of the dialectical, and sounding a bit like Desmond, Barth says that it "presupposes the great truths of both dogmatism as well as self-criticism in their fragmentary nature and relative sufficiency. From the outset, this way takes seriously the positive unfolding of the thought of God on the one side and the critique of the human and all things human on the other."[53] For Barth, the dialectical is the truth of the univocal and the equivocal. But, according to Desmond, this "is distorted, because truncated."[54] It is, in other words, noncomprehensive with respect to being and our experience of being. More fully, Desmond explains:

> There is an immediacy of this metaxological community. It is at work, before we articulate it reflectively in our categories. It is at work in the univocal, the equivocal, the dialectical, but not known explicitly as such, and when stated exclusively in their terms it is distorted, because truncated. The metaxological is the truth of the univocal, the equivocal, the dialectical. They help define the truth of the metaxological, but we risk error when they are absolutized and claimed to cover the entire milieu of being.[55]

Barth hints at something beyond the dialectical when he says that "the possibility that God *himself* speaks when the human speaks of him is not contained in the dialectical way as such. It arises where even this way *comes to an*

---

51. Desmond, *Desire, Dialectic, and Otherness*, 9.
52. Desmond, *Desire, Dialectic, and Otherness*, 10.
53. Barth, "Word of God," 190.
54. Desmond, *Being and the Between*, xii.
55. Desmond, *Being and the Between*, xii.

end."[56] But there is nothing beyond dialectic for Barth, nothing beyond "the necessity and impossibility of our task."[57] That may well be so, but, as Barth himself recognized and yet failed to conceptualize adequately, the possibility that God himself speaks lies beyond the end of the dialectical way.

Desire, it might be said, drives through the middle seeking wholeness, but instead it finds openness. This is what Desmond previously called "a more 'open' reading of Hegel,"[58] or "open whole,"[59] and later "an *open* dialectic,"[60] that is, a metaxologically opened dialectic. Desmond describes this unfolding as "an Augustinian odyssey, embarked on in the wake of Hegel."[61] He explains: "Overall we will follow an itinerary reminiscent of St. Augustine's description of the double movement of his own thought, which proceeded, he said, *ab exterioribus ad interiora, ab inferioribus ad superiora* [from exterior to interior, from inferior to superior]."[62] This movement animates Desmond's fourfold logic and might be taken as shorthand for his metaxological metaphysics. Some might think this too much and others not enough. In any case, I can think of no better way to close than to quote my fellow West Virginian Daniel B. Purinton (1850–1933), who began his book on natural theology where I end mine:

> The current opinion may be true, that authors usually write because of their profound conviction that the world needs their thought, and is waiting for it. The author of this Essay has written because of his conviction that he needed to utter his thought. Having uttered it, he is content. If thereby he may be the means of contributing, even in the slightest degree, to that interest which men ought to feel in the greatest of all truths, his labor will not have been in vain.[63]

---

56. Barth, "Word of God," 194.

57. Barth, "Word of God," 195. He thus concludes: "As we consider our task, it must be equally remembered that only *God* can speak of God. The task of theology is the Word of God. This means the certain *defeat of all* theology and *of every* theologian" (196).

58. William Desmond, *Art and the Absolute: A Study of Hegel's Aesthetics* (State University of New York Press, 1986), xix.

59. Desmond, *Art and the Absolute*, 77; cf. Desmond, *Desire, Dialectic and Otherness*, 93.

60. William Desmond, *Philosophy and Its Others: Ways of Being and Mind* (State University of New York Press, 1990), 5.

61. Desmond, *Desire, Dialectic, and Otherness*, 17.

62. Desmond, *Desire, Dialectic, and Otherness*, 17. See also 238n32.

63. D. B. Purinton, *Christian Theism: Its Claims and Sanctions* (Putnam, 1889), iv.

Afterword

This book has for the most part been concerned with what I refer to as the "Descriptive Responsibility." Failure to meet this responsibility is the greatest challenge facing natural theology today, and this because the lack of specificity can easily make model-specific objections seem like project objections. The only way to move beyond this recurring false perception (and to understand natural theology in all its forms) is to fulfill the "Descriptive Responsibility" regularly and repeatedly.

After the descriptive challenge, I would argue that the greatest challenge facing natural theology is the want of a good metaphor. Since Augustine, theologians have commonly referred to "the two books"—the book of nature (i.e., God's works) and the book of Scripture (i.e., God's words). These complementary sources are two texts that can be read with knowledge of God as the result. The notions of general revelation and special revelation correspond to these two books, with natural religion drawing upon the former, and revealed (or historical) religion drawing upon the latter. But this metaphor skews the conversation from the outset, for how can a metaphorical book ever prove valuable alongside a literal one? What I mean to say is that the two books metaphor begs the question. It puts natural theology at a disadvantage, for in the end it is the book of Scripture that communicates more clearly with actual words. On this line of thinking, natural theology is the second volume (containing only plates) of a two-volume set found on the shelves of a local charity shop. If only we had volume 1, then we could make sense of volume 2. Without volume 1, what use is volume 2? In fact, if we have volume 1, do we really need volume 2? Perhaps that is why these volumes are so commonly found on the charity shop shelf.[1] It is time to leave Augustine's metaphor of the two books behind. It is no longer useful in a constructive sense. In its place, I would—after having fulfilled the Descriptive Responsibility with respect to natural theology—suggest that we abandon "natural" and "revealed" theology and, in their place, draw upon Gérard Genette's notion of the paratext to speak of "paratextual theology." And here we come to the "Prescriptive Possibility," for upon hearing this new designation, one can't help but ask: What might that look like?

Briefly, according to Genette, "The paratext is what enables a text to become a book."[2] It is "a *threshold*, or—a word Borges used apropos of a preface—a 'vestibule' that offers the world at large the possibility of either stepping inside or turning back."[3] More concretely, the name of the author, titles, dedications and inscriptions, epigraphs, notes, and so on are paratextual elements "at the service of a better reception for the text and a more pertinent reading of it."[4] The individual features are not particularly relevant for us, and in any case, as Genette explains: "The ways and means of the paratext change continually, depending on period, culture, genre, author, work, and edition, with varying degrees of pressure, sometimes widely varying."[5] These paratextual elements may be "around the text and either within the same volume or at a more respectful (or more prudent) distance."[6] The previously mentioned concrete features are examples of the former, and interviews, conversations, letters, diaries, and so forth are examples of the latter.[7] Relevant to the discussion here is that the paratext precedes, accompanies and mediates the text. "It is an 'undefined zone' between the inside and the outside," says

---

1. Here again, I disagree with Barth. See Barth, *Church Dogmatics* III.1, 414.
2. Gérard Genette, *Paratexts: Thresholds of Interpretation*, trans. Jane E. Lewin (Cambridge University Press, 1997), 1. I am grateful to Garrick V. Allen for introducing me to Genette.
3. Genette, *Paratexts*, 2.
4. Genette, *Paratexts*, 2.
5. Genette, *Paratexts*, 3. Add to this the fact that I am using paratext in a metaphorical sense where my concern has more to do with relation (i.e., between what has historically been referred to as "the two books") than it does with particular paratextual features. That said, Genette speaks of nontextual paratexts including illustrations, the material that goes into the making of a book as well as the purely factual (7).
6. Genette, *Paratexts*, 4.
7. Genette, *Paratexts*, 5. Genette refers to these as "peritext" (i.e. the former) and "epitext" (i.e. the latter), and together, these make up the paratext. Genette also mentions prenatal, "*prior* paratexts," e.g., "prospectuses, announcements of forthcoming publications," etc.

Genette.[8] This is significant with reference to the traditional opposition of natural to revealed (or historical) theology. While the two books metaphor allowed for and perhaps even encouraged such opposition (i.e., between separate books), the paratextual is more hospitable and all encompassing. The paratext stands in relation, but the relation is more intimate because it not only precedes but also mediates and accompanies. The function of the paratext is, one might say, Trinitarian, for the Father precedes, the Son mediates, and the Spirit accompanies. It is also thoroughly incarnational, insofar as the paratext mediates the text in time and space. The paratext is that without which we have no access to the text and that through which we come to understand the text. To make the connection even more explicit, there is no so-called revealed theology without so-called natural theology. But neither of these does justice to God and his revelation, which is not only christologically mediated but also naturally and culturally mediated. Revelation comes in flesh through the material. Revelation is in this sense paratextual. Text/paratext is a bookish metaphor that is, from my perspective, continuous with, but more promising than, Augustine's two books metaphor. It moves beyond, without leaving behind, nature and science, emphasizing culture and art. I hope to write another book developing this idea further, but it will likely be some time before that hope is realized.

---

8. Genette, *Paratexts*, 2.

Bibliography

Abraham, William J. *Crossing the Threshold of Divine Revelation*. Eerdmans, 2006.

Allen, Garrick V., Christopher R. Brewer, and Dennis F. Kinlaw III, eds. *The Moving Text: Interdisciplinary Perspectives on David Brown and the Bible*. SCM, 2018.

Allen, James. *Inference from Signs: Ancient Debates About the Nature of Evidence*. Clarendon, 2001.

Anderson, James. "If Knowledge Then God: The Epistemological Theistic Arguments of Alvin Plantinga and Cornelius Van Til." *Calvin Theological Journal* 40 (2005): 49–75.

Balthasar, Hans Urs von. *The Theology of Karl Barth*. Translated by Edward T. Oakes, SJ. Ignatius, 1992.

Bansnee, Jules. "Thomas Aquinas's Proofs of the Existence of God Presented in Their Chronological Order." In *Philosophical Studies in Honor of the Very Reverend Ignatius Smith, O. P.*, edited by John K. Ryan. Newman, 1952.

Barnett, S. J. *The Enlightenment and Religion: The Myths of Modernity*. Manchester University Press, 2003.

Barr, James. *Biblical Faith and Natural Theology*. Clarendon, 1993.

Barth, Karl. *Anselm: Fides quarens intellectum. Anselm's Proof of the Existence of God in the Context of His Theological Scheme*. Translated by Ian W. Robinson. SCM, 1960.

Barth, Karl. *Church Dogmatics*. Edited by T. F. Torrance and G. W. Bromiley. 4 vols. in 13 parts. T&T Clark, 1932–67.

Barth, Karl. *The Epistle to the Romans*. 6th ed. Translated by Edwin C. Hoskyns. Oxford University Press, 1933.

Barth, Karl. "Fate and Idea in Theology." In *The Way of Theology in Karl Barth: Essays and Comments*, translated by George Hunsinger, edited by H. Martin Rumscheidt. Pickwick, 1986.

Barth, Karl. *The Knowledge of God and the Service of God According to the Teaching of the Reformation: Recalling the Scottish Confession of 1560. The Gifford Lectures Delivered in the University of Aberdeen in 1937 and 1938.* Translated by J. L. M. Haire and Ian Henderson. Hodder & Stoughton, 1938.

Barth, Karl. "No!" In *Natural Theology: Comprising "Nature and Grace" by Professor Dr. Emil Brunner and the Reply "No!" by Dr. Karl Barth*, translated by Peter Fraenkel. Centenary, 1946.

Bauckham, Richard. "First Steps to a Theology of Nature." *Evangelical Quarterly* 58 (1986): 229–44.

Bavinck, Herman. *The Doctrine of God.* Translated by William Hendricksen. Eerdmans, 1951.

Begbie, Jeremy. "The Future: Looking to the Future: A Hopeful Subversion." In *For the Beauty of the Church: Casting a Vision for the Arts*, edited by W. David O. Taylor. Baker, 2010.

Begbie, Jeremy. "Incarnation, Creation, and New Creation: T. F. Torrance and a Theological Re-Visioning of the Arts." *Participation* 11 (2023): 61–79.

Begbie, Jeremy. *Music, Modernity, and God: Essays in Listening.* Oxford University Press, 2013.

Begbie, Jeremy. "Natural Theology and Music." In *The Oxford Handbook of Natural Theology*, edited by Russell Re Manning. Oxford University Press, 2013.

Benes, Tuska. *The Rebirth of Revelation: German Theology in an Age of Reason and History, 1750–1850.* University of Toronto Press, 2022.

Bennett-Hunter, Guy. *Ineffability and Religious Experience.* Pickering & Chatto, 2014.

Berger, Peter L. *Adventures of an Accidental Sociologist: How to Explain the World Without Becoming a Bore.* Prometheus, 2011.

Berger, Peter L. "The Desecularization of the World: A Global Overview." In *The Desecularization of the World: Resurgent Religion and World Politics*, edited by Peter L. Berger. Eerdmans, 1999.

Berger, Peter L. *A Far Glory: The Quest for Faith in an Age of Credulity.* Free, 1992.

Berger, Peter L. *The Heretical Imperative: Contemporary Possibilities of Religious Affirmation.* Anchor, 1980.

Berger, Peter L. *The Many Altars of Modernity: Toward a Paradigm for Religion in a Pluralist Age.* De Gruyter, 2014.

Berger, Peter L. *Redeeming Laughter: The Comic Dimension of Human Experience.* De Gruyter, 1997.

Berger, Peter L. *A Rumour of Angels: Modern Society and the Rediscovery of the Supernatural*. Anchor, 1970.

Berger, Peter L. *The Sacred Canopy: Elements of a Sociological Theory of Religion*. Anchor, 1969.

Berger, Peter L., and Thomas Luckmann. *The Social Construction of Reality: A Treatise in the Sociology of Knowledge*. Anchor, 1967.

Berkouwer, G. C. *General Revelation*. Eerdmans, 1955.

Beversluis, John. "Reforming the 'Reformed' Objection to Natural Theology." *Faith and Philosophy* 12 (1995): 189–206.

Brewer, Christopher R. "David W. Brown (1948–)." In *Twentieth Century Anglican Theologians: From Evelyn Underhill to Esther Mombo*, edited by Stephen Burns, Bryan Cones, and James Tengatenga. Wiley-Blackwell, 2021.

Brewer, Christopher R. "From Apparently Finite to Infinite: Conceptual Art and Natural Theology." In *Christian Theology and the Transformation of Natural Religion: From Incarnation to Sacramentality; Essays in Honour of David Brown*, edited by Christopher R. Brewer. Peeters, 2018.

Brewer, Christopher R. "Rolling with Release into the Future: William Desmond's Donation to a Natural Theology of the Arts." In *William Desmond and Contemporary Theology*, edited by Christopher Ben Simpson and Brennan Thomas Sammon. University of Notre Dame Press, 2017.

Brewer, Christopher R. "'Surely the Lord Is in This Place': Jacob's Ladder in Painting, Contemporary Sculpture and Installation Art." In *The Moving Text: Interdisciplinary Perspectives on David Brown and the Bible*, edited by Garrick V. Allen, Christopher R. Brewer, and Dennis F. Kinlaw III. SCM, 2018.

Brown, David. "Butler and Deism." In *Joseph Butler 1692-1752: Philosopher, Theologian, and Pastor*, edited by Christopher Cunliffe. Oxford University Press, 1992.

Brown, David. *Continental Philosophy and Modern Theology: An Engagement*. Blackwell, 1987.

Brown, David. *Divine Generosity and Human Creativity: Theology Through Symbol, Painting and Architecture*. Edited by Christopher R. Brewer and Robert MacSwain. Routledge, 2017.

Brown, David. *The Divine Trinity*. Duckworth, 1985.

Brown, David. "Durham Cathedral and the Jerusalem Temple: Let Sacred Buildings Speak." *International Journal for the Study of the Christian Church* 16 (2016): 93–107.

Brown, David. *God and Enchantment of Place: Reclaiming Human Experience.* Oxford University Press, 2004.

Brown, David. *God and Grace of Body: Sacrament in Ordinary.* Oxford University Press, 2007.

Brown, David. *God and Mystery in Words: Experience through Metaphor and Drama.* Oxford University Press, 2008.

Brown, David. "God and Symbolic Action." In *Divine Action: Studies Inspired by the Philosophical Theology of Austin Farrer,* edited by Brian Hebblethwaite and Edward Henderson. T&T Clark, 1990.

Brown, David. *God in a Single Vision: Integrating Philosophy and Theology.* Edited by Christopher R. Brewer and Robert MacSwain. Routledge, 2016.

Brown, David. *Gospel as Work of Art: Imaginative Truth and the Open Text.* Eerdmans, 2024.

Brown, David. *Invitation to Theology.* Blackwell, 1989.

Brown, David. "Re-Conceiving the Sacramental: Valuing the Useless." In *The Gestures of God: Explorations in Sacramentality,* edited by Geoffrey Rowell and Christine Hall. Continuum, 2004.

Brown, David. "Sacramentality and Public Theology: Pursuing Stephan van Erp's Vision." *Louvain Studies* 39 (2016): 155–73.

Brown, David. "A Sacramental World: Why It Matters." In *The Oxford Handbook of Sacramental Theology,* edited by Hans Boersma and Matthew Levering. Oxford University Press, 2015.

Brown, David. *Tradition and Imagination: Revelation and Change.* Oxford University Press, 1999.

Brown, Hunter. "Alvin Plantinga and Natural Theology." *International Journal for Philosophy of Religion* 30 (1991): 1–19.

Brunner, Emil. "Nature and Grace." In *Natural Theology: Comprising "Nature and Grace" by Professor Dr. Emil Brunner and the Reply "No!" by Dr. Karl Barth,* translated by Peter Fraenkel. Bles, 1946.

Burling, Hugh. "The Idolatry Argument Against Natural Theology: How It Works and Why It Fails." *Religious Studies* 51 (2015): 401–10.

Butler, Joseph. *The Analogy of Religion: Natural and Revealed to the Constitution and Course of Nature.* Edited by W. E. Gladstone. Clarendon, 1896.

Byrne, Peter. *Natural Religion and the Nature of Religion: The Legacy of Deism.* Routledge, 1989.

Caird, Edward. *The Evolution of Theology in the Greek Philosophers: The Gifford Lectures Delivered in the University of Glasgow in Sessions 1900–1 and 1901–2.* Vol. 1. MacLehose, 1904.

Calvin, John. *Institutes of the Christian Religion.* Edited by John T. McNeill. Translated by Ford Lewis Battles. 2 vols. Westminster, 1960.

Campbell, Douglas A. "Natural Theology in Paul? Reading Rom. 1.19–20." *International Journal of Systematic Theology* 1 (1999): 231–52.

Carroll, Noël. *On Criticism.* Routledge, 2009.

Casserley, J. V. Langmead. *Graceful Reason: The Contribution of Reason to Theology.* Seabury, 1954.

Casserley, J. V. Langmead. *The Retreat from Christianity in the Modern World.* Longmans, Green, 1952.

Clark, Andy, and David Chalmers. "The Extended Mind." *Analysis* 1 (1998): 7–19.

Coakley, Sarah. "Natural Theology and the Flat-plane Fallacy." In *Darwinism and Natural Theology: Evolving Perspectives*, edited by Andrew Robinson. Cambridge Scholars, 2012.

Cobb, John B., Jr. *A Christian Natural Theology: Based on the Thought of Alfred North Whitehead.* 2nd ed. Westminster John Knox, 2007.

Collier, Andrew. *Critical Realism: An Introduction to Roy Bhaskar's Philosophy.* Verso, 1994.

Collier, Andrew. "Natural Theology, Revealed Theology and Religious Experience." In *Transcendence: Critical Realism and God*, edited by Margaret S. Archer, Andrew Collier, and Douglas V. Porpora. Routledge, 2004.

Collins, John J. *Encounters with Biblical Theology.* Fortress, 2005.

Davies, Brian A. "Theology and Natural Theology." *New Blackfriars* 58 (1977): 256–67.

Davis, Stephen T. *God, Reason and Theistic Proofs.* Eerdmans, 1997.

De Cruz, Helen, and Johan De Smedt. *A Natural History of Natural Theology: The Cognitive Science of Theology and Philosophy of Religion.* MIT Press, 2015.

Deely, John. "The Role of Thomas Aquinas in the Development of Semiotic Conciseness." *Semiotica* 152 (2004): 75–139.

Desmond, William. "God, Ethos, Ways." *International Journal for Philosophy of Religion* 45 (1999): 13–30.

Desmond, William. *Art and the Absolute: A Study of Hegel's Aesthetics.* State University of New York Press, 1986.

Desmond, William. *Being and the Between.* State University of New York Press, 1995.

Desmond, William. *Desire, Dialectic, and Otherness: An Essay on Origins*. 2nd ed. Cascade, 2014.

Desmond, William. *Ethics and the Between*. State University of New York Press, 2001.

Desmond, William. *God and the Between*. Illuminations: Theory and Religion. Blackwell, 2008.

Desmond, William. *Godsends: From Default Atheism to the Surprise of Revelation*. University of Notre Dame Press, 2021.

Desmond, William. *The Intimate Strangeness of Being: Metaphysics After Dialectic*. Catholic University of America Press, 2012.

Desmond, William. *Is There a Sabbath for Thought? Between Religion and Philosophy*. Fordham University Press, 2005.

Desmond, William. *Perplexity and Ultimacy*. State University of New York Press, 1995.

Desmond, William. *Philosophy and Its Others: Ways of Being and Mind*. State University of New York Press, 1990.

Dew Jr., James K., and Ronnie P. Campbell Jr., eds. *Natural Theology: Five Views*. Baker Academic, 2024.

Dibelius, Martin. *Studies in the Acts of the Apostles*. Edited by Heinrich Green. Translated by Mary Ling. SCM, 1956.

Dulles, Avery. *Models of Revelation*. Orbis, 1983.

Dupré, Louis. *Symbols of the Sacred*. Eerdmans, 2000.

Eco, Umberto, and Costantino Marmo, eds. *On the Medieval Theory of Signs*. Benjamins, 1989.

Elgin, Catherine Z. *True Enough*. MIT Press, 2017.

Eliade, Mircea. *The Myth of the Eternal Return*. 2nd ed. Translated by Willard R. Trask. Princeton University Press, 2005.

Eliade, Mircea. *Patterns in Comparative Religion*. Translated by Rosemary Sheed. Sheed & Ward, 1958.

Eliade, Mircea. *The Sacred and the Profane: The Nature of Religion*. Translated by Willard R. Trask. Harcourt, 1959.

Evans, C. Stephen. "Apologetics in a New Key: Relieving Protestant Anxieties Over Natural Theology." In *The Logic of Rational Theism: Exploratory Essays*, edited by William Lane Craig and Mark S. McLeod. Edwin Mellon, 1990.

Evans, C. Stephen. *Faith Beyond Reason: A Kierkegaardian Account*. Eerdmans, 1998.

Evans, C. Stephen. "Kierkegaard, Natural Theology, and the Existence of God." In *Kierkegaard and Christian Faith*, edited by Paul Martens and C. Stephen Evans. Baylor University Press, 2016.

Evans, C. Stephen. *Natural Signs and Knowledge of God: A New Look at Theistic Arguments*. Oxford University Press, 2010.

Evans, C. Stephen. *The Quest for Faith: Reason and Mystery as Pointers to God*. InterVarsity, 1986.

Evans, C. Stephen. *Subjectivity and Religious Belief: An Historical Critical Study*. Eerdmans, 1978.

Evans, C. Stephen. *Why Believe? Reason and Mystery as Pointers to God*. Eerdmans, 1996.

Evans, C. Stephen. *Why Christian Faith Still Makes Sense: A Response to Contemporary Challenges*. Baker Academic, 2015.

Evans, C. Stephen, and R. Zachary Manis. *Philosophy of Religion: Thinking About Faith*. 2nd ed. InterVarsity, 2009.

Fenn, W. W. "Concerning Natural Religion." *Harvard Theological Review* 4 (1911): 460–76.

Fergusson, David. *Creation*. Eerdmans, 2014.

Fergusson, David. *Faith and Its Critics: A Conversation*. Oxford University Press, 2009.

Fergusson, David. "Karl Barth's Doctrine of Creation: Church Bells Beyond the Stars." *International Journal of Systematic Theology* 18 (2016): 414–31.

Fergusson, David. "Types of Natural Theology." In *The Evolution of Rationality: Interdisciplinary Essays in Honor of J. Wentzel van Huyssteen*, edited by F. LeRon Shults. Eerdmans, 2006.

Feser, Edward. *Five Proofs for the Existence of God*. Ignatius, 2017.

Fogelin, Robert J. *Hume's Presence in the Dialogues Concerning Natural Religion*. Oxford University Press, 2017.

Fox, Michael V. *Ecclesiastes: The Traditional Hebrew Text with the New JPS Translation/Commentary*. JPS Bible Commentary. Jewish Publication Society, 2004.

Fox, Michael V. "Qohelet's Epistemology." *Hebrew Union College Annual* 58 (1987): 137–55.

Fox, Michael V. *A Time to Tear Down and a Time to Build Up: A Rereading of Ecclesiastes*. Eerdmans, 1999.

Frame, John M. *Cornelius Van Til: An Analysis of His Thought*. P&R, 1995.

Fulton, William. *Nature of God*. T&T Clark, 1927.

Gabriel, Andrew K. *Barth's Doctrine of Creation: Creation, Nature, and the Trinity*. Cascade, 2014.

Garrigou-Lagrange, R. *God: His Existence and Nature; A Thomistic Solution of Certain Agnostic Antinomies*. Translated by Dom Bede Rose. 2 vols. Herder, 1949.

Genette, Gérard. *Paratexts: Thresholds of Interpretation.* Translated by Jane E. Lewin. Cambridge University Press, 1997.

Glacken, Clarence J. *Traces of the Rhodian Shore: Nature and Culture in Western Thought from Ancient Times to the End of the Eighteenth Century.* University of California Press, 1967.

Goodman, Nelson. *Ways of Worldmaking.* Hackett, 1978.

Gorringe, T. J. *Discerning Spirit: A Theology of Revelation.* SCM, 1990.

Gorringe, T. J. *Earthly Visions: Theology and the Challenges of Art.* Yale University Press, 2011.

Guinness, Os. *Signals of Transcendence: Listening to the Promptings of Life.* InterVarsity, 2023.

Gunton, Colin. "The Trinity, Natural Theology, and a Theology of Nature." In *The Trinity in a Pluralistic Age: Theological Essays on Culture and Religion,* edited by Kevin J. Vanhoozer. Eerdmans, 1997.

Harrison, Peter. *"Religion" and the Religions in the English Enlightenment.* Cambridge University Press, 1990.

Hauerwas, Stanley. *With the Grain of the Universe: The Church's Witness and Natural Theology.* Baker Academic, 2001.

Helm, Paul. "John Calvin, the *Sensus Divinitatis,* and the Noetic Effects of Sin." *International Journal for Philosophy of Religion* 43 (1998): 87–107.

Herbert, Edward. *The Autobiography of Edward, Lord Herbert of Cherbury: With Introduction, Notes, Appendices, and a Continuation of the Life.* Edited by Sidney L. Lee. Nimmo, 1886.

Holder, Rodney. *The Heavens Declare: Natural Theology and the Legacy of Karl Barth.* Templeton, 2012.

Hopps, Gavin. *The Extravagance of Music.* Palgrave Macmillan, 2018.

Hume, David. *Dialogues Concerning Natural Religion.* Routledge, 1991.

Hunsinger, George. *How to Read Karl Barth: The Shape of His Theology.* Oxford University Press, 1991.

Jaki, Stnaley L. *Lord Gifford and His Lectures: A Centenary Retrospect.* Scottish Academic Press, 1986.

Jipp, Joshua W. "Paul's Areopagus Speech of Acts 17:16–34 as *both* Critique *and* Propaganda." *Journal of Biblical Literature* 131 (2012): 567–88.

Johnson, Keith L. *Karl Barth and the Analogia Entis.* T&T Clark, 2010.

Johnson, Keith L. "When Nature Presupposes Grace: A Response to Thomas Joseph White, O.P." *Pro Ecclesia* 20 (2011): 264–82.

Jüngel, Eberhard. *Christ, Justice and Peace: Toward a Theology of the State in Dialogue with the Barmen Declaration*. Translated by D. Bruce Hamill and Alan J. Torrance. T&T Clark, 1992.

Juurikkala, Oskari. "The Two Books of God: The Metaphor of the Book of Nature in Augustine." *Augustinianum* 61 (2021): 479–98.

Kearney, Richard. *Anatheism: Returning to God After God*. Columbia University Press, 2010.

Kearney, Richard. "God Who May Be: A Phenomenological Study." *Modern Theology* 18 (2002): 75–85.

Kearney, Richard. "Hermeneutics of the Possible God." In *Givenness and God: Questions of Jean-Luc Marion*, edited by Ian Leask and Eoin Cassidy. Fordham University Press, 2005.

Kearney, Richard. "Ricoeur and Biblical Hermeneutics: On Post-Religious Faith." In *Ricoeur Across the Disciplines*, edited by Scott Davidson. Continuum, 2010.

Keener, Craig S. *The Gospel of Matthew: A Socio-Rhetorical Commentary*. Eerdmans, 2009.

Kerr, Fergus. *After Aquinas: Versions of Thomism*. Blackwell, 2002.

Kort, Wesley A. *Bound to Differ: The Dynamics of Theological Discourses*. Penn State University Press, 1992.

Lampe, G. W. H. "Athens and Jerusalem: Joint Witnesses to Christ?" In *The Philosophical Frontiers of Christian Theology: Essays Presented to D. M. Mackinnon*, edited by Brian Hebblethwaite and Stewart Sutherland. Cambridge University Press, 1982.

Leeuw, G. van der. *Religion in Essence and Manifestation: A Study in Phenomenology*. Translated by J. E. Turner. Vol. 1. Harper & Row, 1963

Levering, Matthew. *Proofs of God: Classical Arguments from Tertullian to Barth*. Baker Academic, 2016.

Lewis, C. S. *Studies in Words*. Cambridge University Press, 1960.

Lifton, Robert Jay. *Thought Reform and the Psychology of Totalism: A Study of "Brainwashing" in China*. Norton, 1961.

Lindsay, Mark R. *Reading Auschwitz with Barth: The Holocaust as Problem and Promise for Barthian Theology*. Clarke, 2014.

Lonergan, Bernard. *Method in Theology*. Edited by Robert M. Doran and John D. Dadosky. Collected Works of Bernard Lonergan 14. University of Toronto Press, 2017.

Long, D. Stephen. *Saving Karl Barth: Hans Urs von Balthasar's Preoccupation.* Fortress, 2014.

López, José, and Gary Potter, eds. *After Postmodernism: An Introduction to Critical Realism.* Athlone, 2001.

Louth, Andrew. *Discerning the Mystery: An Essay on the Nature of Theology.* Clarendon, 1983.

Luhrmann, T. M. *How God Becomes Real: Kindling the Presence of Invisible Others.* Princeton University Press, 2020.

Macquarrie, John. *God-Talk: An Examination of the Language and Logic of Theology.* SCM Press, 1967.

Macquarrie, John. *In Search of Deity: An Essay in Dialectical Theism.* SCM, 1984.

Macquarrie, John. *Principles of Christian Theology.* Rev. ed. SCM, 1977.

Macquarrie, John. *Thinking About God.* SCM, 1975.

MacSwain, Robert. *Saints as Divine Evidence.* Cambridge University Press, 2025.

MacSwain, Robert. "The Tradition of Reason: David Brown, Joseph Butler, and Divine Hiddenness." In *Christian Theology and the Transformation of Natural Religion,* edited by Christopher R. Brewer. Peeters, 2018.

Markus, R. A. "St. Augustine on Signs." *Phronesis* 2 (1957): 60–83.

Mavrodes, George I. *Belief in God.* Random House, 1970.

Mavrodes, George I. *Revelation in Religious Belief.* Temple University Press, 1988.

McCormack, Bruce L. *Karl Barth's Critically Realistic Dialectical Theology: Its Genesis and Development 1909–1936.* Clarendon, 1995.

McGrath, Alister E. "The Natural Sciences and Apologetics." In *Imaginative Apologetics: Theology, Philosophy and the Catholic Tradition,* edited by Andrew Davison. Baker Academic, 2012.

McGrath, Alister E. *The Open Secret: A New Vision for Natural Theology.* Blackwell, 2008.

McGrath, Alister E. *Re-Imagining Nature: The Promise of a Christian Natural Theology.* Wiley-Blackwell, 2017.

McGrath, Alister E. *A Scientific Theology.* 3 vols. T&T Clark, 2002–2003.

McGrath, Alister E. *T. F. Torrance: An Intellectual Biography.* T&T Clark, 1999.

McGrath, Alister E. "Thomas F. Torrance and the Search for a Viable Natural Theology: Some Personal Reflections." *Participatio* 1 (2009): 66–81.

McMaken, W. Travis. "The Impossibility of Natural Knowledge of God in T. F. Torrance's Reformulated Natural Theology." *International Journal of Systematic Theology* 12 (2010): 319–40.

Molnar, Paul D. "Natural Theology Revisited: A Comparison of T.F. Torrance and Karl Barth." *Zeitschrift für dialektische Theologie* 21 (2005): 53–83.

Moltmann, Jürgen. *God in Creation: A New Theology of Creation and the Spirit of God*. Fortress, 1993.

Montell, Amanda. *Cultish: The Language of Fanaticism*. HarperCollins, 2021.

Monti, Anthony. *A Natural Theology of the Arts: Imprint of the Spirit*. Ashgate, 2003.

Monti, Anthony. "'Types and Symbols of Eternity': How Art Points to Divinity." *Theology* 105 (2002): 118–26.

Moore, James A. "The Semiotic of Bishop Berkley–A Prelude to Peirce?" *Transactions of the Charles S. Peirce Society* 20 (1984): 325–42.

Murray, Michael J. "Reason for Hope (in a Postmodern World)." In *Reason for the Hope Within*, edited by Michael J. Murray. Eerdmans, 1999.

Myers, Benjamin. "Alister McGrath's Scientific Theology." In *The Order of Things: Explorations in Scientific Theology*, by Alister E. McGrath. Blackwell, 2006.

Newman, John Henry. *An Essay in Aid of a Grammar of Assent*. University of Notre Dame Press, 1979.

Newman, John Henry. *An Essay on the Development of Christian Doctrine*. University of Notre Dame Press, 1989.

Nichols, Aidan. *A Grammar of Consent: The Existence of God in Christian Tradition*. University of Notre Dame Press, 1991.

Niebuhr, H. Richard. *Christ and Culture*. HarperSanFrancisco, 1951.

Nimmo, Paul T. *Barth: A Guide for the Perplexed*. Bloomsbury, 2017.

Oppy, Graham. "Arguments for the Existence of God." In *The Oxford Handbook of Medieval Philosophy*, edited by John Marenbon. Oxford University Press, 2012.

Oppy, Graham. "Natural Theology." In *Alvin Plantinga*, edited by Deane-Peter Baker. Cambridge University Press, 2007.

Otto, Rudolph. *The Idea of the Holy: An Inquiry into the Non-Rational Factor in the Idea of the Divine and Its Relation to the Rational*. 2nd ed. Translated by John W. Harvey. Oxford University Press, 1950.

Pannenberg, Wolfhart. *Systematic Theology*. Vol. 1. Eerdmans, 1991

Pattison, George. *God and Being: An Enquiry*. Oxford University Press, 2011.

Peirce, Charles Sanders. "Questions Concerning Certain Faculties Claimed for Man." In *Peirce on Signs*, edited by James Hoopes. University of North Carolina Press, 1991.

Plantinga, Alvin. *God and Other Minds: A Study of the Rational Justification of Belief in God*. Cornell University Press, 1967.

Plantinga, Alvin. *God, Freedom, and Evil*. Eerdmans, 1974.

Plantinga, Alvin. *Knowledge and Christian Belief*. Eerdmans, 2015.

Plantinga, Alvin. *The Nature of Necessity*. Oxford University Press, 1974.

Plantinga, Alvin. "The Prospects for Natural Theology." *Philosophical Perspectives* 5 (1991): 287–315.

Plantinga, Alvin. "Reason and Belief in God." In *Faith and Rationality: Reason and Belief in God*, edited by Alvin Plantinga and Nicholas Wolterstorff. University of Notre Dame Press, 1983.

Plantinga, Alvin. "The Reformed Objection to Natural Theology." *Proceedings of the American Catholic Philosophical Association* 15 (1980): 49–63.

Plantinga, Alvin. *Warrant and Proper Function*. Oxford University Press, 1993.

Plantinga, Alvin. *Warranted Christian Belief*. Oxford University Press, 1998.

Plantinga, Alvin. *Warrant: The Current Debate*. Oxford University Press, 1993.

Plantinga, Alvin. *Where the Conflict Really Lies: Science, Religion, and Naturalism*. Oxford University Press, 2011.

Przywara, Erich. *Analogia Entis: Metaphysics; Original Structure and Universal Rhythm*. Translated by John R. Betz and David Bentley Hart. Eerdmans, 2014.

Purinton, D. B. *Christian Theism: Its Claims and Sanctions*. Putnam, 1889.

Raven, Charles E. *Natural Religion and Christian Theology: The Gifford Lectures 1951*. First Series: Science and Religion. Cambridge University Press, 1953.

Re Manning, Russell. "Natural Theology Reconsidered (Again)." *Theology and Science* 15 (2017): 289–301.

Ricoeur, Paul. *The Symbolism of Evil*. Translated by Emerson Buchanan. Beacon, 1967.

Root, Howard E. "Beginning All over Again." In *Soundings: Essays Concerning Christian Understanding*, edited by A. R. Vidler. Cambridge University Press, 1962.

Root, Howard E. "Metaphysics and Religious Belief." In *Prospect for Metaphysics: Essays of Metaphysical Exploration*, edited by Ian Ramsey. Allen & Unwin, 1961.

Root, Howard E. *Theological Radicalism and Tradition: "The Limits of Radicalism" with Appendices*. Edited by Christopher R. Brewer. Routledge, 2018.

Rowe, William L. "Tillich's Theory of Signs and Symbols." *The Monist* 50 (1966): 593–610.

Schleiermacher, Friedrich. *On Religion: Speeches to Its Cultured Despisers.* Translated and edited by Richard Crouter. Cambridge University Press, 1996.

Seow, Choon-Leong. *Ecclesiastes: A New Translation with Introduction and Commentary.* Anchor Bible 18C. Doubleday, 1997.

Sherry, Patrick. "The Religious Roots of Natural Theology." *New Blackfriars* 84 (2003): 301–7.

Sillem, Edward A. *George Berkeley and the Proofs for the Existence of God.* Longmans, Green, 1957.

Simpson, Christopher Ben, ed. *The William Desmond Reader.* State University of New York, 2012.

Smith, John E. "The Permanent Truth in the Idea of Natural Religion: The Dudleian Lecture for 1960." *Harvard Theological Review* 54 (1961): 1–19.

Sommer, Benjamin D. "Nature, Revelation, and Grace in Psalm 19: Towards a Theological Reading of Scripture." *Harvard Theological Review* 108 (2015): 376–401.

Spencer, Stephen R. "Is Natural Theology Biblical?" *Grace Theological Journal* 9 (1988): 59–72.

Steiner, George. *Real Presences.* Faber & Faber, 1989.

Sudduth, Michael. *The Reformed Objection to Natural Theology.* Ashgate, 2009.

Swinburne, Richard. "The Revival of Natural Theology." *Archive di Filosofia* 75 (2007): 303–22.

Swinburne, Richard. "The Vocation of a Natural Theologian." In *Philosophers Who Believe: The Spiritual Journeys of 11 Leading Thinkers,* edited by Kelly James Clark. InterVarsity, 1993.

Swinburne, Richard. *Faith and Reason.* 2nd ed. Oxford University Press, 2005.

Swinburne, Richard. *Revelation: From Metaphor to Analogy.* 2nd ed. Oxford University Press, 2007.

Swinburne, Richard. *The Christian God.* Clarendon, 1994.

Swinburne, Richard. *The Coherence of Theism.* Rev. ed. Oxford University Press, 1993.

Swinburne, Richard. *The Evolution of the Soul.* Rev. ed. Oxford University Press, 2007.

Taylor, Charles. *A Secular Age.* Belknap, 2007.

Temple, William. *Nature, Man and God: Being the Gifford Lectures Delivered in the University of Glasgow in the Academical Years 1932–1933 and 1933–1934.* Macmillan, 1934.

Tice, Terrance. *Schleiermacher.* Abingdon, 2006.

Tietz, Christine. *Karl Barth: A Life in Conflict.* Oxford University Press, 2021.

Tillich, Paul. "The Two Types of Philosophy of Religion." In *Theology of Culture*, edited by Robert C. Kimball. Oxford University Press, 1959.

Tillich, Paul. *The Dynamics of Faith*. Harper & Row, 1957.

Torrance, Alan. "Assessing T. F. Torrance in Dialogue with Paul Molnar." *A Journal for the Theology of Culture* 8 (2012): 77–81.

Torrance, Thomas F. *The Ground and Grammar of Theology: Consonance Between Theology and Science*. T&T Clark, 2001.

Torrance, Thomas F. "The Problem of Natural Theology in the Thought of Karl Barth." *Religious Studies* 6 (1970): 121–35.

Torrance, Thomas F. *Space, Time and Incarnation*. T&T Clark, 1969.

Torrance, Thomas F. *Theological Science*. T&T Clark, 1969.

Turner, Denys. *Reason and the Existence of God*. Cambridge University Press, 2004.

Van Til, Cornelius. *The Defense of the Faith*. Presbyterian and Reformed, 1955.

Wainwright, William J. *Reason, Revelation, and Devotion: Inference and Argument in Religion*. Cambridge University Press, 2016.

Walls, Jerry L., and Trent Dougherty, eds. *Two Dozen (Or So) Arguments for God: The Plantinga Project*. Oxford University Press, 2018.

Ward, Keith. *Religion and Revelation*. Oxford University Press, 1994.

Webb, Clement C. J. *Studies in the History of Natural Theology*. Clarendon, 1915.

White, Thomas Joseph, OP. *Wisdom in the Face of Modernity: A Study in Thomistic Natural Theology*. Sapientia, 2009.

Williams, Rowan. "Dialectic and Analogy: A Theological Legacy." In *Religions*, edited by Nicholas Boyle, Liz Disley, and Nicholas Adams. Vol. 4 of *The Impact of Idealism: The Legacy of Post-Kantian German Thought*. Cambridge University Press, 2013.

Wiman, Christian. *My Bright Abyss: Meditation of a Modern Believer*. Farrer, Straus & Giroux, 2013.

Wolterstorff, Nicholas. "The Migration of the Theistic Arguments: From Natural Theology to Evidentialist Apologetics." In *Rationality, Religious Belief, and Moral Commitment: New Essays in the Philosophy of Religion*, edited by Robert Audi and William J. Wainwright. Cornell University Press, 1986.

Woolford, Thomas. "Natural Theology and Natural Philosophy in the Late Renaissance." DPhil diss., Trinity College, University of Cambridge, 2011.

Wright, N. T. *History and Eschatology: Jesus and the Promise of Natural Theology*. SPCK, 2018.

Wright, N. T. *The New Testament and the People of God*. Vol. 1 of Christian Origins and the Question of God. Fortress, 1992.

Subject Index

actuality, 132
aesthetic experience, 137–38
after and before, 133
Amundsen, Roald, 73–74
analogia entis (analogy of being), 169
analogia fidei (analogy of faith), 169
anatheism, 50, 131
anatheist construct of natural theology,
    129–33
Anselm (Barth), 167
antecedent construct of natural theology,
    129–33
anti-naturalism, 113
anti-Nazism, 3
apologetic function, 68–69
a posteriori arguments, 61, 66
archaic ontology, 103
Areopagus speech, 154
arguments. *See also* natural theology as
    proof/argument (NT2); proofs
  believing in God on basis of, 118
  cosmological, 7, 12–13, 69, 72, 77, 78, 111
  as good, 87
  moral, 7, 69, 111
  natural theology as, 17
  a posteriori, 61, 66
  a priori, 66
  signals as, 102
  sign-informed, 120
  signs as, 114
  teleological, 7, 69, 77, 78, 111
art, 106, 132–33, 136, 138, 149–50, 153

astonishment, 132
atheism, 131
Augustine, 11
autonomous religion, 40
awareness, focal *versus* subsidiary, 137
Balaam, 158
beauty, in the world, 60
before and after, 133
being, as overdetermined, 132
belief
  basic, 67, 79, 81, 82
  of believers, 85–86
  circumstances for, 83–84
  in God, 82–83 (*see also* God)
  as irrational and unreasonable, 80
  justification of, 81, 82
  natural, 67
  natural revelation tag team of, 83–84
  of nonbelievers, 85–86
  rationality of, 85
  theistic, 79, 82, 84, 86
  as warranted, 67, 83
beneficial order, 22
between, the, 64
Bible, 47–48, 154–59. *See also* Word of God
body, defined, 68
brain, 150
capacity, as lacking, 82
Christianity, as religious pluralism, 32–33
Christian natural theology, 22–23,
    138–40. *See also* natural theology as
    Christian natural theology (NT4)

Christian philosophy, restoration of, 72–73
Christology, as material foundation, 169
church, 37, 38–39, 44, 53
Church Dogmatics (Barth), 142, 159–60, 167, 169, 172
civic (political) theology, 11
classical foundationalism, 80–81
clues, types of, 114–15
cognitive capacity, as lacking, 82
Communism, 3
concepts, adoption and types of, 100
condemnation, 91
consequent construct of natural theology, 129–33
Continental Philosophy and Modern Theology (Brown), 51
conversation analogy, 122
cosmic wonder, 22
cosmological argument, 7, 12–13, 69, 72, 77, 78, 111
counter-creation, 138
covenant, 173
creation
art and, 138
centrality of, 161
cosmological arguments and, 12–13
counter, 138
doctrine of, 12–13, 138, 161, 172–74
faith and, 173
God's motivation for, 45
goodness of, 50–51
grace and, 35
key to secret of, 165–78
knowledge of, 174
natural theology as embedded in, 147
nature as distinguished from, 162–63
new, 138
responsive, 138
revelation and, 161
criticism, 37, 131
culture, 9–10, 108
curiosity, 132
deductive proof, 108–9

deism, 20, 31–32, 54
Descriptive Responsibility, 8, 12, 18–19, 86–87, 100, 107
Design Plan, 67
desire, 178
Desire, Dialectic, and Otherness (Desmond), 176
dialectical relation, 176, 177
dialectical theology, 171
Dialogues on Natural Religion (Hume), 70
divine beauty, 45. *See also* God
divine generosity, 45, 46, 106. *See also* God
divine goodness, 35, 36, 45. *See also* God
Divine Trinity, The (Brown), 51
dogmatism, 177
double movement of the thought, 178
dualism, 142, 143–45, 146
Durham Cathedral, 52
easy resistibility principle, 22, 96
Ecclesiastes, 155–56
effective history, 50
effect to cause, 61, 70
Enlightenment, 134, 135
Epicureanism, 161
Epistle to the Romans, The (Barth), 167, 168
equivocal relation, 176, 177
essentialism, 148
ethos
defined, 6, 64
first, 65
in natural theology as proof/argument (NT2), 63–66
ontological, 65–66
reconfigured (second), 64, 65
evidence, 112–13, 114–15, 117. *See also* signs
evidentialist apologetics, 62, 116
evidentialist objection, 112
experience, limitation of, 71
explicit reasoning, 105
faith
after and before of, 133
choice of, 50, 131–32

creation and, 173
importance of, 119
inductive, 102
natural theology and, 2, 130
reason and, 14
as responding to evidence, 117
science and, 144
as seeking understanding, 60
signs and, 120
Thomistic conception of, 80
understanding to, 37
Faith Beyond Reason (Evans), 119
fall, the, 38, 85
father concept, 175
fideism, 119–20
fire, 96
first astonishment, 132
first perplexity, 132
first/primal ethos, 6. *See also* ethos
flexible openness, 136
foundationalism, classical, 80–81
general revelation, 5–6
generative excess, 106
geometry, 142, 143
Germany, 172
gestures, 101–2, 103, 104
Gifford Lectures, 30, 31, 70, 76, 162, 163, 173–74
given signs, 96. *See also* signs
glory, theology of, 130
God. *See also* knowledge of God
   activity of, 50–51
   agency of, 51
   beauty of, 45
   belief in, as immediate, 82–83
   claim of, 120–21
   conceptualizing, 52
   contributions of, 174–75
   covenant of, 173
   as creator, 12–13, 45, 67, 84, 91–92, 173
   death of, 104–5
   denial of, 172
   design plan of, 83

discernment of, 115–16
distance from, 163
doctrine of, 172, 174
encountering, 53
experiential indicators of, 106
generosity of, 45, 46, 106
goodness of, 35, 45, 46
idea of, 61
interaction by, 53–54
material reality and, 54
natural signs of, 7, 22 (*see also* signs)
nature in relation to, 174
nature of, 61
as object of theology, 146
as omnipresent, 47
of possibility, 132
presence of, 115–16, 130, 138
as redeemer, 67, 84, 91–92
residual sense of, 50
revelation of, 35, 49, 142
self-disclosure of, 145
speaking by, 177
as speaking of, 171–72
symbols of, 47
as transcendent Other, 176
as triune, 144
as wholly other, 163–64
God, Freedom, and Evil (Plantinga), 77–78
God and Other Minds (Plantinga), 77
goodness, 45, 50–51, 60
grace, 35, 45, 46
Grammar of Consent, A (Nichols), 108
heaven, 47
hermeneutics, function of, 130–31
hierophany, 103–4
highest being, 72
history, as part of nature, 162
Hitler, Adolf, 172
holy, defined, 48
Holy Spirit, 67, 86, 92
homoousion, 147
human beings
   as affecting belief in God, 89

capacity for knowledge of God by, 92
contributions of, 174–75
intrinsic worth of, 22
as part of nature, 162
prior condition of, 175
as rational, 89
receptivity of, 92
understanding of, 89
will of, 89–90
human freedom, 45, 46, 51
human nature, 68, 108
human reason, 10, 119
ideas, nature of, 107
ignorance, 90
imago Dei, 92
immanent frame, 105
immorality, 90
implicit reasoning, 105
incarnation, 40, 54, 144–45, 147
indication, awareness and, 137
inductive faith, 102
intermediation, 177
interpretation, of thoughts, 97
Invitation to Theology (Brown), 51
Islam, 33
Jacob's ladder, 104, 172
Jesus Christ
beginning with, 159–61
birth of, 156–59
fellowship with, 82
God as revealed through, 12
as historical figure, 161
incarnation of, 54
as key to secret of creation, 165–78
knowledge of God in relation to, 160 (*see also* knowledge of God)
natural theology as including, 161
natural theology as opposed to, 162–63
as revelation, 5, 39, 142
as subject of knowledge of God, 82 (*see also* knowledge of God)
as Word of God, 165
Judaism, 32–33

justification, 81, 82, 112
kitchen analogy, 64–65
knowledge
of creation, 174
motivation of, 121
natural religious, 121
nature of, 107
as sociological, 107
suppression of, 91
vagueness and, 150
warrant for, 83
knowledge of God
attaining, 154
as Creator and Redeemer, 149
natural, 129
in relation to Jesus Christ, 160
structure of, 146
through revelation, 154–55
as true belief, 83
as unrestricted, 96
as widely available, 96
in Word of God, 144
language, function of, 175–76
Lord's Prayer, 47
magi, 156–59
material foundation, 169
McClure, Robert, 73–74
metaphors, 51–52, 136–37
metaphysics, 132
metaxological relation, 176–77
mindfulness, of the ethos, 64
model-specific objection, 19, 118–19, 127–28
moral accountability, 22
moral argument, 7, 69, 111
moral order, mystery of, 115
moving text, 48
mysterium tremendum, 48
mythical (fabulous) theology, 11
natural aetheology, 77, 78
natural cause, 70
natural Christian theology, 134. *See also* natural theology as Christian natural theology (NT4)

natural effect, 70
natural religion. *See also* natural theology as informed by natural religion (NT1)
  corruption of, 32–33
  defined, 29–30
  heresy of, 39–41
  as natural human religiousness, 31
  natural theology and, 20, 30–34
  revealed religion as compared to, 31, 33–34, 40–41
  as transformed, 20
natural revelation, 84
natural signs. *See also* signs
  for existence of God, 7, 22
  given signs as compared to, 96
  interpretation of, 95–96
  as misread, 96
  theistic, 114–21
Natural Signs and Knowledge of God (Reid), 115
natural theology
  antecedent, consequent, and anatheist constructs of, 129–33
  apologetic function of, 14, 17
  basic function of, 36
  challenge of definition of, 15–18
  characteristics of, 148
  as Christian natural theology, 22–23, 138–40
  coexistence function of, 17
  from confessional perspective, 147
  as confident discipline, 109
  connection through, 36
  criticism of, 36, 80, 121–22
  defined, 4, 68, 79, 87, 116, 117, 134, 162, 171
  deistic function of, 17
  development of, 63, 145
  dogmatic function of, 13–14
  as educative, 49–50
  educative function of, 129, 130
  eschatological function of, 129, 132
  as failure, 76
  foundational function of, 17
  function of, 13–15, 17, 36, 87, 114, 123, 129, 130, 132, 146, 174
  general revelation as compared to, 5–6
  hermeneutical function of, 129
  imaginative potential of, 135
  independent character of, 127, 145
  as intrinsic, 146
  key considerations regarding, 8–15
  limitations of, 121
  minimum requirement for, 147–48
  as natural, 13
  natural religion and, 20, 30–34
  as necessary, 162
  negative viewpoints regarding, 2–3
  as not necessary, 75–92, 123
  old-style *versus* new-style, 17
  postmetaphysical approach to, 132
  powers of reason reflection of, 17
  predogmatic function of, 14
  as proof/argument, 21
  purpose of, 123
  as rational, 13
  rejection of, 119, 163
  revealed theology as compared to, 4, 5, 12, 13, 68, 114, 117–18, 122–23, 130
  revealed theology as in, 127, 129, 145
  revelation and, 137, 139
  as revelation-free, 5
  science and, 141
  as signals of transcendence, 22
  symbol of, 51–52
  of theistic natural signs, 114–21
  as theology of nature, 23–24, 136
  of tradition-mediated rationality, 134
  transformation of, 141–50
  types of, 19–24, 119 (*see also specific types*)
  understanding, 4–8
  value of, 123
natural theology as Christian natural theology (NT4)

antecedent, consequent, and anatheist
    constructs of, 129–33
assessment of, 149–50
as correction, 149
introduction to, 22–23, 127–29
overview of, 133–38
Paul Molnar and, 138–40
natural theology as informed by natural
    religion (NT1)
    heresy of natural religion and, 39–41
    introduction to, 20, 29–30
    natural religion and natural theology in,
        30–34
    overview of, 34–39
natural theology as proof/argument (NT2)
    characteristics of, 87
    discussion of, 118–19
    ethos and ways in, 63–66
    failures of, 113
    introduction to, 21, 59–63
    overview of, 66–70
    philosophical critiques of, 70–74
    possibility in, 70
    probity in, 70
    understanding, 73
natural theology as signals of
        transcendence (NT3)
    criticism of, 121
    as hinge of NT1 and NT2, 120
    introduction to, 22, 95–96
    overview of, 101–9
    signs, symbols, and sacraments in,
        96–101
    support for, 115
    value of, 113
natural theology as theology of nature
        (NT5)
    Bible and natural theology in, 154–59
    introduction to, 153–54
    overview of, 159–63
nature
    culture as, 9–10
    defined, 114, 134

as distinguished from creation, 162–63
encountering, 134
first (unworked), 10
history as part of, 162
human, 68
interpretation of, 134–35
of man, 10
meanings of, 9
in natural theology, 8–11
as open secret, 134–35
proper function of, 67
quintessentially human and, 67
in relation to God, 174
second (worked), 10
as sociological, 107
third (human reason), 10
nature-grace debate, 45–46
Nature of Necessity, The (Plantinga), 77–78
Nazism, 4
new creation, 138. *See also* creation
Newtonian dualism, 142
noetic dialectic, 170
nonbelievers, 85–86, 159
Northwest Passage metaphor, 73–74
noumena, 71
noumenal realm, 144
numinous, 48
ontological arguments
    critique of, 71
    division of, 69
    example of, 60–61, 76
    as philosophers' arguments, 66
    Plantinga on, 77, 78
    resurrection of, 61
openness, 178
Open Secret, The (McGrath), 133–34
original sin, 38. *See also* sin
paintings, as parables, 154
parables, 153–54
Pascalian principles, 96
perception, signs in, 97
perplexity, 148
persistent possibility, 92

phenomena, 71
phenomenal realm, 144
philosophical prolegomena, 107
Philosophy of Religion (Evans), 117
physical (natural) theology, 11. *See also*
     natural theology
physicotheological proof, 72
physics, 142, 143
political debate analogy, 122
political (civic) theology, 11
positive theology, 146
possibility, 132
postulary finitism, 105
potency, experience of, 48–49
power, defined, 48–49
prayer, proof and, 60
preambula fidei, 142–43
predogmatic function, 68–69
Prescriptive Possibility, 19, 24–25
primitive naïveté, 37, 131
problem solving, 150
project objection, 19, 118–19, 127–28
proofs. *See also* arguments; natural
     theology as proof/argument (NT2)
  cogency and, 69
  deductive, 108–9
  defined, 21, 59
  differentiation of, 102
  limitations of, 69–70
  as person-relative, 69
  prayer and, 60
  as probing, 70
  pushing for, 109–10
  understanding, 6–7
pure nature, 46
pure *theologia naturalis*, 129–30
Realdialektik, 170
reality, defined, 103
Real Presences (Steiner), 135
reason, 14, 38, 46, 80
reasoning, explicit/implicit, 105
receptivity, 92
rechargeable battery analogy, 65–66

reconfigured ethos (second ethos), 64, 65
Reformed (Calvinist) epistemology, 80–88,
     89, 113
regeneration, of *sensus divinitatus* (sense of
     divinity), 86
Reid, Thomas, 115–19
religion. *See also* natural religion
  essence of, 102
  as inference, 53
  power as basis of, 48–49
  religious experience in, 103
  as revelation, 39
  roots of, 49
  theology and, 31
religious apologetics, 118
religious belief, 112, 114
religious experience, 44, 48, 53–54, 103
religious pluralism, 32–33
remainder concept, 46
responsible fideism, 119–20
responsive creation, 138
revealed religion, natural religion as
     compared to, 31, 33–34, 40–41
revealed theology
  defined, 130
  as mode of presence of God, 130
  as in natural theology, 145
  natural theology as compared to, 4, 5, 12,
     13, 68, 114, 117–18, 122–23, 130
  natural theology as in, 127, 129
revelation
  in the Bible, 47–48, 154
  book of nature and, 35
  book of Scripture and, 35
  creation and, 161
  elements of, 12
  of God, 35, 49, 142
  Jesus Christ as, 5, 39, 142
  man's response to, 175
  natural theology and, 137, 139
  reason and, 46
  religion as, 39
  religious experience as, 48

symbols of, 47
through Jesus Christ, 39
understanding, 47
Roger's Version (Updike), 59
Roman Catholicism, 169
sacramentalism, 54
sacraments, 96–101
Sacred Canopy, The (Berger), 108
sacrifice, 47
sages, 155
salvation, 129, 130
science, 141, 144
scientific method, 143
scientific theology, 133–34
second ethos, 6
second naïveté, 37, 131
second perplexity, 132
secularism, 54
self-criticism, 177
self-mediation, 177
semiotics, defined, 97
sensus divinitatus (sense of divinity), 49,
    83–84, 85–86, 88, 148
signals, 101–2, 105, 115
signs
    as arguments, 114
    characteristics of, 98–99
    as discountable, 117
    as evidence, 113
    faith and, 120
    nature of, 111
    as not participating, 112
    overview of, 96–101
    as pointer, 111, 112
    as proving, 112
    recognition of, 120
    as resistible, 117
    in theistic arguments, 112
    theistic natural, 114–21
sin, 38, 67, 85, 86
smoke, 96
Social Construction of Reality, The (Berger),
    107

social reality, nature of, 107
soft dualism, 68
soul, defined, 68
supernatural cause, 70
Symbolism of Evil, The (Ricoeur), 130–31
symbols
    awareness and, 137
    characteristics of, 98–99
    movement of, 99
    multivalency of, 99
    overview of, 96–101
    participation of, 99
    power of, 99
    re-creation of language via, 130–31
    significance of, 51–52
teleological argument, 7, 69, 77, 78, 111
theism, 69, 78, 87
theistic natural signs, 114–21
theology. *See also* natural theology
    comparative, 147
    confessional, 147
    as determined by its object, 146
    as distinctive science, 143–44, 164
    of glory, 130
    of nature, 161
    positive, 146
    religion and, 31
    task of, 171
theophany, 103
theory of perception, 97
thought form, 169
thoughts, 97, 178
Tower of Babel, 171–72
Tradition and Imagination (Brown), 48
transcendence
    examples of, 101
    gestures as signals of, 104
    natural theology as signal of, 22
    signals of, 104, 105, 115
    wager on, 135
truth, understanding, 153
understanding, faith as seeking, 60
University of Aberdeen, 76

univocal relation, 176, 177
vagueness, 149–50
Vatican Council, 72–73
vocational signposts, 161
warrant, knowledge and belief and, 83
ways, in natural theology as proof/
        argument (NT2), 63–66
wickedness, 89–90
wide accessibility principle, 22, 96
will, wickedness and, 89–90
wonder, 132
Word of God, 92, 144, 165, 172. *See also*
        Bible
worldview, second ethos as, 65

Author Index

Abraham, William J., 6, 34
Allen, Garrick V., 48
Allen, James, 112
Anderson, James, 79
Anselm of Canterbury, 60, 66, 71, 106, 166
Aquinas, Thomas, 17, 45, 53, 61, 66, 72, 79, 97, 98, 106, 173
Aquino, Frederick D., 105
Aristotle, 96, 144, 173
Athanasius, 167
Augustine, 5, 96, 98, 99, 106, 178
Baker, Deane-Peter, 78
Bansnee, Jules, 61
Barnett, S. J., 32
Barr, James, 24, 68, 154, 155–156
Barth, Karl, 2–3, 5–6, 19, 22, 23, 39, 40, 41, 45, 54, 82, 92, 127, 128, 135–136, 138, 139, 140, 142–143, 153, 154, 159–160, 162, 163–164, 165–178
Bauckham, Richard, 138, 161
Bavinck, Herman, 79, 82, 84
Begbie, Jeremy, 9, 16, 23, 54–55, 67, 106, 128, 137, 138
Beintker, Michael, 170
Benes, Tuska, 168
Bennett-Hunter, Guy, 17
Berdyaev, Nicholas, 138
Berger, Peter, 3, 10, 24, 50, 95, 100, 101–103, 104–105, 106, 107, 108, 109, 115
Berkeley, George, 97, 115
Berkouwer, G. C., 5, 6, 35

Beversluis, John, 88–90, 92
Blanshard, Brand, 80
Blount, Charles, 32
Brewer, Christopher R., 6, 43, 46, 48, 63, 80, 81, 104, 162
Brown, David, 2, 4, 5, 6, 10, 19, 20, 21, 24, 33, 34, 35, 36–37, 38, 39, 40, 41, 42–55, 99, 100, 101, 155–157, 161, 162, 174–175, 176
Brown, Hunter, 63
Brunner, Emil, 92, 166, 171, 173
Bulgakov, Sergius, 138
Burling, Hugh, 2
Butler, Joseph, 17, 33–34, 36
Byrne, Peter, 20, 30, 31, 41
Cabot, John, 74
Caird, Edward, 30–31
Calvin, John, 45, 49, 50, 67, 79, 82, 83, 86, 88–91, 148, 157, 173, 175
Cameron, Michael, 96
Campbell, Douglas A., 155
Carroll, Noël, 36
Casserley, J. V. Langmead, 4, 8, 17, 33, 155
Chalmers, David, 50
Chesterton, G. K., 106
Chignell, Andrew, 30
Cicero, 9–10, 108
Clark, Andy, 50, 69
Clark, Kelly James, 69, 82
Clifford, W. K., 80
Coakley, Sarah, 4
Cobb, John, Jr., 127, 128–129

Collier, Andrew, 4, 134

Collins, John J., 154, 155

Craig, William Lane, 15

Cross, F. L., 4

Cruz, Helen De, 31

Cutrone, Emmanuel J., 97

Davies, Brian A., 163–164

Davis, Stephen T., 60

Deely, John, 96, 97, 98

Descartes, René, 61, 159

Desmond, William, 6, 7, 16, 37, 53, 62, 63,
    64–65, 70, 78, 105, 107, 109–110, 131,
    132–133, 148, 176–177, 178

Dibelius, Martin, 154, 155

Dillard, Annie, 60

Dougherty, Trent, 14

Dupré, Louis, 98

Eco, Umberto, 98

Einstein, Albert, 142

Elgin, Catherine Z., 123

Eliade, Mircea, 102, 103, 104

Evans, C. Stephen, 5, 7, 13, 22, 24, 52,
    78, 89, 92, 95–96, 97, 100, 109, 110,
    111–123, 146, 162

Farley, Edward, 17

Faso, Manuel, 115

Fenn, W. W., 29

Fergusson, David, 13, 15, 17, 23, 63, 128,
    173–174

Feser, Edward, 66, 70, 109

Feuerbach, Ludwig, 103

Flew, Anthony, 80

Fogelin, Robert J., 70

Fox, Michael F., 156

Frame, John, 82

Fulton, William, 11

Gabriel, Andrew K., 166, 172, 173

Gadmer, Hans-Georg, 50

Garrigou-Lagrange, R., 21

Genette, Gérard, 35

Gifford, Adam Lord, 70

Gilson, Etienne, 138

Glacken, Clarence J., 10

Goodman, Nelson, 36

Gorringe, T. J., 153–154, 162

Gorringe, Timothy, 135, 138

Gregory of Hyssa, 106

Guinness, Os, 101

Gunton, Colin, 16, 135–136, 161, 162

Harrison, Peter, 32

Hart, Trevor, 138

Hauerwas, Stanley, 162

Hebblethwaite, Brian, 135

Hegel, Georg Wilhelm Friedrich, 178

Helm, Paul, 89, 92

Herbert of Cherbury, Lord, 32

Herbert, Edward, 32

Hirstein, William, 150

Hoopes, James, 97

Hopps, Gavin, 49, 54–55

Horowitz, John, 32

Hume, David, 70–74

Hunsinger, George, 23, 153, 169–170

Jaki, Stanley L., 31

Jipp, Joshua W., 155

John of the Cross, 106

John Paul II (Pope), 32

Johnson, Keith L., 19, 169

Jolivet, Régis, 108

Jung, Carl, 103

Jüngel, Eberhard, 9, 16, 23

Juurikkala, Oskari, 6

Kant, Immanuel, 70–74, 106, 144

Kearney, Richard, 37, 49–50, 131, 132

Keener, Craig S., 157

Kerr, Fergus, 45, 61

Kierkegaard, Søren, 82, 106, 112, 113, 115,
    119–121

Kinlaw, Dennis F., III, 48

Kohler, Dale, 59

Kort, Wesley A., 45

Kung, Hans, 59

Kuyper, Abraham, 82, 138

Lampe, G. W. H., 158, 159

Lentz, Carl, 32

Leo XIII (Pope), 21, 72–73

Levering, Matthew, 21, 66, 70, 109
Lewis, C. S., 9, 167–168
Lifton, Robert Jay, 166
Lindsay, Mark R., 4
Livingstone, E. A., 4
Loades, Ann, 43
Locke, John, 17, 62
Lonergan, Bernard, 1
Long, D. Stephen, 169
Long, Eugene Thomas, 15
López, José, 134
Louth, Andrew, 149
Luckmann, Thomas, 101, 107, 108
Luhrmann, T. M., 50
Luther, Martin, 45
Lyons, Nathan, 110
MacIntyre, Alasdair, 131, 134
Mackintosh, Hugh Ross, 142
Macquarrie, John, 17, 36, 38, 39, 40, 134, 166
MacSwain, Robert, 46, 69
Manis, R. Zachary, 5, 112, 117, 118, 119, 121
Marcel, Gabriel, 106
Maritain, Jacques, 135
Markus, R. A., 96
Marmo, Costantino, 98
Matthew, 156–159
Mavrodes, George I., 5, 7, 69
McCormack, Bruce L., 168–169, 170
McGarrick, Theodore F., 32
McGrath, Alister E., 10, 16, 23, 128, 133–135, 138, 139, 142, 147, 148
McMaken, W. Travis, 23, 139, 140
Molnar, Paul, 23, 128, 138–140
Moltmann, Jürgen, 45, 129, 136, 138, 173–174
Montell, Amanda, 166
Monti, Anthony, 23, 128, 135, 136, 138
Moore, James A., 97
Moreland, J. P., 15
Mounce, William D., 14
Murray, Michael J., 14

Newman, John Henry Cardinal, 34, 63, 100, 105, 106
Nichols, Aiden, 100, 105–106, 107, 108, 109, 115–116
Niebuhr, H. Richard, 20
Nimmo, Paul T., 167, 172
Oppy, Graham, 62, 76
Otto, Rudolph, 48, 102
Packard, Joshua, 50
Pannenberg, Wolfhart, 8–9, 31
Pardi, Paul, 113
Pascal, Blaise, 106
Patte, Daniel, 4
Pattison, George, 18, 135
Paul, 155
Peirce, Charles Sanders, 97–98
Pereboom, Derk, 30
Philo, 70–71
Plantinga, Alvin, 14, 63, 66, 67, 68, 73, 75–92, 112–113, 146, 162
Plato, 144
Poinsot, John, 97, 98
Polanyi, Michael, 136, 137
Polkinghorne, John, 136, 138
Potter, Gary, 134
Przywara, Erich, 169
Pseudo-Dionysius, 45
Purinton, Daniel B., 178
Qoheleth, 155–156
Rahner, Karl, 46
Ramachandran, V. S., 150
Raven, Charles E., 5, 9, 35, 36
Re Manning, Russell, 10, 12, 15, 101, 131, 154
Reid, Thomas, 22, 95, 100, 112
Ricoeur, Paul, 37, 53, 54, 98–99, 106, 130–131
Root, Howard, 1, 2, 12, 38, 39, 63, 144
Rosenfeld, Sophia, 9
Rowe, William L., 98
Rowland, Christopher, 154
Rowling, J. K., 2
Ruskin, John, 135

Russell, Bertrand, 80
Schleiermacher, Friedrich, 45, 100, 102, 103, 115
Schwöbel, Christoph, 171–172
Scott, Nathan A., 135
Scotus, Duns, 45
Scriven, Michael, 80
Sennett, James F., 76
Seow, Choon-Leong, 156
Sharp, Ronald A., 135
Sherry, Patrick, 12–13, 138, 159
Sillem, Edward A., 97
Simpson, Christopher Ben, 63, 64
Smedt, Johan De, 31
Smith, John E., 29, 34–35, 36
Sölle, Dorothee, 45
Solovyov, Vladimir, 138
Sommer, Benjamin D., 154
Soskice, Janet Martin, 136–137
Spencer, Stephen R., 153
Stang, Nicholas F., 144
Steiner, George, 135, 138
Struck, Peter T., 9
Sudduth, Michael, 6, 13, 14, 19, 54, 62, 68–69, 118
Swinburne, Richard, 21, 66, 67, 68, 73, 75
Taylor, Charles, 37, 53, 105, 148
Temple, William, 12
Tice, Terrance, 102

Tietz, Christine, 164, 167
Tillich, Paul, 61, 98, 163
Tindal, Matthew, 17
Torrance, Alan, 139–140
Torrance, James, 139
Torrance, Thomas F., 5, 22, 127, 129, 133, 134, 136, 138–139, 141–150, 162
Turner, Denys, 49, 72–73
Updike, John, 59
van der Leeuw, Gerard, 10, 48–49
Van Til, Cornelius, 79, 82, 86
Varro, Marcus Terentius, 11
von Balthasar, Hans Urs, 138, 168, 169
Wainwright, William J., 7
Walls, Jerry L., 14
Ward, Keith, 147
Warfield, B. B., 79
Webb, Clement C. J., 8–9, 11, 30, 32
Weber, Max, 37, 53
West, Peter, 115
White, Thomas Joseph, 2, 61
Whitehead, Alfred North, 128
Williams, Thomas, 60, 169
Wiman, Christian, 24, 50
Wolterstorff, Nicholas, 7, 62, 113, 116, 138
Woolford, Thomas, 14, 38
Wright, N. T., 121, 134, 136–137, 160–161, 162